Rapid Java Persistence and Microservices

Persistence Made Easy Using Java EE8, JPA and Spring

Raj Malhotra

Apress®

Rapid Java Persistence and Microservices: Persistence Made Easy Using Java EE8, JPA and Spring

Raj Malhotra
Faridabad, Haryana, India

ISBN-13 (pbk): 978-1-4842-4475-3   ISBN-13 (electronic): 978-1-4842-4476-0
https://doi.org/10.1007/978-1-4842-4476-0

Managing Director, Apress Media LLC: Welmoed Spahr
Acquisitions Editor: Steve Anglin
Development Editor: Matthew Moodie
Coordinating Editor: Mark Powers

Cover designed by eStudioCalamar

Cover image designed by Freepik (www.freepik.com)

Distributed to the book trade worldwide by Springer Science+Business Media New York, 233 Spring Street, 6th Floor, New York, NY 10013. Phone 1-800-SPRINGER, fax (201) 348-4505, e-mail orders-ny@springer-sbm.com, or visit www.springeronline.com. Apress Media, LLC is a California LLC and the sole member (owner) is Springer Science + Business Media Finance Inc (SSBM Finance Inc). SSBM Finance Inc is a **Delaware** corporation.

For information on translations, please e-mail editorial@apress.com; for reprint, paperback, or audio rights, please email bookpermissions@springernature.com.

Apress titles may be purchased in bulk for academic, corporate, or promotional use. eBook versions and licenses are also available for most titles. For more information, reference our Print and eBook Bulk Sales web page at http://www.apress.com/bulk-sales.

Any source code or other supplementary material referenced by the author in this book is available to readers on GitHub via the book's product page, located at www.apress.com/9781484244753. For more detailed information, please visit http://www.apress.com/source-code.

Printed on acid-free paper

To my beloved Guru Ji

Table of Contents

About the Author

Raj Malhotra is a passionate, hands-on, experienced leader with a proven track record and more than 14 years of experience. With proven experience in architecting large-scale software systems with complex performance and availability requirements, he has delivered innovative products and solutions across various domains and has diverse experience in multiple functional and technical domains. He has worked with startups, enterprises, and service-based companies and has built systems capable of handling millions of operations/second with complex workflows.

Please contact me for any queries of sharing feedback at mraj6046@gmail.com.

About the Technical Reviewer

Manuel Jordan Elera is an autodidactic developer and researcher who enjoys learning new technologies for his own experiments and for creating new integrations. Manuel won the Springy Award – Community Champion and Spring Champion, 2013. In his little free time, he reads the Bible and composes music on his guitar. Manuel is known as `dr_pompeii`. He has tech reviewed numerous books for Apress, including *Pro Spring, 4th Edition* (2014), *Practical Spring LDAP* (2013), *Pro JPA 2, Second Edition* (2013), and *Pro Spring Security* (2013). Read his 13 detailed tutorials about many Spring technologies, contact him through his blog at `http://www.manueljordanelera.blogspot.com`, and follow him on his Twitter account, `@dr_pompeii`.

Acknowledgments

I want to thank the whole team at Packt for all their support in making my dream come true. Special thanks to Manuel and Chris, as reviewers, they helped me and shaped my writing as a professional. Thanks to Steve for giving me this opportunity and Mark for supporting me with patience in the entire duration.

I want to thank my wife, Divya, for giving me the inspiration, belief, and constant encouragement to pursue my passion of writing. I also want to thank my father Lt. Shri R. S. Malhotra and my mother Kailash Malhotra who gave me their unconditional support so that I could devote all my spare time to writing. Finally, big thanks to my Guru Ji, who gave me the idea to share whatever I have learned from this big world, to the world again.

PART I

Java Ecosystem Review and Persistence Quick Start

CHAPTER 1

Introduction

Welcome to *Rapid Java Persistence and Microservices*. In the past few years, we have seen a constant rise in new technologies coming out. Especially for newcomers, it has become harder to become an all-around developer or even decide which programming language to learn first. Programmers often want to learn a language like Java so that they can work in any domain and do anything, including web development, Big Data, mobile development, machine learning, etc. This is not easy and a few issues that further complicate this goal include:

- There are many frameworks and technologies in every programming language.

- Competition is fierce and time-to-market is very brief.

- There is a bigger and ever-growing need for scalability and data storage.

- Complicated deployments, release management, and automation affect our decisions.

This book covers Java-based backend development through various frameworks, which should make development a lot easier, faster, and more efficient. This book is for impatient developers and architects who do not want to read too much theory, hundreds of concepts, and repeated text. Instead, this book is a quick tool to help you refresh concepts using to-the-point explanations and concrete real-world examples.

Before moving to the main part of the book, this chapter looks at some of the benefits of Java, explains what this book provides, covers the current issues in Java, and discusses the kinds of practical problems and solutions covered in this book.

© Raj Malhotra 2019
R. Malhotra, *Rapid Java Persistence and Microservices*, https://doi.org/10.1007/978-1-4842-4476-0_1

Why Java and Why This Book

So, what makes Java a good development solution, and why is this book the one developers should use?

The answer to the first question, in my opinion, includes these benefits of Java:

- Enterprise-level business application development.

- Long-term reliable solutions that remain stable.

- Superior readability and maintainability.

- A very strong community that gives you a lot of power and solutions to problems.

- Syntactical shortcuts in languages may only help in the short term.

Given the benefits of Java, here are a few good reasons to read this book:

- We cover all data access variations in simplified form through Java. These variations include RDBMS access via ORMs, JDBC, and NoSQLs.

- As an architect, you'll want to refresh your understanding of all key and advanced concepts quickly in order to design better decisions and address development issues.

- Some developers are moving to languages other than Java for development and to frameworks other than Spring. They feel that Java has become too large and that frameworks like Spring Data JPA, Hibernate, and so forth are slow in development. Due to their difficulty to learn, time-to-market increases. We will simplify this process through a rapid-fire overview of JPA and the various needed solutions in short form.

- There are many misleading examples being thrown on to the Internet that use obsolete ways of comparing Java to other languages. This book is in a quick notes-like format, which will also help guide you.

- A few years back, developers faced difficulty in clearing interviews only in Java. Let's think about the situation now and consider what all developers have to be knowledgeable of:

  - Java, with all its concepts and APIs.

  - The latest frameworks, with their pros and cons.

- SQL and RDBMS concepts.

- NoSQL concepts and their production issues.

- Enterprise and full text search-related solutions like ElasticSearch and Solr.

- Big Data and machine learning concepts.

- Reactive development.

- Security mechanisms for an API to the middle layer and data-level security.

- Headless computing or architectures.

Why not have solutions for all these fields and layers through one single language? We all need quick solutions and code with examples. A lot of information is available on the web, but it's not without its problems:

- Many online articles are obsolete. They may take you through unnecessary trials and experiments.

- They often include unnecessary explanations. To-the-point quick solutions are required.

Considering the success of Java 8 and other language frameworks like Django, writing only the minimum lines of code is what everyone needs. Even if the shortcuts look dirty or opinionated, this is what we need at times in today's world. Even if the concepts are good, we don't want to go through thousands of concepts just to achieve a small thing.

Current Issues with the Java Ecosystem

Along with the benefits of the wide and mature Java ecosystem, there are a few challenges to be aware of. The following list outlines the most important challenges:

- Java has become huge. From Java 8 to Java 11, there are many new concepts and API facilities and they all take time to master.

- There are many frameworks to choose from, for every layer and system.

- Along with Java, there are many JVM language options, including Scala, Closure, Groovy, Kotlin, and Jython.

- These are some important aspects of the current state of Java persistence to consider:

  - There is a large set of options to choose from for fresh development.

  - For an early stage developer, options start with JDBC. There are also various lightweight libraries, such as Apache DBUtils, Sql2o, Yank, JDBI, and the Spring JDBC template.

  - Next we have the ORM frameworks, such as Hibernate and EclipseLink, and data-mapping persistence frameworks like MyBatis.

  - Next comes Spring-supported J2EE specification APIs, such as EJB and JPA.

  - We also have a few smarter options today, such as JOOQ, Querydsl, and the Spring Data abstraction layer.

Real-World Problems and Solutions

We will see in this book all the real-world practical problems from an architect's experience. I will try to guide you, with my experience, on how to get started. The book goes through all the necessary concepts and shows solutions to complex problems.

Here is a brief history of the major changes in tech stacks for enterprise development that I've encountered in my 14 years of experience:

- It all started with C, C++, VB, messaging systems (like the MQ series), and databases (RDBMS). Messaging is probably the oldest technology I have seen. It is still the most popular way for scaling your architecture.

- Java, messaging, applets, etc. Java came to the rescue for enterprise web development through J2EE and JMS.

- Java Web Services (SOAP) and MVC frameworks. Struts, SOAP, Spring, etc., made things easier.

- REST services. Many more MVC and web frameworks, and SOA expansion. The SOA world had two sides—through web services and through MOM (message oriented middleware, such as IBM Message Broker, Tibco Rendezvous, etc.).

- Portal technologies (especially Weblogic Portal) and Content Management Systems (Documentum and Filenet).

- Upgraded open source messaging systems (AMQP, ActiveMQ, RabbitMQ, ZeroMQ, etc.) and frameworks (Protobuf, etc.), plus more web frameworks (Play, JSF, etc.).

- HTML5 (Bootstrap, AngularJS, Ember.js, etc.). This includes Thymeleaf and other templating technologies, CSS3, Bootstrap and JavaScript world evolution, NoSQL databases, functional programming (Scala, etc.), and cloud technologies (such as AWS).

- NodeJS, Python, etc. This includes Polyglot programming, deployment evolution through Docker, Chef, etc., and the analytics revolution through Big Data.

- Reactive programming, HTTP2, WebSockets, etc.

- Microservices with polyglot systems and cloud-automated deployments. There are too many technologies and possibilities right now, but these include RESTful microservices, headless architectures/function as a service, event driven/reactive services, and WebSocket-based connected services.

- GraphQL has now started disrupting the RESTful world. However, there are many caveats and the community is looking for other possibilities as well.

Summary

Having described the state of the Java ecosystem and the overall problems due to the vast variety of technologies that exist, we will start our journey in this book by introducing different frameworks for developing microservices as well as bigger applications in the next chapter. After that, we will take a deep dive into the most important layer of any application—*persistence*. After that, we will see all the challenges in the microservices architecture in Part II of the book.

CHAPTER 2

Developing Microservices with Java

Most development happening today is through a *microservices architecture*. In the microservices architectural approach, an application is developed through a bunch of small modular services. Each of these services run as a separate process and communicates with others via different patterns. This is not a new invention and we have seen it already with different nomenclature, for example, with SOA and MOM. When many of the web giants—including Amazon, Netflix, Twitter, and PayPal—successfully adopted the microservice architecture, it started gaining popularity.

There are a number of reasons for the rapid evolution of this architectural style:

- Legacy systems are very hard to rebuild. They have to be broken down into domains or functional areas and new pluggable systems have to replace the legacy slowly.

- Code versioning and deployment issues when multiple features have to be developed.

- It's easier to evolve a system with smaller independent services rather than a single giant application.

- Experimentation and diversity of tech stacks is easier with microservices. Code for different services can be written in different languages.

- Emerging technologies have made us rethink the way we build software systems.

- The microservice architecture enables easier continuous delivery and it's easy to understand as it follows the single responsibility principle.

- The services are aligned to business domains or features.

© Raj Malhotra 2019
R. Malhotra, *Rapid Java Persistence and Microservices*, https://doi.org/10.1007/978-1-4842-4476-0_2

- It's hard to test a single big application. When there are multiple system components, you can focus more on testing critical ones first.

- For a faster time-to-market, we need rapid-fire development of features in parallel. This helps the progress be more visible.

Different Ways of Creating Microservices

When we talk about microservices, we often talk about RESTful endpoints focused on a particular feature. However, developers have many different ways of creating microservices. There are a couple of ways to create microservices in the Java world, as follows:

- Independent RESTful endpoint-based applications as services related to a particular feature in the system.

- Headless service development such as AWS Lambda, also referred to as Function as a Service (FaaS).

- Messaging or event-based services such as clustered Vert.x vertices (Reactive framework in Java) that are deployed on different machines and communicate via event busses.

- Should OSGi modules also be treated as microservices? OSGi bundles are also sometimes referred as services running within a single JVM and a single constraint within their classloader boundaries.

Various Microservices Libraries in Java

When migrating from a monolithic to a microservices architecture, there are a number of concepts, problems, and technology options available that can make it difficult to think about the technology roadmap. As a result, people sometimes overthink the situation and overdevelop the solution when designing a new application in a microservice architecture.

For example, leaders sometimes want their teams to apply all the principles of the microservices architecture just by referring to the articles or innovations of bigger successful companies. A very common example within the Java world is implementing Netflix OSS tools in a small set of services. Architects often wonder if all these tools are required for a system with just a handful of services. Within Netflix, these frameworks handle huge loads with complicated system requirements and hundreds of microservices. If you have a system of 8-10 services, you should be a little cautious when choosing libraries during the initial development.

The Spring framework in the Java ecosystem has the most extensive support for microservices libraries. Table 2-1 identifies a number of libraries with use cases and conceptual needs that require specific handling when dealing with microservices.

Table 2-1. *Useful Libraries and Example Use Cases*

Library	Use Cases	Examples of Tools
Configuration Management	Distributed and secure configuration management	Spring Cloud Config, Consul, Vault
Service Registry and Discovery	Location service nodes based on registered service names	Spring Cloud - Netflix Eureka, Consul
Dynamic Routing and Load Balancer	Load balancing client requests with a live dashboard of nodes	Netflix Eureka and Netflix Ribbon
Distributed Tracing	Tracing the request end-to-end, if request flows through a couple of services	Spring Sleuth - Zipkin, ELK, Dapper
System, JVM, and API Monitoring	Performance degradation, risk and crash analysis	Spring Boot Admin, Datadog, New Relic
Security	Password and digest auth OAUTH and JWT SAML Single Sign On (SSO) Magic Links Captcha CORS OWASP (Injection, XSS, CSRF, etc.) Social login integrations SSL based authentication	Apache Shiro (a general library), Spring Security for Spring, pac4j for the Spark framework Dropwizard has its own classes for authentication and authorization

(*continued*)

Table 2-1. (*continued*)

Library	Use Cases	Examples of Tools
Logs	Centralized logs management for distributed services	Spring Sleuth, ELK (ElasticSearch, Logstash, Kibana), Splunk
Circuit Breaker	Avoiding continuous failure of service-to-service calls through a backup endpoint	Netflix Hystrix, Resilience4j, Sentinel
API Gateway	Acting as an entry point and handling security, URL naming concerns, etc.	Zuul, Nginx, cloud-provided API gateways
Documentation	Service versions, field-wise descriptions, and dependencies	Swagger, RAML, GraphQL

Here are a few more questions to ask when building your microservice approach:

- If you have a small number of services with simple use cases (basically a simple business logic and mostly CRUD), consider whether you need tools from Netflix OSS, like Eureka, Ribbon, Feign, Zuul, and Hystrix.

- How do you define the service boundaries? If they are too tiny and there are too many, can comfortably combine some of them based on functionality?

- What stage of development are you in? Do you need to focus more on product engineering, infrastructure management, or on scaling your application? These are all different and require special focus.

- Are you ready for new technology offerings as they come? WebSockets, RSocket, and GraphQL are the latest examples.

Microservices with Various Java Frameworks

A new generation of Java frameworks enables you to easily package a complete web app, with the embedded container of your choice in a self-runnable JAR file. This was a revolutionary movement from heavyweight J2EE containers to a lightweight smaller version. We will look at a couple of frameworks, starting with simple ones, up to a Spring Boot example. The Spring Framework has been around for over a decade and has become nearly the de facto standard framework for developing Java applications.

There are three major frameworks I see in use today:

- Spark (`http://sparkjava.com/`)

- Dropwizard (`https://www.dropwizard.io/1.3.8/docs/`)

- Spring Boot (`http://spring.io/`)

We consider each of these frameworks in the following sections. You will need Java 8 or higher with Gradle 5 to run all the examples. I have specifically kept the examples based on Java 8—with minimal use of functional programming and few newer language constructs such as Lambdas and Streams API—to keep the readability verbose and easy. I also show all the `import` statements in the text for full clarity.

Spark Framework

For newcomers, I recommend starting with the Spark Framework. This is the quickest way to build and play with RESTful services. As per the introduction on the website:

> *"Spark Framework is a simple and expressive Java/Kotlin web framework DSL built for rapid development. Spark's intention is to provide an alternative for Kotlin/Java developers that want to develop their web applications as expressive as possible and with minimal boilerplate. With a clear philosophy Spark is designed not only to make you more productive, but also to make your code better under the influence of Spark's sleek, declarative and expressive syntax."*

You just need to create a Maven- or Gradle-based project with a single Gradle dependency as `com.sparkjava:spark-core:2.8.0` in `build.gradle` (see Listing 2-1). Beyond that, with a simple five lines of code, you can run and access the URL at `http://localhost:4567/hello`.

A Gradle application can be created from the command line using a simple command, as follows:

```
gradle init --type java-application
```

Listing 2-1. Build.gradle

```
plugins {
    id 'java'
}

java {
    group = 'com.example'
    version = '1.0'
    sourceCompatibility = JavaVersion.VERSION_11
    targetCompatibility = JavaVersion.VERSION_11
}

repositories {
    mavenCentral()
}

dependencies {
    compile "com.sparkjava:spark-core:2.8.0"
}
```

As the next step, run the class shown in Listing 2-2, and your first microservice is up and running.

Listing 2-2. Bootstrapping Code

```
import static spark.Spark.*;

public class HelloWorld {
    public static void main(String[] args) {
        get("/hello", (req, res) -> "Hello World");
    }
}
```

You can quickly implement all other HTTP methods very easily, as follows:

```
get("/", (request, response) -> {
    return "Hello World";
});
```

```
post("/", (request, response) -> {
    // businessService.createResource(request.getInput("input"));
});

put("/", (request, response) -> {
    // businessService.updateResource(request.getInput("input"));
});

delete("/", (request, response) -> {
    // businessService.deleteResource(request.getInput("input"));
});
```

Although this looks clean, beyond this point, you may need extra libraries to support other complex application needs. Spark is a wonderful and clean Java framework, but it requires much more work beyond just creating a good RESTful layer. This has integration with the Spring Framework also, but that is an extra burden on top of another framework.

For data access, this framework promotes using the sql2o library. Yank and JDBI could also be used. You can start creating simple applications—either REST-based or MVC with support—for nearly all templating engines like Thymeleaf and Handlebars.

Dropwizard

Dropwizard is a packaged set of micro frameworks and libraries. All the most popular and standard supported frameworks for all needs in a web application are bundled together. Just including one dependency of Dropwizard can bring in support for Jetty, Jersey, Jackson, Guava, Liquibase, YAML, etc.

Let's see a Hello World app with this framework in action. We first need to create a Gradle-based project that can be run via any IDE and from any command line.

Note   You may need to set up Java 8 (minimum) and Gradle 5 to run all the examples in this book. All code in working condition can be downloaded from the GitHub repository.

After creating the Gradle file, we have to create four base classes to initiate an app:

- Configuration class

- Model class

- Resource class

- Application class

Additionally, we need a Maven or Gradle script and a YML file for actual configuration values.

Gradle Project

First create a new Gradle project from the command line (IDEs can also optionally be used) using the following command:

```
gradle init --type java-application
```

This will create all the necessary source folders, along with the default `build.gradle` file, which can then be overridden by the code shown in Listing 2-3.

Listing 2-3. Build.gradle

```
plugins {
    id 'java'
    id "com.github.johnrengelman.shadow" version "5.0.0"
}

group 'com.example'
version '1.0'

java {
    sourceCompatibility = JavaVersion.VERSION_1_8
    targetCompatibility = JavaVersion.VERSION_1_8
}
// optionally sourceCompatibility = JavaVersion.VERSION_11 can also be used
repositories {
    mavenCentral()
}
```

```
jar {
    manifest {
        attributes 'Main-Class': 'com.example.blogs.BlogApplication'
    }
}

dependencies {
    compile group: 'io.dropwizard', name: 'dropwizard-core', version: '1.3.7'
    compile('org.projectlombok:lombok:1.18.6')
    testCompile group: 'junit', name: 'junit', version: '4.12'

    annotationProcessor 'org.projectlombok:lombok:1.18.6'
}
```

Configuration Class

Add a configuration handler class as the carefully initialized object with values binded from the supplied YAML file while running the application (see Listing 2-4).

Listing 2-4. Configuration Class

```
package com.example.blogs.config;

import com.fasterxml.jackson.annotation.JsonProperty;
import io.dropwizard.Configuration;
import org.hibernate.validator.constraints.NotEmpty;

public class BlogAppConfig extends Configuration {

    @NotEmpty
    @JsonProperty
    private String blogName;

    public String getBlogName() {
        return blogName;
    }

    public void setBlogName(String blogName) {
        this.blogName = blogName;
    }
}
```

Model Class

Model classes hold the properties for providing requests and responses to the web layer (see Listing 2-5).

Listing 2-5. Configuration Class

```
package com.example.blogs.model;

import lombok.Data;
import org.hibernate.validator.constraints.Length;

@Data
public class Post implements Serializable {

    private Long id;

    @Length(min = 5, max = 300)
    private String content;

    public Post(Long id, String content)    {
        this.id = id;
        this.content = content;
    }
}
```

Resource Class

The resource class (see Listing 2-6) serves as the RESTful endpoint implementation.

Listing 2-6. Resource Class

```
package com.example.blogs.api;

import com.codahale.metrics.annotation.Timed;
import com.example.blogs.model.Post;

import javax.ws.rs.GET;
import javax.ws.rs.Path;
import javax.ws.rs.Produces;
import javax.ws.rs.QueryParam;
```

```java
import javax.ws.rs.core.MediaType;
import java.util.Optional;

@Path("/post")
@Produces(MediaType.APPLICATION_JSON)
public class PostResource {

    private String blogName;

    public PostResource(String blogName)    {
        this.blogName = blogName;
    }

    @GET
    @Timed
    public Post getRandomPost(@QueryParam("name") Optional<String> name) {
        return new Post(1l, name.orElse("This is a random post name") + "
        from " +
blogName );
    }

}
```

Application Class

This class acts as the entry point for the application and initializes all the user-defined components (see Listing 2-7).

Listing 2-7. Application Class

```java
package com.example.blogs;

import com.example.blogs.api.PostResource;
import com.example.blogs.config.BlogAppConfig;
import io.dropwizard.Application;
import io.dropwizard.setup.Bootstrap;
import io.dropwizard.setup.Environment;
import lombok.extern.slf4j.Slf4j;
```

```java
@Slf4j
public class BlogApplication extends Application<BlogAppConfig> {

    @Override
    public String getName() {
        return "BlogApplication";
    }

    @Override
    public void initialize(Bootstrap<BlogAppConfig> bootstrap) {
        log.info("Application initialized");
    }

    @Override
    public void run(BlogAppConfig configuration, Environment environment)
    throws
Exception {
        log.info("Application started");
        final PostResource resource = new PostResource(configuration.
        getBlogName());
        environment.jersey().register(resource);
    }

    public static void main(String[] args) throws Exception {
        new BlogApplication().run(args);
    }

}
```

YAML File: Application.yml

This file holds all the user-defined properties along with values that can change outside of the code.

```
blogName: Sample Blog
```

At this point, we are done with the codebase for the Hello World application. Let's see an example and run it.

Running the Application

From the IDE, pass in the application arguments, as `server application.yml`, and put `application.yml` in the root directory of the project. Figure 2-1 shows an example from Idea IntelliJ.

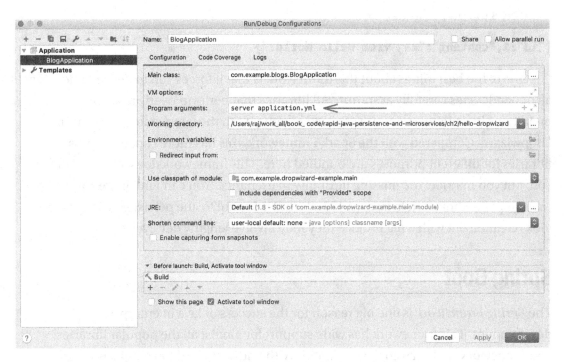

Figure 2-1. *Configuration settings in Idea IntelliJ*

Now just run the `BlogApplication` class from the IDE. In order to run it from the command line, you need to add a plugin to Gradle to create a fat JAR. We use the Shadow (`https://github.com/johnrengelman/shadow`) plugin, as shown earlier in the `build.gradle` file.

The command to create a shadow JAR is:

gradle shadowJar

Run the app from the command line:

java -jar ./build/libs/dropwizard-example-1.0-all.jar server application.yml

After application startup, you can visit this URL in the browser: `http://localhost:8080/post?name=Raj`.

Or you can use the CURL tool from the terminal as follows:

```
curl -X GET http://localhost:8080/post?name=Raj
```

Here's the output from CURL:

```
{"id":1,"content":"Raj from Hello World!"}
```

One of the best things about this framework is that it forces you to declare and assign all dependencies carefully at startup. All libraries that perform nearly all necessary operations in a microservice are grouped together with the latest stable versions in Dropwizard. Compared with the Spark Framework, this has more capabilities, as more libraries for different purposes are bundled here. This framework does a lot of stuff for you, but you may feel the missing flexibility in exchange. You can't integrate some of the most popular choices in Java, even JPA. With JDBI or sql2o, the persistence framework looks cleaner, but with a big project, they may involve lengthy dev cycles.

Spring Boot

The *Spring Framework* is one big reason for the success of Java in enterprise development. This framework has wide support for almost all the popular libraries and frameworks in Java web development. With Spring Boot, we can quickly create self-runnable microservices within minutes. In the past, we had to spend a lot of development time in an application writing boilerplate code for wiring Spring infra components only. Now, most of the common stuff is preconfigured for us.

Here are a few highlights of Spring Boot:

- It also has a curated list of libraries bundled, just like Dropwizard, but these are mostly preconfigured.

- It's easy to get things up and running quickly.

- It's very flexible to override configuration, libraries, and frameworks.

- There is a very strong community to provide solutions to various problems that may arise.

Let's look at a sample Hello World application along with the foundation class for our use cases. This class will act as the starting point for our sample web application. If you want to change or override anything, you have the option of a properties file, a YAML file, and Java-based configuration.

To start a new application with Spring Boot, we will be implementing an interface called CommandLineRunner. This will enable us to start running a few sample cases just after the web container has started. In other words, this class helps us bootstrap the application.

Let's define our Application class. This tiny single class serves as the starting point and as a RESTful endpoint for the Spring Boot application (see Listing 2-8).

Listing 2-8. Application Class

```java
package com.example.hello;

import lombok.extern.slf4j.Slf4j;
import org.springframework.boot.CommandLineRunner;
import org.springframework.boot.SpringApplication;
import org.springframework.boot.autoconfigure.SpringBootApplication;
import org.springframework.web.bind.annotation.GetMapping;
import org.springframework.web.bind.annotation.RestController;

@SpringBootApplication
@RestController
@Slf4j
public class HelloApplication implements CommandLineRunner {

    public static void main(String[] args) {
        SpringApplication.run(HelloApplication.class, args);
    }

    @Override
    public void run(String... args) throws Exception {
        log.info("App started");
    }

    @GetMapping("/hello")
    public String hello() {
        return "Hello World";
    }
}
```

Here is the `application.properties` file:

```
server.servlet.context-path=/library
```

We also need to add a property to the `{rootSrcPath}/main/resources/` `application.properties` file, as shown. With this property, we are setting the context path for the application. There are many such properties to customize. We will not be discussing all of them and I suggest you read the basics from the Spring documentation.

The Spring Framework community provides an extra facility so that the initial project setup doesn't have to be done manually. The `http://www.start.spring.io` site gives you the quick, ready-to-start initial setup, with all the Spring dependencies listed.

Just download a quick app and provide the `groupId` and `artifactId` onscreen. Set up and run the main class from any IDE and access the URL as `http://localhost:8080/` `library/hello`.

Alternatively, the CURL command is:

```
curl -X GET http://localhost:8080/library/hello
```

This is the output:

```
Hello World
```

The `CommandLineRunner` interface doesn't have to be implemented; the application can run directly within the `main` method, as `SpringApplication.run(Application.` `class, args)`. This interface is used in case you want to run or trigger more code after the embedded container starts. In Spring Boot, most things are configured by convention.

Spring Boot loads the configuration by default from `application.properties` or `application.yml` in the classpath.

The `@Sl4j` annotation is from the open source project Lombok. This annotation generates a final static log, an Sl4j-based field in the compiled class.

Consider these two special comments about why the Spring Framework is used in this book:

- With a huge community and years of hard work, the Spring Framework very consistently supports hundreds of libraries and frameworks. This is quite challenging.

- The speed of upgrades and speed of adapting to any trending technologies is very good with the community.

To be specific, if you want the most controlled, optimal dev setup, Dropwizard should be your first choice; otherwise, Spring is the preferred choice.

Summary

We have just seen three popular frameworks to start with. From now on, we will see most of examples using the Spring Framework, as it offers the most comprehensive solutions for various needs of any enterprise system. We can create a microservice from a bigger macroservice or from a monolithic application using Spring Boot.

CHAPTER 3

Basic Persistence with Spring

The intent of this chapter is to explain easy and convenient Java persistence with optimal choices for performance. We will recap the various options and show examples of important use cases. Persistence, in my opinion, is the most important layer in any application.

Starting with ORM frameworks, we have seen a lot of love and hate for ORMs in the past decade, yet they are still heavily used by the community. ORMs provide a lot of choices in the Java ecosystem for database interaction. Let's start by discussing the first popular choice—Spring Data JPA—and take a quick recap of Hibernate.

Spring Data JPA is a very useful DSL (Domain Specific Language) based module that provides maximum reduction to boilerplate code for interacting with databases. Using Spring Data on top of JPA/Hibernate provides a consistent API for interacting with relational and NoSQL databases. There are three important steps we need to follow while developing applications with Spring Data JPA:

1. Define the domain models or entities. When starting a new project, you need to decide whether entities should be defined first or should be generated later from the database. The best way I see to design with JPA is to have a SQL definition of your database initially and then create the table-by-table model classes after that. Even if this involves two steps, this might be more useful than generating Java models from DB tables. SQL scripts need not have all their constraints defined initially. Based on the first application run, relationships (foreign keys) will be updated in the database automatically by JPA.

© Raj Malhotra 2019
R. Malhotra, *Rapid Java Persistence and Microservices*, https://doi.org/10.1007/978-1-4842-4476-0_3

2. Define the repositories with any necessary customization. Customization can be done when you know your access patterns; otherwise, this is mostly done on an incremental need basis.

3. Use these models and repositories along with optimizing the queries and/or convert to native whenever required. Based on the performance requirements, native queries can also be utilized.

By the end of this chapter, you should have good understanding of the following Spring Data JPA concepts:

- Basic entity definitions with:

    - `@OneToOne`

    - `@OneToMany`

    - `@ManoToOne`

    - `@ManyToMany` and lazy loading

    - Usage of `Cascade.ALL` and when to avoid it

    - Usage of Lombok's `@ToString` and `@EqualsAndHashCode`

    - Usage of Jackson's `@JsonIgnore`

- PostgreSQL with JPA, especially when:

    - Using enums

    - Using UUID

    - Fetching, storing, and querying arrays

- Basic usage:

    - JPA query example with pagination

    - The usage and advantages of a common base repository

Spring Data JPA Introduction

Spring Data is an umbrella project that simplifies Java persistence through a very lean and consistent API that works on top of JDBC, JPA, and other NoSQL product APIs. Spring Data JPA is a subset of Spring Data and drastically reduces the effort needed to do CRUD operations. For a simple application, the major effort now goes into defining the models because no lengthy boilerplate DAOs have to be written. Let's recap the problems we had in using ORMs and how Spring Data JPA helps:

- Prior to Spring Data JPA, we had to implement the DAO layer by writing lot of generic boilerplate code to handle common select and update operations. Now, merely using its DSL, the interface method definitions are enough.

- No need for the EntityManager API anymore, although you can still autowire it anytime.

- Same consistent API for RDBMS and NoSQLs.

- Readability and ease of use increases as less code has to be written. The same factor makes it more reliable as well as less error-prone.

- With continuous improvements by the community, Spring Data now offers pure JDBC and a mapper-based solution.

- Keeping the core API the same allows integration with MyBatis, QueryDSL, JOOQ, and other JDBC libraries along with customization support. As an architect, I have always found a conceptual difference while developing with ORMs versus JDBC solutions:

  - ORMs are based on the object per table pattern and thus there is a lot of thinking required to query in that form and fulfill requests in a normalized database.

  - JDBC solutions give you the simplicity and flexibility to create SQL queries by combining any random tables through joins and simply map the results back to any POJO class. The only time the object per query method works here is when the database is denormalized using flat tables.

There are three interfaces in Spring Data API on the top:

- `CrudRepository`

- `PagingAndSortingRepository`, which extends `CrudRepository`

- `JpaRepository`, which extends `PagingAndSortingRepository`

All these three interfaces work with JPA entities only. CrudRepository mainly provides basic CRUD functions. PagingAndSortingRepository provides methods to do pagination and sort records. JpaRepository provides JPA-related methods, such as flushing the persistence context and deleting records in a batch. Listing 3-1 shows the source code for CrudRepository.

Listing 3-1. Repository Definition

```
package org.springframework.data.repository;

import java.util.Optional;

@NoRepositoryBean
public interface CrudRepository<T, ID> extends Repository<T, ID> {

        <S extends T> S save(S entity);
        <S extends T> Iterable<S> saveAll(Iterable<S> entities);
        Optional<T> findById(ID id);
        boolean existsById(ID id);
        Iterable<T> findAll();
        Iterable<T> findAllById(Iterable<ID> ids);
        long count();
        void deleteById(ID id);
        void delete(T entity);
        void deleteAll(Iterable<? extends T> entities);
        void deleteAll();
}

@NoRepositoryBean
public interface PagingAndSortingRepository<T, ID> extends
 CrudRepository<T, ID> {
        Iterable<T> findAll(Sort sort);
        Page<T> findAll(Pageable pageable);
}

@NoRepositoryBean
public interface JpaRepository<T, ID> extends PagingAndSortingRepository<T, ID>,
QueryByExampleExecutor<T> {
    List<T> findAll();
```

```
    List<T> findAll(Sort var1);
    List<T> findAllById(Iterable<ID> var1);
    <S extends T> List<S> saveAll(Iterable<S> var1);
    void flush();
    <S extends T> S saveAndFlush(S var1);
    void deleteInBatch(Iterable<T> var1);
    void deleteAllInBatch();
    T getOne(ID var1);
    <S extends T> List<S> findAll(Example<S> var1);
    <S extends T> List<S> findAll(Example<S> var1, Sort var2);
}
```

The beauty of the Spring Data JPA lies in the way it derives queries from the tables by just defining the repository method names. This capability comes from the Spring Data Query DSL. Consider this example of a sample UserRepository interface:

```
@Repository
public interface UserRepository extends CrudRepository<User, Long> {
    void deleteByUsername(String username);
    Optional<User> findByUsername(String username);

    @Query("select u from User u")
    Stream<User> streamAll();
}
```

All findBy{fieldName}, deleteBy* methods will get their implementation by the framework itself. Java 8 Optional and Streams are also supported.

Spring Data JPA Example

It's often said that ORM/JPA and Hibernate are hard for newcomers. To see what all is involved with the most common cases, we will create a blog application in this chapter, taking PostgreSQL as the database. In recent years, PostgreSQL has become the default choice because of its many recent innovations and upgrades by the community.

The @OnetoMany and @ManyToone Annotations

We will start by creating an example application that covers the first two points from the previous list. The code structure for this applications will be as follows:

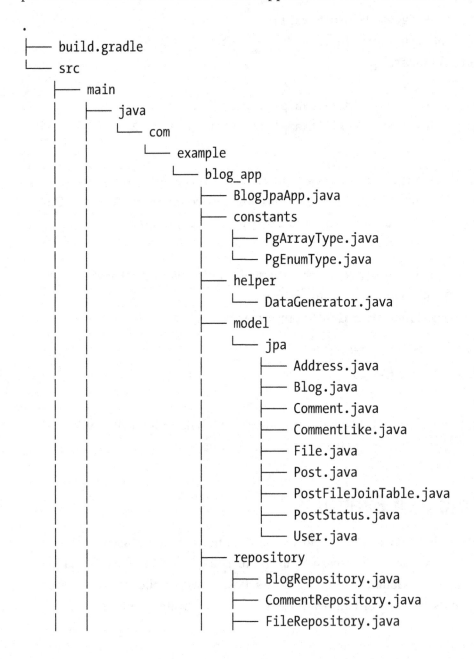

```
.
├── build.gradle
└── src
    ├── main
    │   ├── java
    │   │   └── com
    │   │       └── example
    │   │           └── blog_app
    │   │               ├── BlogJpaApp.java
    │   │               ├── constants
    │   │               │   ├── PgArrayType.java
    │   │               │   └── PgEnumType.java
    │   │               ├── helper
    │   │               │   └── DataGenerator.java
    │   │               ├── model
    │   │               │   └── jpa
    │   │               │       ├── Address.java
    │   │               │       ├── Blog.java
    │   │               │       ├── Comment.java
    │   │               │       ├── CommentLike.java
    │   │               │       ├── File.java
    │   │               │       ├── Post.java
    │   │               │       ├── PostFileJoinTable.java
    │   │               │       ├── PostStatus.java
    │   │               │       └── User.java
    │   │               ├── repository
    │   │               │   ├── BlogRepository.java
    │   │               │   ├── CommentRepository.java
    │   │               │   ├── FileRepository.java
```

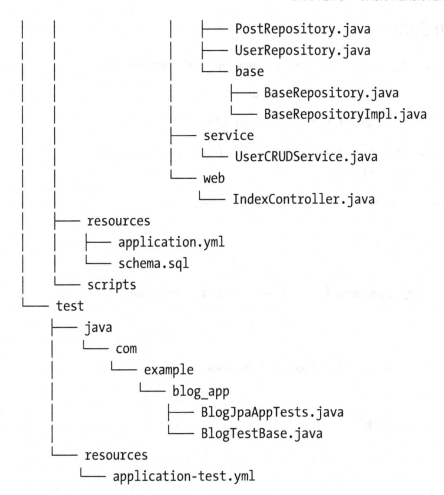

```
|   |                       |       ├── PostRepository.java
|   |                       |       ├── UserRepository.java
|   |                       |       └── base
|   |                       |           ├── BaseRepository.java
|   |                       |           └── BaseRepositoryImpl.java
|   |                       ├── service
|   |                       |   └── UserCRUDService.java
|   |                       └── web
|   |                           └── IndexController.java
|   ├── resources
|   |   ├── application.yml
|   |   └── schema.sql
|   └── scripts
└── test
    ├── java
    |   └── com
    |       └── example
    |           └── blog_app
    |               ├── BlogJpaAppTests.java
    |               └── BlogTestBase.java
    └── resources
        └── application-test.yml
```

Creating the Blog App

First, go to start.spring.io or create a new Gradle app called blog-app-jpa-ch3 with the groupId set to com.example and the artifactId set to blog-app.

If you switch to the full version at start.spring.io, nearly all the Spring libraries and frameworks are shown. Select Web, Lombok, JPA, JDBC, and PostgreSQL, and then generate a project.

Application Setup

Before we start writing the code, let's set up the project using these steps:

1. Set up dependencies in build.gradle.

2. Create and execute SQL statements for table creation.

3. Create a database in PostgreSQL and map its access details to application.yml.

These steps are detailed in Listings 3-2 through 3-4.

Listing 3-2. Build.gradle

```
plugins {
    id 'org.springframework.boot' version '2.1.3.RELEASE'
    id 'java'
}

apply plugin: 'io.spring.dependency-management'

bootJar {
    baseName = 'blog-app'
    version = '1.0'
}

repositories {
    mavenCentral()
}

dependencies {

    compile('org.springframework.boot:spring-boot-starter-web')
    compile('org.springframework.boot:spring-boot-starter-jdbc')
    compile('org.springframework.boot:spring-boot-starter-data-jpa')
    compile("org.springframework.boot:spring-boot-starter-data-mongodb")

    compile('org.postgresql:postgresql:42.2.5')

    testCompile('junit:junit:4.12')
    testCompile('org.springframework.boot:spring-boot-starter-test')
```

```
    compile("org.projectlombok:lombok:1.18.6")
    annotationProcessor("org.projectlombok:lombok:1.18.6")
}
```

Listing 3-3. Schema at {project-root}/resources/schema.sql

```sql
CREATE EXTENSION IF NOT EXISTS "uuid-ossp"; -- This is required to enable
UUID extension

drop table if exists blog cascade;
drop table if exists post cascade;
drop table if exists comment cascade;
drop table if exists comment_like cascade;
drop table if exists file cascade;
drop table if exists post_files cascade;
drop table if exists "user" cascade; -- since user is a keyword in
postgresql, double quotes are used here

-- DROP statements end here

Create table if not exists blog (
  id serial primary key not null,
  guid uuid default uuid_generate_v4(),
  name varchar(150),
  about text,
  published_at timestamp
);

create table if not exists post  (
  id serial primary key not null,
  blog_id int,
  title varchar(150),
  content text,
  "user" int
);

create table if not exists comment  (
  id serial primary key not null,
  parent_id int,
```

```
  content text,
  post_id int
);

create table if not exists "user"  (
  id serial primary key not null,
  username varchar(150),
  password varchar(150),
  email varchar(150),
  is_active boolean,
  activated_at timestamp DEFAULT (current_timestamp AT TIME ZONE 'UTC')
);

create table comment_like (id  bigserial not null, comment_id int8, post_id
int8, user_id int8, primary key (id));
create table file (id bigserial not null, name varchar(255), primary key (id));
create table post_files (post_id int8 not null, file_id int8 not null,
primary key (file_id, post_id));
```

Listing 3-4. {project-root}/resources/application.yml

```
server:
  port: 8080
  servlet:
    contextPath: /blog
spring:
  application:
    name: blog-service
  jpa:
    show-sql: false
    hibernate:
      ddl-auto: update
      jdbc.lob.non_contextual_creation: true
    generate-ddl: true
  datasource:
    username: postgres
    password: postgres
```

```
    url: jdbc:postgresql://localhost:5432/blogs
    driverClassName: org.postgresql.Driver

logging:
  file: logs/blogging-service.log
  level:
    org.hibernate.SQL: ERROR
    org.springframework.data: DEBUG
```

In the preceding code, I included most of the common attributes to get things up and running quickly with PostgreSQL. Note that we have not yet defined the relationships in the SQL file, as they will be auto-generated from the JPA entity models in the next step. We just added the ddl-auto: update property in the file. Figure 3-1 shows the entity relationship (ER) diagram.

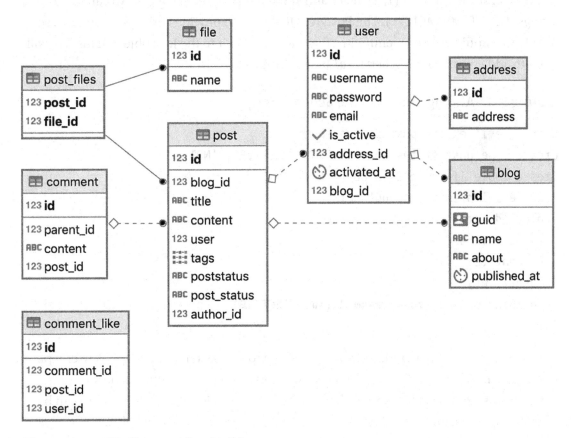

Figure 3-1. *ER diagram for the blog app*

Enums as Datatypes in Postgresql and Mapping in JPA

Often there is a need to store literal constants in the database as strings and map them to enumerations in Java. We will be using Java enum types in the upcoming examples, so let's take a minute to look at their correct usage in this section.

If we map and store Java enums as ordinal in a PostgreSQL database, as an example through POST entity definition, they should be easy to deal with. If we want to store enum values (string literals) as is through JPA, we need an extra step, as described in this section. For example, if we have the following enum in the Java code:

```
public enum PostStatus implements Serializable {
    ACTIVE(1), NOT_ACTIVE(2);
}
```

We can store numbers (1, 2) in DB and keep mapping them back or we can store strings (ACTIVE, NOT_ACTIVE). The PostgreSQL database provides ENUM as a datatype, so ideally we should create an enum in a database to map it to the Java object fields. We will need to add enums to the schema.sql (see Listing 3-5).

Listing 3-5. Adding Enums to the Schema Script

```
drop type if exists post_status_enum;
Create type post_status_enum as ENUM ('ACTIVE', 'NOT_ACTIVE');
create table if not exists post (
  id serial primary key not null,
  blog_id int,
  title varchar(150),
  content text,
  "user" int,
  postStatus post_status_enum default 'ACTIVE'
);
```

In order to map them to Java enums, we need to define a new user type. A user type is a feature in Hibernate that defines custom datatypes. Listing 3-6 shows how this is done for this example. Once that is defined, a @Type (see Listing 3-8) annotation can be used on top of the enum fields to map them to the code and database fields.

Listing 3-6. Defining a Custom Type as a Hibernate User Type to Map Enums

```
package com.example.blog_app.constants;

import org.hibernate.HibernateException;
import org.hibernate.engine.spi.SharedSessionContractImplementor;
import org.hibernate.usertype.EnhancedUserType;
import org.hibernate.usertype.ParameterizedType;
import org.postgresql.util.PGobject;

import java.io.Serializable;
import java.sql.PreparedStatement;
import java.sql.ResultSet;
import java.sql.SQLException;
import java.sql.Types;
import java.util.Properties;
public class PgEnumType implements EnhancedUserType, ParameterizedType {

    private Class<Enum> enumClass;

    public void setParameterValues(Properties parameters) {
        String enumClassName = parameters.getProperty("enumClassName");
        try {
            enumClass = (Class<Enum>) Class.forName(enumClassName);
        } catch (ClassNotFoundException cnfe) {
            throw new HibernateException("Enum class not found", cnfe);
        }
    }
    public Object assemble(Serializable cached, Object owner)
            throws HibernateException {
        return cached;
    }

    public Object deepCopy(Object value) throws HibernateException {
        return value;
    }
```

```java
    public Serializable disassemble(Object value) throws HibernateException {
        return (Enum) value;
    }

    public boolean equals(Object x, Object y) throws HibernateException {
        return x == y;
    }

    public int hashCode(Object x) throws HibernateException {
        return x.hashCode();
    }

    @Override
    public Object nullSafeGet(ResultSet rs, String[] names,
SharedSessionContractImplementor session, Object owner) throws
HibernateException,
SQLException {
        Object object = rs.getObject(names[0]);
        if (rs.wasNull()) {
            return null;
        }

        if (object instanceof PGobject) {
            PGobject pg = (PGobject) object;
            return Enum.valueOf(enumClass, pg.getValue());
        }

        if (object instanceof String) {
            return Enum.valueOf(enumClass, String.valueOf(object));
        }

        return null;
    }
    @Override
    public void nullSafeSet(PreparedStatement st, Object value, int index,
SharedSessionContractImplementor session) throws HibernateException,
SQLException {
```

```java
        if (value == null) {
            st.setNull(index, Types.VARCHAR);
        } else {
            st.setObject(index, ((Enum) value), Types.OTHER);
        }
    }

    public boolean isMutable() {
        return false;
    }

    public Object replace(Object original, Object target, Object owner)
            throws HibernateException {
        return original;
    }

    public Class returnedClass() {
        return enumClass;
    }

    public int[] sqlTypes() {
        return new int[]{Types.VARCHAR};
    }

    public Object fromXMLString(String xmlValue) {
        return Enum.valueOf(enumClass, xmlValue);
    }

    public String objectToSQLString(Object value) {
        return '\"' + ((Enum) value).name() + '\"';
    }

    public String toXMLString(Object value) {
        return ((Enum) value).name();
    }
}
```

Note the three methods:

- setParameterValues: We are reading a property named enumClassName and loading its target class by reflection.

- nullSafeGet: In the PostgreSQL API, custom datatypes can be retrieved as a PGobject and the enum value can be mapped through this object.

- nullSafeSet: This method resets the enum value in PreparedStatement.

We will use this code in the next section and show the outcome.

Data Models and Repositories

We need to define Java entity or domain objects to map the tables in DB as per the ER diagram shown in Figure 3-1. In this section, we will see what is involved in creating the domain layer through JPA. We will start the example by using the @OneToMany annotation to define the BLOG object (see Listing 3-7) and using the @ManyToOne annotation for the POST object (see Listing 3-8).

Listing 3-7. BLOG Object Definition

```
package com.example.blog_app.model.jpa;

import com.fasterxml.jackson.annotation.JsonIgnore;
import lombok.*;

import javax.persistence.*;
import java.time.LocalDateTime;
import java.util.Set;
import java.util.UUID;

@Data              // generates getters, setters, equals, toString &
                      hashCode we well
@Builder           // generater builder for the fields within
@NoArgsConstructor // generates a no argument constructor
@AllArgsConstructor // generates a constructor with all arguments
@ToString(exclude = {"posts"}) // generates toString method, skipping
                                   passed field as name
```

```java
// generates equals and hashCode methods, skipping passed fields
@EqualsAndHashCode(exclude = {"posts"}) @Entity
public class Blog  implements Serializable {

    @Id
    @GeneratedValue(strategy = GenerationType.IDENTITY)
    private Long id;

    /*
    'guid' is useful to hide incremental 'id' from all external
    communications for
    security reasons.
    'id' would be faster to index and query while doing pagination,
    filtering etc.
     */
    @org.hibernate.annotations.Type(type = "pg-uuid")
    UUID guid;

    private String name;
    private String about;
    private LocalDateTime publishedAt;

    @JsonIgnore
    @OneToMany(fetch = FetchType.LAZY, cascade = CascadeType.ALL,
            orphanRemoval = true, mappedBy = "blog")
    private Set<Post> posts;
}
```

Key observations about the preceding blog code:

- In order to use UUID in the PostgreSQL database, we need to enable it in the schema through the SQL statement, as mentioned in the schema.sql file (i.e., CREATE EXTENSION IF NOT EXISTS uuid-ossp).

- Since we are running the SQL script separately, schema.sql need not be run by Spring upon startup. Therefore, we have kept ddl-auto: update. This will only run alter commands and not create one until ddl-auto is set to create or create-drop.

- With Lombok annotations on top of `class`, we have made it very readable by reducing boilerplate code of getters, setters, equals, `hashCode`, and `toString` methods.

- The annotation `@org.hibernate.annotations.Type(type = "pg-uuid")` is required to support mapping of UUIDs in PostgreSQL to the Java UUID class.

- We can easily support `LocalDateTime` now, mapping to timestamp in the datatype in the DB.

- The annotations `@JsonIgnore`, `@ToString(exclude = {"posts"})`, and `@EqualsAndHashCode(exclude = {"posts"})` help in ignoring lazy loaded related objects from serialization, generated `toString`, equals, and `hashCode` object comparison methods.

- As good practice, it is better not to send back an incremental ID and primary key to the client for any object. Thus, GUIDs (Global Unique Identifiers) can be used. However, performance can be slow, as indexing big random characters is going to be slow. To overcome this, we use both IDs.

Similarly we will have the definitions of POST (see Listing 3-8) and USER objects (see Listing 3-9).

Listing 3-8. POST Object and PostEnum Definitions

```
package com.example.blog_app.model.jpa;

import com.fasterxml.jackson.annotation.JsonIgnore;
import lombok.*;

import javax.persistence.*;
import java.util.Set;

@Data
@Builder
@NoArgsConstructor
@AllArgsConstructor
@ToString(exclude = {"blog", "user"})
@EqualsAndHashCode(exclude = {"blog", "user"})
```

```java
@Entity
public class Post  implements Serializable {

    @Id
    @GeneratedValue(strategy = GenerationType.IDENTITY)
    private Long id;
    private String title;
    private String content;

    @Column(name = "post_status")
    @Type(type = "com.example.blog_app.constants.PgEnumType",
            parameters = {@org.hibernate.annotations.Parameter(name =
            "enumClassName", value = "com.example.blog_app.model.jpa.
            PostStatus")})
    // @Enumerated(EnumType.ORDINAL) // Use this otherwise to store it as
    integer
    PostStatus postStatus;

    @ManyToOne(fetch = FetchType.LAZY, cascade = CascadeType. REFRESH)
    @JoinColumn(name = "blog_id")
    private Blog blog;

    @JsonIgnore
    @ManyToOne(fetch = FetchType.LAZY, cascade = CascadeType.REFRESH)
    @JoinColumn(name = "author_id")
    private User user;
}

package com.example.blog_app.model.jpa;
import java.io.Serializable;

public enum PostStatus implements Serializable {

    ACTIVE(1), NOT_ACTIVE(2);
    int status;

    PostStatus(int status)  {
        this.status = status;
    }
}
```

Listing 3-9. USER Object Definition

```java
package com.example.blog_app.model.jpa;

import lombok.*;
import javax.persistence.*;
import java.util.Set;

@Data
@Builder
@NoArgsConstructor
@AllArgsConstructor
@ToString(exclude = {"posts"})
@EqualsAndHashCode(exclude = {"posts"})
@Entity(name = "`user`")
public class User  implements Serializable {

    public User(String username, String password, String email)   {
        this.username = username;
        this.password = password;
        this.email = email;
    }

    @Id
    @GeneratedValue(strategy = GenerationType.IDENTITY)
    private Long id;

    private String username;
    private String password;
    private String email;
    private Boolean isActive;

    @OneToMany(fetch = FetchType.LAZY, cascade = CascadeType
.ALL, mappedBy = "user", orphanRemoval = true)
    private Set<Post> posts;

}
```

As facilitated by Spring Data, interface definitions are enough to define the DAO layer (see Listing 3-10).

Listing 3-10. Repository Interface Definitions

```
package com.example.blog_app.repository;

import com.example.blog_app.model.jpa.Blog;
import com.example.blog_app.model.jpa.Post;
import org.springframework.data.jpa.repository.JpaRepository;

public interface PostRepository extends JpaRepository<Post, Long> {}

package com.example.blog_app.repository;

import com.example.blog_app.model.jpa.User;
import com.example.blog_app.repository.base.CustomRepository;

public interface UserRepository extends CustomRepository<User, Long> {
    void deleteByUsername(String username);
}

package com.example.blog_app.repository;

import com.example.blog_app.model.jpa.Blog;
import org.springframework.data.jpa.repository.JpaRepository;

public interface BlogRepository extends JpaRepository<Blog, Long> {
}
```

Notes:

- Define datatypes for fields as objects rather than primitives, as they may create issues in handling nulls.

- The user entity is surrounded by quotes in its definition, such as @Table(name = "`user`"). This is needed, as user is a keyword in PostgreSQL. The same character is used in the schema.sql file.

- We defined the @OneToMany annotation in the Blog and User objects.
  There are a couple of conventions to follow when defining this
  relationship. Consider the User -> Post object as an example here:

```
USER
@OneToMany(fetch = FetchType.LAZY, cascade = CascadeType.ALL,
        mappedBy = "user", orphanRemoval = true)
private Set<Post> posts;

POST
@JsonIgnore
@ManyToOne(fetch = FetchType.LAZY, cascade = CascadeType.REFRESH)
@JoinColumn(name = "author_id")
private User user;
```

- – As per best practice from the Hibernate docs, always define
    associations as Lazy first.

- – As per best practice from the Hibernate docs, define bidirectional
    associations, as the navigation is easier on both sides. However,
    they are bit harder to define and keep in sync. As an example,
    while adding a new POST, both entities (POST and Blog) will
    require a refresh to keep the objects in memory in sync.

- – The parent object (User) has an attribute set to mappedBy=user
    that maps the user field in the child object, which is POST here.
    This is required only when the relationship is bidirectional.

- – CascadeType.ALL will trigger all cascade events when the parent
    entity is deleted or updated to the child objects in memory. For
    example, when a user is deleted, all related POST rows become
    orphans. orphanRemoval=true further removes those related
    rows from the database.

- – On the opposite side, child or POST entities have to be annotated
    with Cascade.REFRESH so that just the parent object is refreshed
    when any child object is deleted or updated.

- We have ignored lazily loaded fields through @ToString and @EqualsAndHashCode for Lombok. This will ignore relationship fields in the generated code for the toString(), equals(), and hashCode() methods.

- @JsonIgnore is used on top of the related fields to ignore them during serialization and deserialization.

Using CascadeType.ALL and What to Avoid

The meaning of CascadeType.ALL is that the persistence context will propagate (cascade) all EntityManager operations (PERSIST, REMOVE, REFRESH, MERGE, and DETACH) to the related entities.

Detailed Cascade type descriptions are as follows:

- PERSIST: If the parent entity is persisted into the persistence context, the related entity will also be persisted.

- MERGE: If the parent entity is merged into the persistence context, the related entity will also be merged.

- REFRESH: If the parent entity is refreshed in the current persistence context, the related entity will also be refreshed.

- DETACH: If the parent entity is detached from the persistence context, the related entity will also be detached.

- REMOVE: If the parent entity is removed from the current persistence context, the related entity will also be removed.

- ALL: All descriptions are applied to related entities.

Cascading is the most sensitive setting, as in the case of update and removal, unexpected behavior can also happen. As an example with CascadeType.REMOVE, sometimes you may want child table rows to exist even when the parent is being deleted, especially for some other relationships with other tables.

Let's look at a negative example to explain the impact of using CascadeType.All with the changes in the entity associations code from the previous section (see Listing 3-11).

Listing 3-11. Entity Changes to Reflect Illegal Deletions in Database

```
public class Blog  implements Serializable {
    @OneToMany(fetch = FetchType.LAZY, cascade = CascadeType.ALL,
            orphanRemoval = true, mappedBy = "blog")
    private Set<Post> posts;
}

public class Post  implements Serializable {

    @ManyToOne(fetch = FetchType.LAZY, cascade = CascadeType.ALL)
    @JoinColumn(name = "blog_id")
    private Blog blog;

    @ManyToOne(fetch = FetchType.LAZY, cascade = CascadeType.ALL)
    @JoinColumn(name = "author_id")
    private User user;
}

public class User  implements Serializable {

    @OneToMany(fetch = FetchType.LAZY, cascade = {CascadeType.ALL},
     mappedBy = "user", orphanRemoval = true)
    private Set<Post> posts;
}
```

Notes:

- We marked cascade=CascadeType.ALL for all the associations in the code.

- Any deletion to the POST entity object will trigger a deletion to the related Blog object, which will further trigger a deletion of all related POST and USER objects. Ultimately, it's a mess to delete everything.

- Deleting the POST entity will also trigger deletion of all related users, even if the users from those are connected to other posts.

In order to test the code both positively and negatively, we have to define two supporting classes—DataGenerator (see Listing 3-12) and TestCase (see Listing 3-13). This class generates sample blogs, along with users and their posts.

Listing 3-12. Sample DataGenerator Class and Missing Pieces

```
package com.example.blog_app.helper;

import com.example.blog_app.model.jpa.Blog;
import com.example.blog_app.model.jpa.Post;
import com.example.blog_app.model.jpa.PostStatus;
import com.example.blog_app.model.jpa.User;
import com.example.blog_app.repository.BlogRepository;
import com.example.blog_app.repository.PostRepository;
import com.example.blog_app.repository.UserRepository;
import lombok.extern.slf4j.Slf4j;
import org.springframework.beans.factory.annotation.Autowired;
import org.springframework.stereotype.Service;

import org.springframework.transaction.annotation.Transactional;
 import java.time.LocalDateTime;
import java.util.ArrayList;
import java.util.Arrays;
import java.util.List;
import java.util.UUID;

@Service
@Slf4j
public class DataGenerator {

private AtomicBoolean initialized = new AtomicBoolean(false);

List<String> blogNames = Arrays.asList("PartyBlog", "ScienceBlog");

    @Autowired
    BlogRepository blogRepository;

    @Autowired
    UserRepository userRepository;

    @Autowired
    PostRepository postRepository;

    @Transactional
    public void generateSampleData()      {
```

```
    this.initialized.compareAndSet(false, true);

        log.info("data being generated");
        List<Blog> blogs = new ArrayList<>();

        User user1 = new User( "Akira", "password", "none@none.com");
        User user2 = new User( "Lisa", "password", "none@none.com");
        User user3 = new User( "James", "password", "none@none.com");

        userRepository.save(user1);
        userRepository.refresh(user1);
        userRepository.save(user2);
        userRepository.refresh(user2);
        userRepository.save(user3);
        userRepository.refresh(user3);

        blogNames.forEach(name->{

            Blog blog = Blog.builder()
                    .name(name)
                    .guid(UUID.randomUUID())
                    .about("Sample blog")
                    .publishedAt(LocalDateTime.now()).build();

            blogRepository.save(blog);
            blogRepository.refresh(blog); //populate generated id
            blogs.add(blog);

            Post post1 = Post.builder()
                    .title("Lorem Ispum1")
                    .content("Sample content1")
                    .user(user1)
                    .blog(blog)
                    .postStatus(PostStatus.ACTIVE)
                    .build();

            Post post2 = Post.builder()
                    .title("Lorem Ispum2")
                    .content("Sample content2")
```

```
                    .user(user2)
                    .blog(blog)
                    .postStatus(PostStatus.ACTIVE)
                    .build();

            Post post3 = Post.builder()
                    .title("Lorem Ispum3")
                    .content("Sample content3")
                    .user(user3)
                    .blog(blog)
                    .postStatus(PostStatus.ACTIVE)
                    .build();
            postRepository.save(post1);
            postRepository.save(post2);
            postRepository.save(post3);

        });
        log.info("data generated");

    }
}

package com.example.blog_app.repository;

import com.example.blog_app.model.jpa.Blog;
import com.example.blog_app.repository.base.BaseRepository;

public interface BlogRepository extends BaseRepository<Blog, Long> {
}

public interface UserRepository extends BaseRepository<User, Long> {
}
```

Note BaseRepository can be ignored for the time being and will be explained in Section 3.2.7. For the time being, this can be assumed to be JpaRepository.

The preceding code creates two entries in the blog table—PartyBlog and ScienceBlog—with three users and each user creating three posts. Let's now define a TestCase class that will help us test the workings of these entity definitions (see Listing 3-13). Just for simplicity, the TestCase class (BlogJpaAppTests) extends a base test case class (BlogTestBase), which holds all the needed autowired components to keep the actual test class clean.

Listing 3-13. TestCase Base Class and BlogJpaAppTests Class

```
package com.example.blog_app;

import com.example.blog_app.helper.DataGenerator;
import com.example.blog_app.repository.BlogRepository;
import com.example.blog_app.repository.FileRepository;
import com.example.blog_app.repository.PostRepository;
import com.example.blog_app.repository.UserRepository;
import com.example.blog_app.service.UserCRUDService;
import org.springframework.beans.factory.annotation.Autowired;
import org.springframework.boot.test.web.client.TestRestTemplate;
import org.springframework.stereotype.Component;

@Component
public class BlogTestBase {

    @Autowired
    DataGenerator dataGenerator;

    @Autowired
    UserRepository userRepository;

    @Autowired
    UserCRUDService userCRUDService;

    @Autowired
    PostRepository postRepository;

    @Autowired
    BlogRepository blogRepository;
```

```
    @Autowired
    FileRepository fileRepository;

    @Autowired
     protected TestRestTemplate restTemplate;
}

package com.example.blog_app;

import com.example.blog_app.helper.DataGenerator;
import com.example.blog_app.repository.PostRepository;
import com.example.blog_app.repository.UserRepository;
import com.example.blog_app.service.UserCRUDService;
import lombok.extern.slf4j.Slf4j;
import org.junit.Assert;
import org.junit.Test;
import org.junit.runner.RunWith;
import org.springframework.beans.factory.annotation.Autowired;
import org.springframework.boot.test.context.SpringBootTest;
import org.springframework.boot.test.web.client.TestRestTemplate;
import org.springframework.test.annotation.Commit;
import org.springframework.test.context.ActiveProfiles;
import org.springframework.test.context.junit4.SpringRunner;
import org.springframework.transaction.annotation.Transactional;

import javax.annotation.PostConstruct;

import static org.assertj.core.api.Assertions.assertThat;

@RunWith(SpringRunner.class)
@SpringBootTest(webEnvironment = SpringBootTest.WebEnvironment.RANDOM_PORT)
@ActiveProfiles("test")
@Slf4j
public class BlogJpaAppTests extends BlogTestBase {
// Using BlogTestBase, just to abstract all declarations and keep test
case clean

private boolean generateData = true; // Update to generate sample data
```

```
@PostConstruct
public void init()  {
    log.info("Checking if already initialized");
    if(dataGenerator.getInitialized().get() == false && generateData)
        dataGenerator.generateSampleData();
}

    @Test
    @Transactional()
    @Commit
    public void testOneToManyDeletion() {
        log.info("Deleted user : {}", "Akira");
        userCRUDService.deleteUser("Akira");
            log.info("Printing all users");
        userRepository.findAll().stream().forEach(u->
                log.info("User: {}, {}", u.getId(), u.getUsername())
        );
        long count = userRepository.findAll().stream().filter(u ->
                "Akira".equals(u.getUsername())).count();
        Assert.assertEquals(0l, count); // should be 0 by now
    }
}
```

With the entity mappings in this code, this test case is going to delete all the data in the database, as explained previously. Let's see the corrections in the relationship fields to the Blog, Post, and User and the entities (see Listing 3-14).

Listing 3-14. Corrections in Entity Classes for Correct Cascade Operations

```
public class Blog {

    @OneToMany(fetch = FetchType.LAZY, cascade = CascadeType.ALL,
        orphanRemoval = true, mappedBy = "blog")
    private Set<Post> posts;

    @JsonIgnore
    @OneToMany(fetch = FetchType.LAZY, cascade = CascadeType.ALL,
        orphanRemoval = true)
```

```
        @JoinColumn(name = "blogId")
        private Set<User> users;
}

public class Post {

        // notice, cascade is removed thus no. operations will be cascaded down
        // Cascading will only happen from parent to child with this code
        // This could have been CascadeType.REFRESH as well
        @ManyToOne(fetch = FetchType.LAZY)
        @JoinColumn(name = "blog_id")
        private Blog blog;

        @ManyToOne(fetch = FetchType.LAZY) // same changes as above
        @JoinColumn(name = "author_id")
        private User user;
}

public class User {
        @OneToMany(fetch = FetchType.LAZY, cascade = {CascadeType.PERSIST,
CascadeType.MERGE, CascadeType.REMOVE}, mappedBy = "user", orphanRemoval =
true)
        private Set<Post> posts;
}
```

The previous block of code specifically mentions all cascade operations separately. Alternatively, they can also be used together:

```
public class User {
        @OneToMany(fetch = FetchType.LAZY, cascade = {CascadeType.ALL,
        mappedBy = "user", orphanRemoval = true)
        private Set<Post> posts;
}
```

Deletion issues are not very common, because in enterprise applications, data is not supposed to be hard deleted and hence no delete operations happen.

An @ManyToMany Example

We need to modify the POST entity and introduce a new entity called File (see Listing 3-15). That way, one POST can have multiple files (attachments) and one file can be linked to multiple POSTs. As an example, once a file is uploaded to the system, users should be able to attach it to any POST.

Listing 3-15. File Entity Definition and POST Entity Changes

```
package com.example.blog_app.model.jpa;

import com.fasterxml.jackson.annotation.JsonIgnore;
import lombok.*;

import javax.persistence.*;
import java.util.Set;

@Data
@Builder
@NoArgsConstructor
@AllArgsConstructor
@ToString(exclude = {"posts"})
@EqualsAndHashCode(exclude = {"posts"})
@Entity
public class File {

    @Id
    @GeneratedValue(strategy = GenerationType.IDENTITY)
    private Long id;
    private String name;

    @JsonIgnore
    @ManyToMany(cascade = {CascadeType.MERGE,CascadeType.REFRESH},
    fetch = FetchType.LAZY)
    @JoinTable(
        name = "post_files",joinColumns = {
        @JoinColumn(name = "file_id", referencedColumnName = "id")},
        inverseJoinColumns={
```

```
            @JoinColumn(name = "post_id", referencedColumnName = "id")})
    private Set<Post> posts;

}

package com.example.blog_app.model.jpa;

import com.fasterxml.jackson.annotation.JsonIgnore;
import lombok.*;
import org.hibernate.annotations.Type;

import javax.persistence.*;
import java.io.Serializable;
import java.util.Set;

@Data
@Builder
@NoArgsConstructor
@AllArgsConstructor
@ToString(exclude = {"blog", "user", "files"})
@EqualsAndHashCode(exclude = {"blog", "user", "files"})
@Entity
public class Post implements Serializable {

    @Id
    @GeneratedValue(strategy = GenerationType.IDENTITY)
    private Long id;
    private String title;
    private String content;

    @Column(name = "post_status")
    @Type(type = "com.example.blog_app.constants.PgEnumType",
        parameters = {@org.hibernate.annotations.Parameter(name =
        "enumClassName", value = "com.example.blog_app.model.jpa.
        PostStatus")})
    PostStatus postStatus;

    @ManyToOne(fetch = FetchType.LAZY)
    @JoinColumn(name = "blog_id")
    private Blog blog;
```

```
@JsonIgnore
@ManyToOne(fetch = FetchType.LAZY)
@JoinColumn(name = "author_id")
private User user;

@JsonIgnore
@ManyToMany(cascade = {CascadeType.MERGE,CascadeType.REFRESH},
fetch = FetchType.LAZY)
@JoinTable(
    name = "post_files",joinColumns = {
        @JoinColumn(name = "post_id", referencedColumnName = "id")},
    inverseJoinColumns={
        @JoinColumn(name = "file_id", referencedColumnName = "id")})
private Set<File> files;
}
```

In order to validate that this code is working, let's add one more method to our existing test case, shown in Listing 3-16. This method will create two new File objects, add them to a new POST object, and then save the POST object. With the association mappings, the File objects will be saved automatically along with the POST objects.

Listing 3-16. Test Case Updates

```
public class BlogJpaAppTests extends BlogTestBase {

/*
 By default Spring Framework rollbacks the updates made to database while
running test cases. Keeping annotation @Transactional to enable Spring
transaction support and @Commit specifically  to keep data persisted in the
DB after test run so that we can verify the results later from database as
well. I suggest the reader to try both variations.
*/
@Test
@Transactional
@Commit
public void testManyToManyWithPostAndFiles() {
```

```java
Post post = postRepository.findById(11).get();

File file = new File();
file.setName("main_image");
fileRepository.save(file);

File file1 = new File();
file1.setName("second_image");
fileRepository.save(file1);
fileRepository.refresh(file);
fileRepository.refresh(file1);

Set<File> files = post.getFiles();
if(files == null)
    files = new HashSet<>();
files.add(file);
files.add(file1);

post.setFiles(files);
postRepository.save(post);

List<File> allFiles = fileRepository.findAll();
allFiles.forEach(f->{
    Set<Post> posts = f.getPosts();
    posts.forEach(p->{
        log.info("Post : {} attached with file : {}", p.getTitle(),
        f.getName());
    });
});

post.getFiles().forEach(f->{
    log.info("File: {} attached to Post: {}", f.getName(), post.
    getTitle());
});
}
```

Running the Application

In order to see the queries that Hibernate is running in the background, we need to enable a property in the `application.yml` file before running the app, as follows:

```
spring:
  jpa:
    show-sql: true
```

After this change, when the test case runs, the queries will also be logged on the console, as shown in Figure 3-2.

Figure 3-2. *Console output for the test case run*

```
> gradle clean build
> gradle test

<<Skipping generic Spring Boot output>>
com.example.blog_app.BlogJpaAppTests        : File: main_image attached to
                                              Post: Lorem Ispum1

com.example.blog_app.BlogJpaAppTests        : File: second_image attached to
                                              Post: Lorem Ispum1
```

As a recap, we created two new File objects and saved them. We then added these persistent objects to the POST entity object and saved it. After that, we fetched all the File objects and listed its parent POST. Similarly, we listed the child File objects from the POST entity object.

Notes:

- We have just seen an @ManyToMany association example through a third table named post_files, but the related fields are directly embedded within each other. This is the advantage we talked about earlier—that navigation on both sides become easier.

- As per the Hibernate docs, the @ManyToMany annotation is rarely a good choice because it treats both sides as unidirectional associations.

- A better alternate is to have the @OneToMany associations to the link table in both entities. For our example, POST and File entities should have a @OneToMany association to the PostFile entity.

- There is also an approach to define @ManyToMany via an embeddable or composite key. We are skipping this as this is also a rare and complicated approach.

The @OneToOne Annotation

The @OneToOne associations are quite simple to understand and implement. The owning entity refers to the related entity through the reference column. The other entity refers to the owning entity through the mappedBy attribute. This is the case of bidirectional association. Let's look at an example with the User and Address objects (see Listing 3-17).

Listing 3-17. OneToOne Association Example

```
package com.example.blog_app.model.jpa;

import lombok.*;

import javax.persistence.*;
import java.io.Serializable;
import java.time.LocalDateTime;
import java.util.Set;
```

```java
@Data
@Builder
@NoArgsConstructor
@AllArgsConstructor
@ToString(exclude = {"posts"})
@EqualsAndHashCode(exclude = {"posts"})
@Entity
@Table(name = "`user`")
public class User implements Serializable {

    @Id
    @GeneratedValue(strategy = GenerationType.IDENTITY)
    private Long id;
    private Integer addressId;
    @OneToOne(cascade = CascadeType.ALL, fetch = FetchType.LAZY)
    @JoinColumn(name = "addressId", insertable = false, updatable = false)
    private Address address;
}

package com.example.blog_app.model.jpa;

import javax.persistence.*;

@Entity
public class Address {

    @Id
    @GeneratedValue(strategy = GenerationType.IDENTITY)
    private Long id;
    private String address;

    @OneToOne(mappedBy = "address")
    private User user;
}
```

Notes:

- If you define the referenced column in the same table where you are defining @JoinColumn, you need to mention the name attribute instead of referencedColumnName.

- That means the User table owns and is responsible for the relationship.

- If you create a field in an entity class by the name of the referenced column, you need to mark that field as not insertable and updatable in @JoinColumn.

- The other entity using mappedBy attributes denotes these entities as not responsible for the relationship and looks for the configuration of reference in the mapped field of the related entity.

Handling Array Types in PostgreSQL

PostgreSQL allows table columns to be defined as variable-length multidimensional arrays. Arrays of any built-in or user-defined base type, enum type, composite type, range type, or domain can be created. With Spring Data JPA, this can be implemented with Hibernate's UserType, just like we did to enable enums in Java. Let's see an example, with only the minimal code snippet (see Listing 3-18).

Listing 3-18. PgArrayType Definition

```
public class PgArrayType<T extends Serializable> implements UserType {

    @Override
    public Object nullSafeGet(ResultSet resultSet, String[] names,
    SharedSessionContractImplementor sharedSessionContractImplementor,
    Object o) throws
    HibernateException, SQLException {

        if (resultSet.wasNull()) {
            return null;
        }
        if (resultSet.getArray(names[0]) == null) {
            return new String[0];
        }

        Array array = resultSet.getArray(names[0]);
        @SuppressWarnings("unchecked")
```

```
      T javaArray = (T) array.getArray();
      return javaArray;
  }

  @Override
  public void nullSafeSet(PreparedStatement preparedStatement, Object
  value,
  int index, SharedSessionContractImplementor
  sharedSessionContractImplementor) throws
  HibernateException, SQLException {

    Connection connection = preparedStatement.getConnection();
    if (value == null) {
      preparedStatement.setNull(index, SQL_TYPES[0]);
    } else {
      @SuppressWarnings("unchecked")
      T castObject = (T) value;
      Array array = connection.createArrayOf(JDBCType.VARCHAR.getName(),
      (Object[]) castObject);
      preparedStatement.setArray(index, array);
    }
  }
}
```

There are a few other methods I skipped since they look very similar to PgEnumType, such as assemble() and disassemble(). The full working source code can be downloaded from the GitHub repo.

We also need to add an array type column in the POST table and add a @Type annotation to the top of the entity field (see Listing 3-19).

Listing 3-19. Schema and Entity Changes for Array Types

```
create table if not exists post (
  id serial primary key not null,
  blog_id int,
  title varchar(150),
  content text,
```

```
  "user" int,
  tags varchar[],
  postStatus post_status_enum default 'ACTIVE'
);

public class Post implements Serializable {
    @Id
    @GeneratedValue(strategy = GenerationType.IDENTITY)
    private Long id;

    @Type(type = "com.example.blog_app.constants.PgArrayType")
    private String[] tags;
}
```

These code arrays can seamlessly be stored and retrieved from PostgreSQL tables. To query these, native SQL will be required because this is a database-specific feature and JPA does not support it yet. There are various specific array functions provided by PostgreSQL to query them in SQL. Let's extend our BlogApp test case (see Listing 3-20) to test this.

Listing 3-20. TestCase and Sample SQL to Query Arrays

```
public class BlogJpaAppTests extends BlogTestBase {
    @Test
    @Transactional
    @Commit
    public void testForArrayTypes() {
        Post post = Post.builder()
            .title("Sample Title for arrays")
            .content("Sample content for arrays")
            .postStatus(PostStatus.ACTIVE)
            .tags(new String[] {"sample", "text"})
            .build();
        postRepository.save(post);
    }
}
```

The sample SQL to query this array would be as follows:

select * **from** post **where** tags @> '{text}'::**varchar**[];

Here is the output:

```
Name          |Value                    |
-----------   |-------------------------|
id            |43                       |
blog_id       |                         |
title         |Sample Title for arrays  |
content       |Sample content for arrays|
user          |                         |
tags          |{sample,text}            |
poststatus    |ACTIVE                   |
post_status   |ACTIVE                   |
author_id     |                         |
```

JPQL Queries and Pagination with Spring Data JPA

With Spring Data JPA, hardly any extra effort is required to run JPQL (Java Persistence Query Language) queries and map the results back to lists, entity objects, or optional return types. In order to run a custom query over a repository method, a @Query annotation is provided by Spring (see Listing 3-21). Any valid JPQL can be passed as a value for the annotation.

Listing 3-21. JPQL Query Example

```
@Query("Select p.id, p.title from Post p")
Optional<List<Post>> findPostWithIdAndTitle();
```

In order to provide pagination support, a PageRequest class, which is the implementation of the Pageable interface, is provided. This PageRequest object takes the page number and page size and sorts the direction and sort field.

The findAll() method in the PagingAndSortingRepository interface accepts this and returns a Page class return type, which can further return a List type through the getContent() method.

```
postRepository.findAll(PageRequest.of(page: 1,size: 10)).getContent();
```

The Pageable interface is injectable into any custom repository method and can directly return a List return type. As an example, see Listing 3-22.

Listing 3-22. Pageable Example

```
@Query("Select p.id, p.title from Post p")
List<Post> findPostWithIdAndTitle(PageRequest pageRequest);
```

The PageRequest class contains a Sort class, which further contains the Direction and Order static inner classes. Next, the previous navigation is available in the Page class.

Using a Common Base Repository

Many big applications need a base repository implementation in order to create common methods, like refreshing after saving. As a result, we populate the primary key ID and sometimes other auto-generated columns in the database. Ideally, JPA does this by default, but in case of transactions, the entity is populated back until the transaction ends or a commit happens because that is where flush() happens internally.

People may argue that the saveAndFlush() method can be used instead of save(). Calling saveAndFlush() earlier and having the method end manually may not be the right choice in a transaction, because that will hit Hibernate's internal optimizations. Developers can also call a find() or load() method after it has been saved, but there is often a need to save and read with multiple entities in a single method and a single transaction.

As an example, we used this technique in Section 3.2.5 in the DataGenerator class. We have its usage in DataGenerator, but let's now see how to write this base repository implementation (see Listing 3-23).

Listing 3-23. Base Repository Definition

```
package com.example.blog_app.repository.base;

import org.springframework.data.jpa.repository.JpaRepository;
import org.springframework.data.repository.NoRepositoryBean;

import java.io.Serializable;
```

```java
@NoRepositoryBean
public interface BaseRepository<T, ID extends Serializable> extends
JpaRepository<T, ID> {
    void refresh(T t);
}
```

```java
package com.example.blog_app.repository.base;

import org.springframework.data.jpa.repository.support.JpaEntityInformation;
import org.springframework.data.jpa.repository.support.SimpleJpaRepository;

import javax.persistence.EntityManager;
import org.springframework.transaction.annotation.Transactional;
import java.io.Serializable;

public class BaseRepositoryImpl<T, ID extends Serializable> extends
SimpleJpaRepository<T, ID> implements BaseRepository<T, ID> {

    private final EntityManager entityManager;

    public BaseRepositoryImpl(JpaEntityInformation entityInformation,
    EntityManager entityManager) {
        super(entityInformation, entityManager);
        this.entityManager = entityManager;
    }
    @Override
    @Transactional
    public void refresh(T t) {
        entityManager.refresh(t);
    }
}
```

```java
package com.example.blog_app.repository;

import com.example.blog_app.model.jpa.Blog;
import com.example.blog_app.repository.base.BaseRepository;

public interface BlogRepository extends BaseRepository<Blog, Long> {
}
```

Notes:

- Spring Data internally uses the `SimpleJpaRepository` class as the generic implementation to manage dynamic repository definitions of the custom repositories defined by the developer.

- We have a `BaseRepository` interface annotated with `@NoRepositoryBean`, which is a Spring convention to define a superclass for all repositories.

- We defined the `BaseRepositoryImpl` class as the definition of `BaseRepository`, which extends the `SimpleJpaRepository` class. We also added a `refresh()` method in this class.

- The `EntityManager` instance is already available to this object.

- All repositories extending this new `BaseRepository` interface will have access to all non-private common methods.

- If we remove this from the repositories, the `DataGenerator` class will not work. This is because we are inserting multiple entities in a transaction and using them within the method itself before the transaction commits at the end of the `DataGenerator.generateSampleData` method.

Summary

We learned about various options that work with different types of associations in JPA. Along with that, the examples in this chapter showed the correct usage of Jackson and Lombok annotations. We also explored using enums, UUIDs, and using array datatypes with PostgreSQL through JPA. At last, we saw a brief explanation of the Pagination API. In the next chapter, we will see advanced usage of the Spring Data JPA for important use cases related to performance, lazy loading issues, and so on.

PART II

Solving Advanced Persistence Problems and Microservices Communication Challenges

CHAPTER 4

Common Use Cases with JPA

So far, we have seen the basic setup of JPA along with Spring Data. In this chapter, we go through typical industry use cases and solutions with Spring Data JPA:

- Multi datasource interaction

- Solving the N+1 problem

- Native queries with results mapped to DTOs using constructor

- Native queries with results mapped to projections

- The Spring Converter Service role in native queries

- Concepts like entity lifecycle, ACID properties, CAP Theorem, and isolation levels

We will be creating a new application called eshop in this chapter. All subsections of this chapter update the code incrementally. The code structure of the application looks like this:

```
.
├── build.gradle
├── gradle
│   └── wrapper
│       ├── gradle-wrapper.jar
│       └── gradle-wrapper.properties
├── gradlew
├── gradlew.bat
```

© Raj Malhotra 2019
R. Malhotra, *Rapid Java Persistence and Microservices*, https://doi.org/10.1007/978-1-4842-4476-0_4

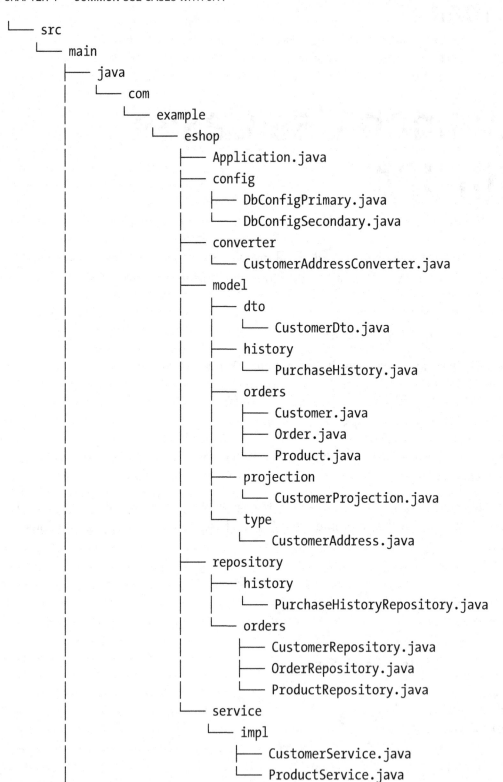

```
└── src
    └── main
        ├── java
        │   └── com
        │       └── example
        │           └── eshop
        │               ├── Application.java
        │               ├── config
        │               │   ├── DbConfigPrimary.java
        │               │   └── DbConfigSecondary.java
        │               ├── converter
        │               │   └── CustomerAddressConverter.java
        │               ├── model
        │               │   ├── dto
        │               │   │   └── CustomerDto.java
        │               │   ├── history
        │               │   │   └── PurchaseHistory.java
        │               │   ├── orders
        │               │   │   ├── Customer.java
        │               │   │   ├── Order.java
        │               │   │   └── Product.java
        │               │   ├── projection
        │               │   │   └── CustomerProjection.java
        │               │   └── type
        │               │       └── CustomerAddress.java
        │               ├── repository
        │               │   ├── history
        │               │   │   └── PurchaseHistoryRepository.java
        │               │   └── orders
        │               │       ├── CustomerRepository.java
        │               │       ├── OrderRepository.java
        │               │       └── ProductRepository.java
        │               └── service
        │                   └── impl
        │                       ├── CustomerService.java
        │                       └── ProductService.java
```

```
└── resources
    ├── application.properties
    └── application.yml
```

22 directories, 24 files

Multi-Datasource Interaction

This key feature in Spring Data JPA differentiates Java and Spring from other language frameworks, as this is not a basic need but a rare and potential feature in enterprise applications. Sometimes an application must talk to different databases at the same time. Let's create an ecommerce online bookshop as an example. We will be creating and storing customer, product, and orders data in MySQL and purchase history in PostgreSQL for the same microservice.

Functionally, we will simulate a flow to save new customer and product objects in the first step. Then we will purchase that product and use MySQL as the datastore. For the same purchase, we will store purchase history in a PostgreSQL database for analytics. Technically, this is going to involve:

- Creating separate datasource properties for connections.

- Creating two datasource and `entityManager` factory beans.

- Creating data or domain models and repositories, in different packages, for clarity. Entity classes and repositories are not required to be in different packages, but it's better to keep it consistent.

Let's the build the example application for our use case now.

Application Setup

Create a new application called `eshop-ch4` from `http://www.spring.io` with the following dependencies in the `build.gradle` file:

```
dependencies {
    compile ([
        "org.springframework.boot:spring-boot-starter-web",
        "org.springframework.boot:spring-boot-starter-jdbc",
```

```
            "org.springframework.boot:spring-boot-starter-data-jpa"
    ])
    compile ([
        "mysql:mysql-connector-java:8.0.15",
        "org.postgresql:postgresql:42.2.5",
        "org.projectlombok:lombok:1.18.6"
    ])
    testCompile("junit:junit")
    annotationProcessor 'org.projectlombok:lombok:1.18.6'
}
```

Datasource Configuration

All of the datasource-related properties are defined in application.yml or application.
properties, but we also need to define datasource Java beans in the Java config for our
use case. For a single datasource, the Java beans configuration step is not required and the
properties in the config are sufficient. The following code defines two distinct database
configurations comprised of datasource beans (LocalEntityManagerFactory) and
transaction managers, respectively. Listing 4-1 defines the configuration for the primary
datasource and Listing 4-2 relates to the secondary datasource.

Listing 4-1. Primary Database Configuration

```
package com.example.eshop.config;

import lombok.extern.slf4j.Slf4j;
import org.springframework.beans.factory.annotation.Qualifier;
import org.springframework.boot.autoconfigure.EnableAutoConfiguration;
import org.springframework.boot.context.properties.ConfigurationProperties;
import org.springframework.boot.jdbc.DataSourceBuilder;
import org.springframework.boot.orm.jpa.EntityManagerFactoryBuilder;
import org.springframework.context.annotation.Bean;
import org.springframework.context.annotation.Configuration;
import org.springframework.context.annotation.Primary;
import org.springframework.data.jpa.repository.config.
EnableJpaRepositories;
import org.springframework.jdbc.core.JdbcTemplate;
```

```java
import org.springframework.orm.jpa.JpaTransactionManager;
import org.springframework.orm.jpa.LocalContainerEntityManagerFactoryBean;
import org.springframework.transaction.PlatformTransactionManager;

import javax.persistence.EntityManagerFactory;
import javax.sql.DataSource;
import java.util.HashMap;
import java.util.Map;

@Configuration
@EnableAutoConfiguration
@EnableJpaRepositories(
        entityManagerFactoryRef = "entityManagerFactory",
        transactionManagerRef = "transactionManager",
        basePackages = { "com.example.eshop.repository.orders" })
@Slf4j
public class DbConfigPrimary {

   @Bean(name = "dataSource")
   @Primary
   @ConfigurationProperties(prefix = "spring.datasource.orders")
   public DataSource dataSourcePrimary() {
      return DataSourceBuilder.create().build();
   }

   @Primary
   @Bean(name = "entityManagerFactory")
   public LocalContainerEntityManagerFactoryBean entityManagerFactory(
         EntityManagerFactoryBuilder builder, @Qualifier("dataSource")
         DataSource dataSource)
   {
      return builder
            .dataSource(dataSource)
            .packages("com.example.eshop.model.orders")
            .persistenceUnit("orders")
            .properties(jpaProperties())
            .build();
   }
```

```java
    @Primary
    @Bean(name = "transactionManager")
    public PlatformTransactionManager transactionManager(
            @Qualifier("entityManagerFactory") EntityManagerFactory
                                                entityManagerFactory
    ) {
        return new JpaTransactionManager(entityManagerFactory);
    }

    private Map<String, Object> jpaProperties() {
        Map<String, Object> props = new HashMap<String, Object>();
        props.put("hibernte.ejb.naming_strategy", "org.hibernate.cfg.
        ImprovedNamingStrategy");
        props.put("hibernate.dialect", "org.hibernate.dialect.
        MySQL5InnoDBDialect");
        props.put("hibernate.hbm2ddl.auto", "create-drop");

        return props;
    }
}
```

The secondary configuration in Listing 4-2 looks like the previous one, only with constants and properties lookup changes.

Listing 4-2. Secondary Database Configuration

```java
package com.example.eshop.config;

import lombok.extern.slf4j.Slf4j;
import org.springframework.beans.factory.annotation.Qualifier;
import org.springframework.boot.context.properties.ConfigurationProperties;
import org.springframework.boot.jdbc.DataSourceBuilder;
import org.springframework.boot.orm.jpa.EntityManagerFactoryBuilder;
import org.springframework.context.annotation.Bean;
import org.springframework.context.annotation.Configuration;
import org.springframework.data.jpa.repository.config.
EnableJpaRepositories;
import org.springframework.orm.jpa.JpaTransactionManager;
```

```java
import org.springframework.orm.jpa.LocalContainerEntityManagerFactoryBean;
import org.springframework.transaction.PlatformTransactionManager;

import javax.persistence.EntityManagerFactory;
import javax.sql.DataSource;
import java.util.HashMap;
import java.util.Map;

@Configuration
@EnableJpaRepositories(
        entityManagerFactoryRef = "entityManagerFactoryHistory",
        transactionManagerRef = "transactionManagerHistory",
        basePackages = { "com.example.eshop.repository.history" })
@Slf4j
public class DbConfigSecondary {

    @Bean(name = "dataSourceHistory")
    @ConfigurationProperties(prefix = "spring.datasource.history")
    public DataSource dataSourceSecondary() {
        return DataSourceBuilder.create().build();
    }

    @Bean(name = "entityManagerFactoryHistory")
    public LocalContainerEntityManagerFactoryBean entityManagerFactory(
            EntityManagerFactoryBuilder builder, @Qualifier("dataSourceHistory")
            DataSource dataSource)
    {
        log.info("Secondary EM initialized");
        return builder
            .dataSource(dataSource)
            .packages("com.example.eshop.model.history")
            .persistenceUnit("history")
            .properties(jpaProperties())
            .build();

    }
```

```
  @Bean(name = "transactionManagerHistory")
  public PlatformTransactionManager transactionManager(
       @Qualifier("entityManagerFactoryHistory") EntityManagerFactory
       entityManagerFactory
  ) {
     return new JpaTransactionManager(entityManagerFactory);
  }

   private Map<String, Object> jpaProperties() {
       Map<String, Object> props = new HashMap<String, Object>();
       props.put("hibernte.ejb.naming_strategy", "org.hibernate.cfg.
       ImprovedNamingStrategy");
       props.put("hibernate.dialect", "org.hibernate.dialect.
       PostgreSQLDialect");
       props.put("hibernate.hbm2ddl.auto", "create-drop");
       return props;
   }
}
```

Notes:

- We are distinguishing the classes at three levels through packages in the code:

  a) On the top we are distinguishing the repository locations through the basePackages attribute in @EnableJpaRepositories annotation, as follows:

  - (From Listing 4-1.)

    ```
    @EnableJpaRepositories(
        entityManagerFactoryRef = "entityManagerFactory",
        transactionManagerRef = "transactionManager",
        basePackages = { "com.example.eshop.repository.orders" })
    ```

  - (From Listing 4-2.)

    ```
    @EnableJpaRepositories(
        entityManagerFactoryRef = "entityManagerFactoryHistory",
        transactionManagerRef = "transactionManagerHistory",
        basePackages = { "com.example.eshop.repository.history" })
    ```

b) DatasourceBuilder will look for properties with the spring.
    datasource.orders and spring.datasource.history
    prefixes in the primary and secondary configurations.

c) EntityManagerFactoryBuilder will build the bean
    using different packages, as marked in the line builder.
    packages("com.example.eshop.model.orders").

–   We also defined two distinct names for persistence units in this code.
    For example, the builder.persistenceUnit("orders") line in
    Listing 4-1 and the builder.persistenceUnit("history") line in
    Listing 4-2.

–   Defining transactionManager is quite self-explanatory except for the
    usage of @Qualifier, which is used in Spring to distinguish two
    beans with the same name or same types.

–   We are also using the @Primary annotations to declare beans as
    default datasources within the same Spring context.

Data Models and Repositories

As mentioned, we will define two separate packages for the models and repositories
to keep it clean. Listing 4-3 refers to the model classes for the primary and secondary
datasources.

Listing 4-3. Domain Model Definitions

```
package com.example.eshop.model.orders;

import java.io.Serializable;
import java.time.LocalDateTime;
import java.util.List;
import java.util.Set;
import javax.persistence.*;
import com.fasterxml.jackson.annotation.JsonIgnore;
import lombok.*;
```

```java
@Data
@Entity
@ToString(exclude = {"orders"})
@EqualsAndHashCode(exclude = {"orders"})
public class Customer implements Serializable {

    @Id
    @GeneratedValue(strategy=GenerationType.IDENTITY)
    private Long customerId;
    private String name, email, password;
    private LocalDateTime dateAdded;

    @JsonIgnore
    @OneToMany(fetch = FetchType.LAZY)
    @JoinColumn(name = "customerId")
    Set<Order> orders;
}

@Data
@Entity
public class Product implements Serializable {

    @Id
    @GeneratedValue(strategy=GenerationType.IDENTITY)
    private Long productId;
    private String name;
    private Integer price, quantity;
}

@Data
@Entity
@Table(name="CustomerOrder")
public class Order implements Serializable {

    @Id
    @GeneratedValue(strategy=GenerationType.IDENTITY)
    private Long orderId;
```

```java
    private Long productId, customerId;
    private int quantity, price;
}

package com.example.eshop.model.history;

@Data
@Entity
@Table(name="PurchaseHistory")
public class PurchaseHistory implements Serializable {

    @Id
    @GeneratedValue(strategy=GenerationType.IDENTITY)
    private Long id;
    private Long customerId, productId;
    private Date createdDate;
}
```

Listing 4-4 refers to the repositories for the primary and secondary datasources.

Listing 4-4. Repository Definitions

```java
package com.example.eshop.repository.orders;

import com.example.eshop.model.orders.Customer;
import org.springframework.data.jpa.repository.JpaRepository;
import org.springframework.data.jpa.repository.Query;

import java.util.List;
import java.util.Optional;

public interface CustomerRepository extends JpaRepository<Customer, Long>{ }

public interface OrderRepository extends JpaRepository<Order, Long>{ }

public interface ProductRepository extends JpaRepository<Product, Long> { }

package com.example.eshop.repository.history;
public interface PurchaseHistoryRepository extends
JpaRepository<PurchaseHistory, Long>{ }
```

Data model definitions are quite self-explanatory. We do not need any custom methods for our use case and thus we have the blank repository definitions in Listings 4-3 and 4-4.

Service Definitions

To support our use case, we need to define two service classes to handle the business logic, as shown in Listing 4-5.

Listing 4-5. Service Definition

```java
package com.example.eshop.service.impl;

import com.example.eshop.model.history.PurchaseHistory;
import com.example.eshop.model.orders.Product;
import com.example.eshop.repository.history.PurchaseHistoryRepository;
import com.example.eshop.repository.orders.ProductRepository;
import lombok.extern.slf4j.Slf4j;
import org.springframework.beans.factory.annotation.Autowired;
import org.springframework.stereotype.Service;
import org.springframework.transaction.annotation.Transactional;

import com.example.eshop.model.orders.Order;
import com.example.eshop.repository.orders.OrderRepository;

import java.util.Date;
import java.util.List;

@Service
@Slf4j
public class ProductService {

    @Autowired
    OrderRepository orderRepository;

    @Autowired
    ProductRepository productRepository;

    @Autowired
    PurchaseHistoryRepository purchaseHistoryRepository;
```

```java
@Transactional
public Boolean purchase(Long productId, Long customerId, int quantity,
int price) {
    Boolean success = Boolean.TRUE;
    Order order = new Order();
    order.setCustomerId(customerId);
    order.setProductId(productId);
    order.setPrice(price);
    order.setQuantity(quantity);
    orderRepository.save(order);
    return success;
}

@Transactional
public void saveHistory(Long customerId, Long productId)    {
    PurchaseHistory ph = new PurchaseHistory();
    ph.setCustomerId(customerId);
    ph.setProductId(productId);
    ph.setCreatedDate(new Date());
    purchaseHistoryRepository.save(ph);
}

public void registerNewProducts() {
    Product product = new Product();
    product.setName("Superb Java");
    product.setPrice(400);
    product.setQuantity(3);
    productRepository.save(product);
}

public List<Product> findAll() {
    return productRepository.findAll();
}
}
package com.example.eshop.service.impl;
```

```java
import com.example.eshop.model.orders.Customer;
import com.example.eshop.repository.orders.CustomerRepository;
import lombok.extern.slf4j.Slf4j;
import org.springframework.beans.factory.annotation.Autowired;
import org.springframework.stereotype.Service;
import org.springframework.transaction.annotation.Isolation;
import org.springframework.transaction.annotation.Propagation;
import org.springframework.transaction.annotation.Transactional;

import java.time.LocalDateTime;
import java.util.List;

@Service
@Slf4j
public class CustomerService {

    @Autowired
    CustomerRepository customerRepository;

    @Transactional(propagation=Propagation.REQUIRED,
    isolation=Isolation.DEFAULT)
    public void registerNewCustomers() {
        Customer customer = new Customer();
        customer.setName("Raj Malhotra");
        customer.setEmail("raj.malhotra@example.com");
        customer.setPassword("password");
        customer.setDateAdded(LocalDateTime.now());
        customerRepository.saveAndFlush(customer);
        log.info("All registered customers: " + customerRepository.findAll());
    }

    public List<Customer> findAll()     {
        return customerRepository.findAll();
    }
}
```

Just calling these service class methods will save transaction details in MySQL and its history in PostgreSQL within the same microservice. At last we need to define configuration properties. We will define the JPA related one in the `application.properties` file and the rest in `application.yml`, just to keep it more readable.

Notes:

- CustomerService has the methods to register a new example customer and fetch all the customers.

- ProductService has the methods to register new products, perform the purchase operation for the customer, and save the history of this transaction.

Application Configuration

In Listing 4-6, we enable auto-creation of the database on application startup. All the tables should be dropped after the app stops.

Listing 4-6. Configuration Files

application.properties

```
spring.datasource.orders.jdbcUrl=jdbc:mysql://localhost:3306/db1
spring.datasource.orders.username=root
spring.datasource.orders.password=mysql
spring.datasource.orders.driver-class-name: com.mysql.jdbc.Driver
spring.datasource.orders.dialect=org.hibernate.dialect.MySQL5InnoDBDialect

spring.datasource.history.jdbcUrl=jdbc:postgresql://localhost:5432/db2
spring.datasource.history.username=postgres
spring.datasource.history.password=postgres
spring.datasource.history.dialect=org.hibernate.dialect.PostgreSQLDialect

spring.jpa.hibernate.ddl-auto=create-drop
spring.jpa.properties.hibernate.jdbc.lob.non_contextual_creation: true
```

application.yml

```
server:
  context-path: /eshop
  port: 8080

spring:
  jpa:
    hibernate.ddl-auto: create-drop
    show-sql: true
    generate-ddl: true
```

We have seen most of these properties in the previous chapter, except for spring.jpa.properties.hibernate.jdbc.lob.non_contextual_creation. This is used to suppress a warning message that is started by the PostgreSQL JDBC driver. Implicitly, the java.sql.Connection is loaded in the JDBC driver class and does not cover the JDBC4 LOB creation methods.

Application Class

To validate this code, we create the Application class and execute service methods in the code in sequence (see Listing 4-7).

Listing 4-7. Application Class

```
package com.example.eshop;

import com.example.eshop.model.orders.Customer;
import com.example.eshop.repository.history.PurchaseHistoryRepository;
import com.example.eshop.repository.orders.CustomerRepository;
import com.example.eshop.repository.orders.OrderRepository;
import com.example.eshop.service.impl.CustomerService;
import com.example.eshop.service.impl.ProductService;
import lombok.extern.slf4j.Slf4j;
import org.springframework.beans.factory.annotation.Autowired;
import org.springframework.boot.CommandLineRunner;
import org.springframework.boot.SpringApplication;
import org.springframework.boot.autoconfigure.SpringBootApplication;
```

```java
import java.util.List;

@SpringBootApplication
@Slf4j
public class Application implements CommandLineRunner {

    @Autowired
    ProductService productService;
    @Autowired
    CustomerService customerService;

    @Autowired
    OrderRepository orderRepository;
    @Autowired
    CustomerRepository customerRepository;
    @Autowired
    PurchaseHistoryRepository purchaseHistoryRepository;

    public static void main(String[] args) throws Exception {
        SpringApplication.run(Application.class, args);
    }

    @Override
    public void run(String... strings) throws Exception {
        customerService.registerNewCustomers();
        productService.registerNewProducts();
        productService.purchase(1l, 1l, 2, 400);
        productService.saveHistory(1l, 1l);

        log.info("Customers {}", customerService.findAll());
        log.info("Products {}", productService.findAll());
        log.info("Orders {}", orderRepository.findAll());
        log.info("PurchaseHistory {}", purchaseHistoryRepository.findAll());
    }
}
```

Running the Application

Run the Gradle application from the command line using this command:

```
> gradle bootRun
```

```
<<Skipping generic Spring Boot output>>
com.example.eshop.Application : Customers [Customer(customerId=1,
name=Raj Malhotra, email=raj.malhotra@example.com, password=password,
dateAdded=2019-02-13T13:53:26)]
com.example.eshop.Application : Products [Product(productId=1, name=Superb
Java, price=400, quantity=3)]
com.example.eshop.Application : Orders [Order(orderId=1, productId=1,
customerId=1, quantity=2, price=400)]
com.example.eshop.Application : PurchaseHistory [PurchaseHistory(id=1,
customerId=1, productId=1, createdDate=2019-02-13 13:53:26.447)]
```

We have the log statements showing successful registration of the new customer
(Raj Malhotra) and product (Suberb Java). The next statement shows a successful order
made in MySQL. Finally, the last statement shows the history of orders maintained in the
PostgreSQL database.

Let's look at the database tables:

MYSQL:

```
> mysql -u root -pmysql -h localhost
mysql> create database db1;
mysql> use db1;
mysql> Select * from product;
+-----------+-------------+-------+----------+
| productId | name        | price | quantity |
+-----------+-------------+-------+----------+
|         1 | Superb Java |   400 |        3 |
+-----------+-------------+-------+----------+
```

PostgreSQL:

```
> psql "dbname=postgres host=localhost user=postgres password=postgres
port=5432"
```

```
> postgres=# create database db2;
> postgres=# \c db2;
> db2=# Select * from purchasehistory;
 id |        createddate        | customerid | productid
----+---------------------------+------------+-----------
  1 | 2019-03-31 20:58:53.433   |          1 |          1
```

In the following sections, we cover the application logs only in output.

Solving the N+1 Problem

A common problem we generally hear about with respect to ORMs is the N+1 problem. This is a misconception that N+1 problem happens only with ORMs. Rather, this is a generic data access issue that can happen while fetching data from RDBMS. Considering the example from the previous section, if we want to fetch a list of users along with their written posts, by default Hibernate is going to fire one query to fetch all the users and then N queries to fetch POSTs of each returned user object. This scenario is called the N+1 problem. If you are fetching data via JDBC in the form of a parent object list containing a child object list, the same problem persists there. There are three ways to query with JPA on entities with associations to overcome this problem:

- Fetch using the left fetch join clause in JPQL

- Fetch user objects first and then fetch POST objects for these users separately

- Fetch as a single combined result mapped to DTOs with a native query

Fetching by Using the Left Fetch Join Clause in JPQL

This method is going to add a left outer join in the generated query, resulting in a Cartesian product of the joined tables. ORM will further map the results back to parent and child entity lists. To see this in action, we need to change the CustomerRepository code from the previous section. In Listing 4-8, we add a new custom method with a JPQL query and execute it from the Application class as an example.

Listing 4-8. CustomerRepository and Application Changes

```java
public interface CustomerRepository extends JpaRepository<Customer, Long>{
        /* N+1 example */
            @Query("Select c from Customer c left join fetch c.orders")
            List<Customer> findCustomersWithOrderDetails();
}

@SpringBootApplication
@Slf4j
public class Application implements CommandLineRunner {

            @Autowired
            ProductService productService;

            @Autowired
            CustomerService customerService;

            @Autowired
            OrderRepository orderRepository;

            @Autowired
            CustomerRepository customerRepository;

            @Autowired
            PurchaseHistoryRepository purchaseHistoryRepository;

@Override
public void run(String... strings) throws Exception {
   customerService.registerNewCustomers();
   productService.registerNewProducts();
   productService.purchase(1l, 1l, 2, 400);
   productService.saveHistory(1l, 1l);

   log.info("Customers {}", customerService.findAll());
   log.info("Products {}", productService.findAll());
   log.info("Orders {}", orderRepository.findAll());
   log.info("PurchaseHistory {}",
       purchaseHistoryRepository.findAll());
           nPlusOneExample();
       }
```

```
public void nPlusOneExample()    {
    List<Customer> customerList =
    customerRepository.findCustomersWithOrderDetails();
    log.info("Customers List with Order Details: {}",
    customerList);
  }
}
```

Running the Eshop Application Again

When we run the previous code, it is going to generate a single Hibernate query instead of multiple ones and print the query in the console:

```
> gradle bootRun
<<Skipping generic Spring Boot output>>
```

com.example.eshop.Application : Starting Application on Rajs-MacBook-Pro. local with PID 38997 (started by raj in /Users/raj/work_all/book_ code/ rapid-java-persistence-and-microservices/ch4/eshop-ch4)

Hibernate: select distinct customer0_.customerId as customer1_0_0_, orders1_.orderId as orderId1_1_1_, customer0_.dateAdded as dateAdde2_0_0_, customer0_.email as email3_0_0_, customer0_.name as name4_0_0_, customer0_.password as password5_0_0_, orders1_.customerId as customer2_1_1_, orders1_.price as price3_1_1_, orders1_.productId as productI4_1_1_, orders1_.quantity as quantity5_1_1_, orders1_. customerId as customer2_1_0__, orders1_.orderId as orderId1_1_0__ from Customer customer0_ left outer join CustomerOrder orders1_ on customer0_. customerId=orders1_.customerId

com.example.eshop.Application : Customer Order Details: [Customer(customerId=1, name=Raj Malhotra, email=raj. malhotra@example.com, password=password, dateAdded=2019-03-31T15:16:40, customerAddress=null, orders=[Order(orderId=1, productId=1, customerId=1, quantity=2, price=400)])]

The preceding query is going to generate a flat resultset comprised of all the fields combined from the joined tables. Hibernate is going to filter out the repeating rows/ columns and map the left to the respective objects.

Fetching the User Objects First and Then Fetching the Post Objects for These Users Separately

As an easy alternative, we can fetch the user object list in the first step and then the related POST objects list in the second query. There are two problems with this approach:

- The second query will have to be run using an IN clause, which is not considered good practice. The IN clause in databases are generally rewritten using OR clauses, which may cause the database to reparse and rebuild the execution plan each time arguments change. If the target column is indexed and there are only a few arguments, you still should get decent performance.

- Client code will have to iterate over two separate lists.

Fetching as a Single Combined Result Mapped to DTOS with a Native Query

With this technique, a custom query can be executed with outer joins and the results can be mapped to a single object list. This means there is no nested parent-child object structure and a few fields may have the same values throughout the list.

JPA Querying with Constructor Mapping

There are multiple solutions for mapping back results from a JPA query to any entity object or entity objects list in JPA 2.2. The simplest of them is using a constructor provided by any custom POJO. Let's see an example in Listing 4-9.

Listing 4-9. DTO and CustomerRepository

```
package com.example.eshop.model.dto;

import lombok.Data;
```

```java
@Data
@AllArgsConstructor
public class CustomerDto {
    private Integer id;
    private String name;
}

public interface CustomerRepository extends JpaRepository<Customer, Long>{

    // Query example with Constructor mapping
    @Query(value = "Select new com.example.eshop.model.dto.CustomerDto(c.id,
    c.name) from Customer c")
    List<CustomerDto> findCustomers();
}

@SpringBootApplication
@Slf4j
public class Application implements CommandLineRunner {
@Override
    public void run(String... strings) throws Exception {
        constructorMappingExample();
    }

    public void constructorMappingExample() {
        List<CustomerDto> customersList = customerRepository.
        findCustomers();
        log.info("Customers List with Constructors mapped query results
        : {}", customersList);
    }
}
```

Notes:

- We added a new class CustomerDto to the codebase. This class does not have entity annotations and exactly maps to the needs of the frontend app with specific attributes only. This class is also expected to have a constructor with all fields that are required to be populated by query results mapping.

- We also added a new method in `CustomerRepository` with a custom query on top of it through the @Query annotation.

- In the JPQL query, we directly created a new Java object through its `com.example.eshop.model.dto.CustomerDto(c.id, c.name)` constructor.

Running the Eshop Application Again for the Constructor Mapping Use Case

Run the application:

```
> gradle clean build
> gradle bootRun
```

```
<<Skipping generic Spring Boot output>>
```

```
com.example.eshop.Application : Customers List with Constructors mapped
query results: [CustomerDto(id=1, name=Raj Malhotra)]
```

JPA Querying with Mapping to Projections

Spring Data can also return a projection or a mapped interface of any entity as the result of a JPQL. Projections are simple to implement in Spring Data. The easiest way is by declaring an interface that exposes accessor methods for the properties to be read. These interfaces can be nested as well. Let's see this through the example in Listing 4-10.

Listing 4-10. Projections Example

```
package com.example.eshop.model.projection;

import org.springframework.beans.factory.annotation.Value;

public interface CustomerProjection {
    String getName();
    String getEmail();

    @Value("#{target.name + '_' + target.email}")
    String getCustomerNameWithEmail();
}
```

```java
package com.example.eshop.repository.orders;

import com.example.eshop.model.dto.CustomerDto;
import com.example.eshop.model.orders.Customer;
import com.example.eshop.model.projection.CustomerProjection;
import org.springframework.data.jpa.repository.JpaRepository;
import org.springframework.data.jpa.repository.Query;

import java.util.Collection;
import java.util.List;

public interface CustomerRepository extends JpaRepository<Customer, Long>{

    /* N+1 example */
    @Query("Select c from Customer c left join fetch c.orders")
    List<Customer> findCustomersWithOrderDetails();

    // Query example with Constructor mapping
    @Query(value = "Select new com.example.eshop.model.dto.CustomerDto(c.id,
    c.name) from  Customer c")
    List<CustomerDto> findCustomers();

    // Projection examples
    @Query("Select c from Customer c")
    List<CustomerProjection> findAllCustomers();
    CustomerProjection findOneByName(String name);
}
```

Notes:

- We defined the Projection interface in this code with attributes
  matching names from the original entity object (customer) list,
  returned.

- With this interface definition, Spring creates a proxy of projection
  interfaces on the fly, does the mapping, and returns these proxies as
  output.

- Spring allows providing SpEL (Spring expression language) expres-
  sions on top of these accessor methods to manipulate the results. As
  an example, we have SpEL concatenate the name and email on top of
  the getCustomerNameWithEmail() method. The target field in this
  expression is mapped to the returned object by Spring.

- Projections work just on the basis of returned objects. Thus any
  Spring Data DSL-based method will also work. This is shown through
  the findOneByName(String name) example method in Listing 4-10.

We also need to change the Application class, shown in Listing 4-11, to test the code
in Listing 4-10.

Listing 4-11. Application Class

```
@SpringBootApplication
@Slf4j
public class Application implements CommandLineRunner {

    @Autowired
    CustomerRepository customerRepository;

    public static void main(String[] args) throws Exception {
        SpringApplication.run(Application.class, args);
    }

    @Override
    public void run(String... strings) throws Exception {

        projectionsExample();

        List<CustomerProjection> customers = customerRepository.
        findWithOrders();
        log.info("Customers with Orders");
        customers.forEach(customer -> {
            log.info("Customer Name: {}", customer.
            getCustomerNameWithEmail());
            //log.info("Order: {}", customer.getOrderProjection().getPrice());
        });
```

```java
        log.info("Customer again: {}",
                customerRepository.findOneProjectedByName("Raj Malhotra").
                getCustomerNameWithEmail());
    }

    public void projectionsExample() {
        List<CustomerProjection> customers =
                        customerRepository.findAllCustomers();
        log.info("Customers List with Projections");
        customers.forEach(customer -> {
            log.info("Customer Name: {}",
                    customer.getCustomerNameWithEmail());
        });

        log.info("Find Single Customer : {}",
                customerRepository.findOneByName("Raj Malhotra").
                getCustomerNameWithEmail());
    }
}
```

Running the Eshop Application Again for the Projections Use Case

Run the application:

```
> gradle clean build
> gradle bootRun
```

```
<<Skipping generic Spring Boot output>>
INFO 40196 --- [                main] com.example.eshop.Application             :
No active profile set, falling back to default profiles: default
Hibernate: drop table if exists Customer
Hibernate: drop table if exists CustomerOrder
Hibernate: drop table if exists Product
Hibernate: create table Customer (customerId bigint not null auto_
increment, customerAddress varchar(255), dateAdded datetime, email
varchar(255), name varchar(255), password varchar(255), primary key
(customerId)) engine=InnoDB
```

```
Hibernate: create table CustomerOrder (orderId bigint not null auto_
increment, customerId bigint, price integer not null, productId bigint,
quantity integer not null, primary key (orderId)) engine=InnoDB
Hibernate: create table Product (productId bigint not null auto_
increment, name varchar(255), price integer, quantity integer, primary key
(productId)) engine=InnoDB
INFO 40196 --- [           main] c.e.eshop.config.DbConfigSecondary:
Secondary EM initialized

INFO 40196 --- [           main] com.example.eshop.Application : Customers
List with Constructors mapped query results: [CustomerDto(id=1, name=Raj
Malhotra)]
INFO 40196 --- [           main] com.example.eshop.Application: Customers
List with Projections
INFO 40196 --- [           main] com.example.eshop.Application: Projections
Example, Customer Name With Email: Raj malhotra_raj.malhotra@example.com
INFO 40196 --- [           main] com.example.eshop.Application: Projections
Example, Find Single Customer : Raj Malhotra_raj.malhotra@example.com
```

With this output, we can see that Spring has combined name and email of the returned Customer objects and then has returned the output as a string—Raj Malhotra_raj.malhotra@example.com.

Spring Converter Service

The Spring Framework provides an interesting service that may help you treat a custom class as an entity field. This service will manage its conversion back and forth from database specific datatype to Java-based types. Consider the example in Listing 4-12 to see this in the User class.

Listing 4-12. CustomerAddress Type

```
package com.example.eshop.model.type;

import lombok.Data;
import java.io.Serializable;
```

```
@Data
public class CustomerAddress implements Serializable {
    private String streetAddress;
    private String city;
    private String country;
}
```

Listing 4-12 defines a new class that should be treated as a datatype for our entity model as a composite object. The JDBC driver can handle the native datatypes, but custom classes cannot be mapped to object fields as datatypes. By using the Spring converter service, we can define how the Spring Framework converts/serializes the object fields into a single data element. Further, we can define how they should be decomposed and mapped to the fields object. As an example, we convert the CustomerAddress object fields into a comma-separated string and then convert them back (see Listing 4-13).

Listing 4-13. Type Converter

```
package com.example.eshop.converter;

import com.example.eshop.model.type.CustomerAddress;
import javax.persistence.AttributeConverter;

public class CustomerAddressConverter implements
AttributeConverter<CustomerAddress, String> {

    @Override
    public String convertToDatabaseColumn(CustomerAddress customerAddress) {
        if(customerAddress == null)
            return "";
        return  customerAddress.getStreetAddress() + ", " +
                customerAddress.getCity() + ", " +
                customerAddress.getCountry();
    }

    @Override
    public CustomerAddress convertToEntityAttribute(String value) {
        CustomerAddress customerAddress = null;
```

```
        if(value != null && value.contains(",")) {
            String[] tokens = value.split(",");
            customerAddress = new CustomerAddress();
            customerAddress.setStreetAddress(tokens[0]);
            customerAddress.setCity(tokens[1]);
            customerAddress.setCountry(tokens[2]);
        }
        return customerAddress;
    }
}
```

The convertToDatabaseColumn method converts the object to a string and the convertToEntityAttribute method does the opposite. Let's see how to use this class in Listing 4-14.

Listing 4-14. Customer Entity Changes

```
package com.example.eshop.model.orders;

import java.io.Serializable;
import java.time.LocalDateTime;
import java.util.List;
import java.util.Set;

import javax.persistence.*;

import com.example.eshop.converter.CustomerAddressConverter;
import com.example.eshop.model.type.CustomerAddress;
import com.fasterxml.jackson.annotation.JsonIgnore;
import lombok.*;

@Data
@Entity
@ToString(exclude = {"orders"})
@EqualsAndHashCode(exclude = {"orders"})
public class Customer implements Serializable {

    @Id
    @GeneratedValue(strategy=GenerationType.IDENTITY)
    private Long customerId;
```

```
private String name, email, password;
private LocalDateTime dateAdded;

@Column
@Convert(converter = CustomerAddressConverter.class)
CustomerAddress customerAddress;

@JsonIgnore
@OneToMany(fetch = FetchType.LAZY)
@JoinColumn(name = "customerId")
Set<Order> orders;
}
```

Notice in this code that we added a new field and marked it with an @Convert annotation.

```
@Column
@Convert(converter = CustomerAddressConverter.class)
CustomerAddress customerAddress;
```

While saving and fetching the customer entity, the Spring Data JPA will do this conversion back and forth implicitly.

Important JPA Concepts

Before ending our review of the common use cases and solutions with Spring Data JPA, let's quickly recap some of the concepts that can improve our understanding of the JPA internals.

JPA Managed Entity and Its Lifecycle

Managed entity objects are in-memory instances of entity classes (persistable user-defined classes), which can represent physical objects in the database. We will not go into the details of JPA standard specification, but let's review the managed object's lifecycle, as shown in Figure 4-1, and then continue with our examples.

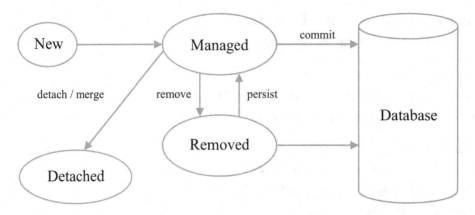

Figure 4-1. *JPA entity object lifecycle*

When an entity object is initially created, its state is New. An entity object becomes Managed when it is persisted to the database. When the Managed object is modified, its change is detected by the owning EntityManager, which is managed by Spring. Changes are propagated to the database upon the commit transaction. When the object is retrieved and marked for deletion, it is marked in the REMOVED state. Any associated objects that are preloaded in memory are also marked for deletion. The last state, called DETACHED, comes when the EntityManager is closed.

Callback methods also provided within the JPA specification that allow users to perform operations before an object enters the respective state. These methods are annotated with the following annotations:

- @PrePersist/@PostPersist

- @PreRemove/@PostRemove

- @PreUpdate/@PostUpdate

- @PostLoad

Use cases:

- One typical use case for these methods is to log or mark timestamps for auditing.

- Another could be to trigger any other functionality upon updating any object.

Isolation Levels, Locking, and Performance

Isolation levels are important for deciding transaction strategies, locking behavior, and given database performance in highly concurrent or high read-write rate based applications involving transactions.

Let's quickly review the data reading-related behaviors in transactions.

Data Read Phenomena

- **Dirty read:** You're permitted to read uncommitted or dirty data. Dirty reads occur when one transaction T1 is changing the record, and the other transaction T2 can read this record before the first transaction has been committed or rolled back. There is a possibility that transaction T1 has read some data that which may not exist anymore because transaction T2 has rolled back. Data integrity is compromised, foreign keys are violated, and unique constraints are ignored.

- **Nonrepeatable read:** This simply means data read in course of a transaction is not always repeatable within the same transaction, if read again. If you read a row at time T1 and try to reread that same row at time T2, the row may have changed within the same transaction by some other transaction. The same rows may have disappeared or updated.

- **Phantom read:** This means that if you execute a query at time T1 and re-execute it at time T2, additional rows may have been added to the database, which may affect your results. This differs from a nonrepeatable read, where in a phantom read, data you have already read has not been changed. Instead, more data might possibly satisfy your query criteria than before.

Isolation Levels

Data isolation levels help ensure the right balance between database performance and maintaining ACID properties while updating data in the database. The higher the isolation level, the lower the performance. Based on these behaviors, the SQL standard defines four isolation levels:

READ_UNCOMITTED

>   Read variations: Dirty reads, non-repeatable reads, phantom reads
>
>   Performance: Highest even in highly concurrent environment
>
>   Locking: None
>
>   Supported by: MYSQL (InnoDB), MSSQL

READ_COMMITTED

>   Read variations: Non-repeatable reads, phantom reads
>
>   Performance: Good even in a highly concurrent environment
>
>   Locking: Shared locks are acquired only for selects or concerned rows
>
>   Supported by: MYSQL (Innodb), MSSQL (default), ORACLE (default), POSTGRESQL (default)

REPEATABLE READ

>   Read variations: Phantom reads
>
>   Performance: Slower, in highly concurrent environment
>
>   Locking: Shared locks are acquired on selected rows; if transaction retries, new changes (any new rows inserted) will be visible
>
>   Supported by: MYSQL (Innodb - default), MSSQL, POSTGRESQL

SERIALIZABLE

Read variations: Phantom reads

Performance: Slowest, in highly concurrent environment

Locking: Shared locks are acquired for whole table; even if transaction retries, new changes (any new rows inserted) will not be visible

Supported by: MYSQL (Innodb), MSSQL, ORACLE, POSTGRESQL

There are two additional non-ANSI/SQL ISO standard isolation levels:

READ-ONLY: Supported by Oracle read-only transactions; we see only those changes that were committed at the time the transaction began. Does not allow INSERT, UPDATE, and DELETE statements.

SNAPSHOT: Similar to Serializable but internally this happens through versioning of data rows per transaction (optimistic concurrency model) and no locking happens. If new versions are found, the transaction is rolled back.

With JPA, we can specify the isolation level through an @Transactional annotation (@Transactional(isolation=Isolation.DEFAULT)), which can help tune the concurrency control based on need.

Table 4-1 shows the possible values we can specify within the @Transactional annotation in Spring for quick reference.

Table 4-1. *Tabular Comparison of Data Read Behavior*

Isolation Level	Dirty Read	Nonrepeatable Read	Phantom Read
Read_Uncommitted	Possible	Possible	Possible
Read_Committed	Not possible	Possible	Possible
Repeatable_Read	Not possible	Not possible	Possible
Serializable	Not possible	Not possible	Not possible

Interesting JPA Properties

With the following properties, we can customize the logging behavior of Hibernate and Spring.

- `spring.jpa.hibernate.show-sql=true`

  This is used by Hibernate to log generated SQL queries in logs.

- `spring.jpa.properties.hibernate.format_sql=true`

  This is used to print SQL in a formatted form.

- `spring.jpa.properties.hibernate.use_sql_comments=true`

  With this property, Hibernate will put comments in all generated SQL statements to hint at what the generated SQL is trying to do.

- `spring.jpa.properties.hibernate.generate_statistics=true`

  With this property, Hibernate will start generating statistics for all the SQL queries executed.

- `logging.pattern.console=[%thread] %-5level %msg%n`

  This is not from JPA; we are just showing this to simplify logging.

Running the Eshop Application for the JPA Properties

After making these changes to the `application.yml` or `application.properties` file in the code for this chapter, we will see the following changes on the console:

```
> gradle clean build
> gradle bootRun

<<Skipping generic Spring Boot output>>

:: Spring Boot ::        (v2.1.3.RELEASE)
[main] INFO  No active profile set, falling back to default profiles: default
[main] INFO  Bootstrapping Spring Data repositories in DEFAULT mode.
[main] INFO  Finished Spring Data repository scanning in 66ms. Found 3
repository interfaces.
```

[main] INFO   Bootstrapping Spring Data repositories in DEFAULT mode.
[main] INFO   Finished Spring Data repository scanning in 6ms. Found 1
repository interfaces.
[main] INFO   Tomcat initialized with port(s): **8080** (http)
[main] INFO   Starting Servlet engine: [Apache Tomcat/**9.0.14**]
[main] INFO   The APR based Apache Tomcat Native library which allows optimal
performance in production environments was not found on the java.library.
path:
[/Users/raj/Library/Java/Extensions:/Library/Java/
Extensions:/Network/Library/Java/Extensions:/System/Library/Java/
Extensions:/usr/lib/java:.]
[main] INFO   Initializing Spring embedded WebApplicationContext
[main] INFO   Root WebApplicationContext: initialization completed in 1967 ms
[main] INFO   HikariPool-1 - Starting...
[main] INFO   HikariPool-1 - Start completed.
[main] INFO   HHH000204: Processing PersistenceUnitInfo [
        name: orders
        ...]
[main] INFO   HHH000412: Hibernate Core {**5.3.7.Final**}
[main] INFO   HHH000206: hibernate.properties not found
[main] INFO   HCANN000001: Hibernate Commons Annotations {**5.0.4.Final**}
[main] INFO   HHH000400: Using dialect: org.hibernate.dialect.
MySQL5InnoDBDialect
[main] INFO   HHH000421: Disabling contextual LOB creation as hibernate.
jdbc.lob.non_contextual_creation is true
Hibernate:
    drop table if exists Customer
Hibernate:
    drop table if exists CustomerOrder
Hibernate:
    drop table if exists Product
Hibernate:
    create table Customer (
       customerId bigint not null auto_increment,
       customerAddress varchar(255),
       dateAdded datetime,

111

```
        email varchar(255),
        name varchar(255),
        password varchar(255),
        primary key (customerId)
    ) engine=InnoDB
```

[main] INFO   HHH000397: Using ASTQueryTranslatorFactory
[main] INFO   Tomcat started on port(s): **8080** (http) with context path "
[main] INFO   Started Application in 5.638 seconds (JVM running for 6.105)
Hibernate:

    /* insert com.example.eshop.model.orders.Customer

```
        */ insert
        into
            Customer
            (customerAddress, dateAdded, email, name, password)
        values
            (?, ?, ?, ?, ?)
```

[main] INFO   Session Metrics {
    16418 nanoseconds spent acquiring 1 JDBC connections;
    0 nanoseconds spent releasing 0 JDBC connections;
    140914 nanoseconds spent preparing 1 JDBC statements;
    730309 nanoseconds spent executing 1 JDBC statements;
    0 nanoseconds spent executing 0 JDBC batches;
    0 nanoseconds spent performing 0 L2C puts;
    0 nanoseconds spent performing 0 L2C hits;
    0 nanoseconds spent performing 0 L2C misses;
    92495 nanoseconds spent executing 1 flushes (flushing a total of 1 entities and 0 collections);
    0 nanoseconds spent executing 0 partial-flushes (flushing a total of 0 entities and 0 collections)
}
Hibernate:

    /* insert com.example.eshop.model.orders.Order

```
        */ insert
        into
            CustomerOrder
```

```
            (customerId, price, productId, quantity)
        values
            (?, ?, ?, ?)
Hibernate:
    /* insert com.example.eshop.model.history.PurchaseHistory
        */ insert
        into
            PurchaseHistory
            (createdDate, customerId, productId)
        values
            (?, ?, ?)
[main] INFO  Customers [Customer(customerId=1, name=Raj Malhotra,
[main] INFO  Customers with Orders
[main] INFO  Customer Name: Raj Malhotra_raj.malhotra@example.com
Hibernate:
    /* select
        generatedAlias0
    from
        Customer as generatedAlias0
    where
        generatedAlias0.name=:param0 */ select
            customer0_.customerId as customer1_0_,
            customer0_.customerAddress as customer2_0_,
            customer0_.dateAdded as dateAdde3_0_,
            customer0_.email as email4_0_,
            customer0_.name as name5_0_,
            customer0_.password as password6_0_
        from
            Customer customer0_
        where
            customer0_.name=?
[main] INFO  Customer again: Raj Malhotra_raj.malhotra@example.com

<============----> 75% EXECUTING [53s]
> :bootRun
```

I skipped a few output lines to avoid repetition. We can see in this output that Hibernate has:

- Printed the formatted queries.

- Added comments to explain the queries.

- Printed the time taken while executing the queries.

These features can be helpful in debugging the application for looking up the generated queries and optimizing them as well.

Summary

In this chapter, we saw solutions for some of the common problems where Spring Data JPA can be very helpful. We skipped the techniques to run Native SQL queries with Spring Data JPA, as I wanted to show the newer solutions available today. In the next chapter, we explore some of the solutions other than JPA for general data access.

CHAPTER 5

Java Persistence Without ORMs

We have so far taken a quick walkthrough of the Spring Data JPA, with mostly positive use cases. There are also a few downsides to use an ORM framework. With today's growing demand for scaling applications, it becomes important to discuss such issues with ORMs. This chapter considers the performance-related problems of ORMs when applications grow to a scale beyond ordinary limits:

- For each operation, the ORM framework has to manage the lifecycle of an entity, leading to extra overhead. As an example, if the entity is transient, persistent, or detached, Hibernate will put extra checks and ensure consistency in all state-changing events.

- The cost of creating SQL queries from JPQL or when operations are performed on entities is additional overhead.

- Database-specific SQL optimizations are hard to manage. Each vendor has certain variations that are hard to support in any ORM. This can limit fine-tuning of queries.

- Along with the domain objects or entities, we also need DTO (data transfer object) classes and we need to do mapping, which affects overall performance. This extra codebase makes maintenance more costly. There are a few general reasons as to why a separate DTO layer is required:

  - DTOs are tied very close to the UI/client layer or use cases and thus they may have extra and/or fewer attributes than the domain model.

  - There is no tight contract between UI data needs and backend data management, which makes a life bit easier.

© Raj Malhotra 2019
R. Malhotra, *Rapid Java Persistence and Microservices*, https://doi.org/10.1007/978-1-4842-4476-0_5

- Sometimes, for security reasons, attributes must be restricted to be sent back to clients, although @JsonIgnore is the option with entities as well.

- Changes in the domain model can happen without changing the DTO classes.

As an alternative to ORMs in Java, we look for solutions that give us the flexibly to fire native queries to SQL databases and help map results back to objects. Within the Spring framework, we have quite a few options to achieve this:

- Spring Data JPA native queries support

- JDBCTemplate

- Spring Data JDBC

Integration with other frameworks is possible, like with MyBatis and JOOQ, but we focus on the ones created by the Spring community. The advantage is consistency in APIs and easier integration. We discussed Spring Data JPA native queries support in a previous chapter. Let's learn about the JDBCTemplate and Spring Data JDBC in the next section.

Spring JDBC Template

The Spring JDBCTemplate is the API created by the Spring Framework that performs native SQL queries on relational databases and maps the results back to custom Java objects. Let's look at a very small example to recreate our Eshop app, connecting it to a MySQL DB. We will query customers, products purchased, and order information in a single query. This result should be mapped to a single DTO class called CustomerOrder using the following steps:

1. Create a Gradle-based application

2. Initialize and run sample SQL queries to fill the Customer, Product, and Order tables.

3. Define a new DTO called CustomerOrder.

4. Run a SQL query and map the results back to the object model; i.e., a list called CustomerOrder.

Let's build an application with the following code structure:

`eshop-jdbc-template-ch5`

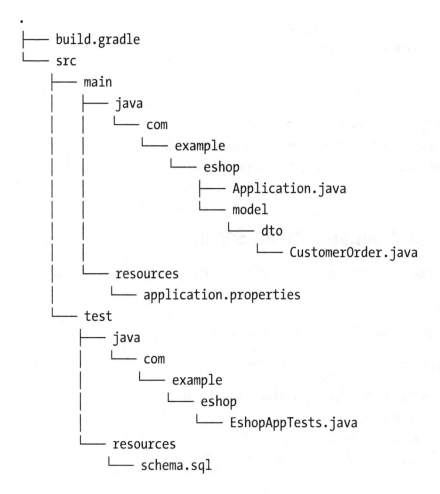

```
.
├── build.gradle
└── src
    ├── main
    │   ├── java
    │   │   └── com
    │   │       └── example
    │   │           └── eshop
    │   │               ├── Application.java
    │   │               └── model
    │   │                   └── dto
    │   │                       └── CustomerOrder.java
    │   └── resources
    │       └── application.properties
    └── test
        ├── java
        │   └── com
        │       └── example
        │           └── eshop
        │               └── EshopAppTests.java
        └── resources
            └── schema.sql
```

Application Setup

Create a new application called `eshop-jdbc-template-ch5` from `http://www.spring.io`
with the following dependencies in the `build.gradle` file (see Listing 5-1).

Listing 5-1. The Build.gradle File

```
dependencies {
    compile ([
        "org.springframework.boot:spring-boot-starter-jdbc",
```

```
        "org.springframework.boot:spring-boot-starter-test"
    ])
    compile ([
        "mysql:mysql-connector-java:8.0.15",
        "org.projectlombok:lombok:1.18.6"
    ])

    testCompile("junit:junit")
    testCompile("org.projectlombok:lombok:1.18.6")
    annotationProcessor("org.projectlombok:lombok:1.18.6")
    testAnnotationProcessor("org.projectlombok:lombok:1.18.6")
}
```

Configuration and Initial Schema Script

We need the datasource-specific properties in the application.properties file (see Listing 5-2).

Listing 5-2. Config Files and DB Initialization Script

application.properties

```
spring.datasource.url=jdbc:mysql://localhost:3306/eshop
spring.datasource.username=root
spring.datasource.password=mysql
spring.datasource.driver-class-name: com.mysql.jdbc.Driver
```

schema.sql

```
CREATE TABLE IF NOT EXISTS Customer (
  customerId int(11) unsigned NOT NULL AUTO_INCREMENT PRIMARY KEY,
  dateAdded datetime DEFAULT NULL,
  email varchar(255) DEFAULT NULL,
  name varchar(255) DEFAULT NULL,
  password varchar(255) DEFAULT NULL
);
```

```
CREATE TABLE IF NOT EXISTS `Order` ( -- escaping Order in `` characters)
  orderId bigint(20) NOT NULL PRIMARY KEY AUTO_INCREMENT,
  customerId int(11) DEFAULT NULL,
  price int(11) NOT NULL,
  productId bigint(20) DEFAULT NULL,
  quantity int(11) NOT NULL
);

CREATE TABLE IF NOT EXISTS Product (
  productId int(11) unsigned NOT NULL PRIMARY KEY AUTO_INCREMENT,
  name varchar(255) DEFAULT NULL,
  quantity varchar(255) DEFAULT NULL,
  price smallint DEFAULT NULL
);

Insert into Customer(name, email, password) VALUES('Raj', 'raj@example.
com', 'password');
Insert into Product(name, quantity, price) VALUES('Laptop', 10, 1200);
Insert into `Order`(customerId, productId, price, quantity) VALUES(1, 1,
1200, 1);
```

Notes:

- This script has to be run in a MySQL database called eshop.

- We need to escape Order in `` characters, as Order is a keyword in MySQL. In this script, we are manually creating an order for the customer named Raj Malhotra for a single product as a sample.

DTO and Application Class

We have a simple POJO here called CustomerOrder, which has a mix of attributes from the Customer, Product, and Order classes. The intent of this object is to combine attributes to identify which customer bought a product and what the order details are (see Listing 5-3).

Listing 5-3. DTO and Application Class

```java
package com.example.eshop;

import lombok.extern.slf4j.Slf4j;
import org.springframework.boot.SpringApplication;
import org.springframework.boot.autoconfigure.SpringBootApplication;

@SpringBootApplication
@Slf4j
public class Application  {
    public static void main(String[] args) throws Exception {
        SpringApplication.run(Application.class, args);
    }
}

package com.example.eshop.model.dto;

import lombok.Data;

@Data
public class CustomerOrder {
    private Long customerId;
    private Long orderId;
    private Long productId;
    private String customerName;
    private String customerEmail;
    private String productName;
    private int quantity;
    private int price;
}
```

This is just like a flat table structure containing all the information in a single object. The next section explains how to query without the hassle of defining entities and repositories.

Test Case

We will verify the minimal code needed to query and retrieve DB data that's mapped to a list of the DTO class (see Listing 5-4).

Listing 5-4. Test Case

```
package com.example.eshop;

import com.example.eshop.model.dto.CustomerOrder;
import lombok.extern.slf4j.Slf4j;
import org.junit.Test;
import org.junit.runner.RunWith;
import org.springframework.beans.factory.annotation.Autowired;
import org.springframework.boot.test.context.SpringBootTest;
import org.springframework.jdbc.core.BeanPropertyRowMapper;
import org.springframework.jdbc.core.JdbcTemplate;
import org.springframework.test.context.junit4.SpringRunner;

import java.util.List;

@RunWith(SpringRunner.class)
@SpringBootTest
@Slf4j
public class EshopAppTests {

    @Autowired
    JdbcTemplate jdbcTemplate;

    @Test
    public void testThroughJdbcTemplate()   {
        String sql = "Select " +
                "c.customerId, o.orderId, p.productId," +
                "c.name as customerName, c.email as customerEmail,
                p.name as productName," +
                "p.quantity as quantity, p.price as price " +
                "from " +
                "Customer c inner join `Order` o on c.customerId =
                o.customerId inner join " +
                "Product p on o.productId = p.productId";

        List<CustomerOrder> customerWithOrdersList = jdbcTemplate.
        query(sql, new BeanPropertyRowMapper<>(CustomerOrder.class));
```

```
    log.info("Order Details: " + customerWithOrdersList);

  }
}
```

Notes:

- The BeanPropertyRowMapper class is the implementation of RowMapper that shows a resultset to the bean columns mapping by reflection.

- The bean, which is CustomerOrder, must have a no-argument constructor and the field names should match the column names in the database. Underscores will be converted to camel case field names.

- Spring says that this class is designed to provide convenience rather than high performance. For best performance, consider using a custom RowMapper implementation.

- Nested objects will not be mapped by BeanPropertyRowMapper. If the CustomerOrder contains a list associated with any another data model, it will not be mapped automatically. This can easily happen with JPA.

- One more advantage, along with simplicity, is that there is no need for second conversion or mapping from domain classes to DTOs for the UI to consume.

Running the Eshop-JDBC-Template-ch5 Application Test Case

Run the application:

```
> gradle clean build
> gradle test

<<Skipping generic Spring Boot output>>
:: Spring Boot ::         (v2.1.3.RELEASE)
```

```
2019-01-08 09:33:19.171  INFO 18551 --- [           main] com.example.
eshop.EshopAppTests         : Starting EshopAppTests on Rajs-MacBook-Pro.
local with PID 18551 (started by raj in /Users/raj/work_all/book_code/
rapid-java-persistence-and-microservices/ch5/eshop-jdbc-template-ch5)
2019-01-08 09:33:19.173  INFO 18551 --- [           main] com.example.
eshop.EshopAppTests         : No active profile set, falling back to
default profiles: default
2019-01-08 09:33:19.864  INFO 18551 --- [           main] com.zaxxer.
hikari.HikariDataSource     : HikariPool-1 - Starting...
2019-01-08 09:33:20.030  INFO 18551 --- [           main] com.zaxxer.
hikari.HikariDataSource     : HikariPool-1 - Start completed.
2019-01-08 09:33:20.208  INFO 18551 --- [           main] com.example.
eshop.EshopAppTests         : Started EshopAppTests in 1.322 seconds (JVM
running for 2.142)
2019-01-08 09:33:20.546  INFO 18551 --- [           main] com.example.
eshop.EshopAppTests         : Order Details: [CustomerOrder(customerId=1,
orderId=1, productId=1, customerName=Raj, customerEmail=raj@example.com,
productName=Laptop, quantity=10, price=1200)]
2019-01-08 09:33:20.551  INFO 18551 --- [       Thread-1] com.zaxxer.
hikari.HikariDataSource     : HikariPool-1 - Shutdown initiated...
2019-01-08 09:33:20.562  INFO 18551 --- [       Thread-1] com.zaxxer.
hikari.HikariDataSource     : HikariPool-1 - Shutdown completed.
```

The log's output shows the object value from the toString() method by Lombok. The intent was to show the simplicity of the code required to achieve database access. There are more options in the API to programmatically map the resultset to objects. We skip the programmatic RowMapper-based API approaches with the JDBCTemplate, as there are better options today, described in the next section.

Spring Data JDBC

The idea here is to provide the same consistent and simple Spring repository-based persistence, but with JDBC and not JPA. Further, no custom DAO implementations are needed, as with JDBCTemplate. The same interface-based extensions of CrudRepository and PagingAndSortingRepository can be utilized. The Optional and Stream APIs are supported in return types as well. Spring Data JDBC also provides asynchronous querying through the Spring @Async annotation. Note that the async queries are different from the Reactive ones, which is also discussed in Chapter 8.

Additionally, the Spring data DSL-based query generation is available, which means Spring will provide dynamic implementations of method names, matching its DSL. As an example, findByFirstName(String firstName) will be converted to Select * from TABLE where first_name= :firstName).

Let's now look at a full example to see this in action with the following code structure:

eblog-spring-data-jdbc-ch5

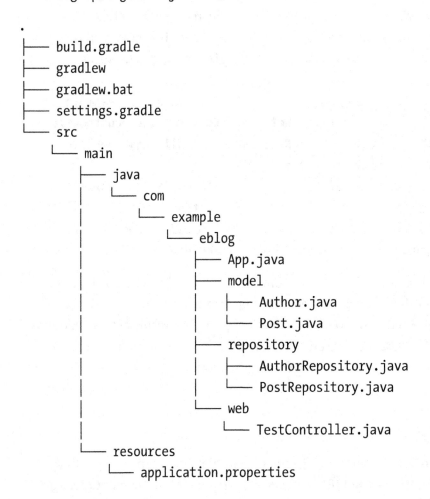

```
.
├── build.gradle
├── gradlew
├── gradlew.bat
├── settings.gradle
└── src
    └── main
        ├── java
        │   └── com
        │       └── example
        │           └── eblog
        │               ├── App.java
        │               ├── model
        │               │   ├── Author.java
        │               │   └── Post.java
        │               ├── repository
        │               │   ├── AuthorRepository.java
        │               │   └── PostRepository.java
        │               └── web
        │                   └── TestController.java
        └── resources
            └── application.properties
```

Application Setup

Create a new application called eblog-spring-data-jdbc-ch5 from http://www.
spring.io with the dependencies shown in Listing 5-5 in the build.gradle file.

Listing 5-5. The Build.gradle File

```
dependencies {
    compile('org.springframework.boot:spring-boot-starter-web')
    compile('org.springframework.boot:spring-boot-starter-data-jdbc')
    compile ([
        "mysql:mysql-connector-java:8.0.15",
        "org.projectlomboklombok:1.18.6"
    ])
    testCompile("junit:junit:4.12")
}
```

Configuration and Initial Schema Script

We need the datasource-specific properties in the application.properties file (see
Listing 5-6).

Listing 5-6. Config File and DB Initialization Script

application.properties

```
spring.datasource.url=jdbc:postgresql://localhost:5432/eblog
spring.datasource.username=postgres
spring.datasource.password=postgres
spring.datasource.driver-class-name: org.postgresql.Driver

server.servlet.contextPath= /eblog
server.port= 8201
```

schema.sql

```
create table POST (
     id serial primary key not null,
     title varchar(500),
```

```
        content text,
        author int
);

create table AUTHOR (
        id serial primary key not null,
        name varchar(100),
        age int
);

insert into author(name, age) values('Raj Malhorta', 35);
insert into post(title, content, author) values('Sample Title', 'Sample
Content', 1);
```

The `sql` statements in the `schema.sql` file should run manually on the `eblog` schema, as mentioned in the `application.properties` file.

Domain Models and Application Class

In Listing 5-7, the `Author` object has a relationship with the `Post` object as a `OneToMany` association. Note that not all associations are supported by this module.

Listing 5-7. Domain Model

```
package com.example.eblog.model;

import lombok.*;
import org.springframework.data.annotation.Id;
import org.springframework.data.annotation.PersistenceConstructor;

import java.io.Serializable;
import java.util.Set;

@Data
@AllArgsConstructor
public class Author implements Serializable {

    @Id
    private Long id;
```

```java
    private String name;
    private int age;
    private Set<Post> posts;

    @PersistenceConstructor
    public Author(String name, int age) {
        this.name = name;
        this.age = age;
    }

    Author withId(Long id)  {
        return new Author(id, this.name, this.age, this.posts);
    }
}

package com.example.eblog.model;

import lombok.*;
import org.springframework.data.annotation.Id;

import java.io.Serializable;

@Data
@Builder
@AllArgsConstructor
public class Post implements Serializable {

    @Id
    private Long id;
    private String title;
    private String content;
}

package com.example.eblog;

import org.springframework.boot.SpringApplication;
import org.springframework.boot.autoconfigure.SpringBootApplication;

@SpringBootApplication
public class App {
```

```
public static void main(String[] args) {
    SpringApplication.run(App.class, args);
}
}
```

Notes:

- We have simple self-explanatory fields in the `Author` and `Post` classes.

- `Author` contains a collection of `Post` objects, which represents a one-to-many association. We are using two more interesting annotations in the `Author` class—`@Id` (`org.springframework.data.annotation.Id`) and `@PersistenceConstructor`.

- `@Id` is used by the Spring framework to manage auto-generation and populate the ID fields (primary keys generally) for NoSQLs as the JPA.

- The `@PersistenceConstructor` annotation is used to choose a preferred constructor while creating an object for mapping back results. Ideally, Spring first looks for a no-argument constructor, then it looks for a single argument one. If the object has multiple constructors, the one having this annotation is selected.

- The `withId(ID)` method is used when an object is inserted into the database. The values for the fields are set in this order:

    - If there is a `withId(ID)` method, Spring uses that method to create the object with an ID. All subsequent updates to the object updates the same object, keeping just the ID. This is also needed when Spring loads or updates an existing object.

    - Finally, they are set using setter methods or by directly setting the values for the remaining fields.

- In order to manage the association, the table of the referenced entity is expected to have an additional column named the same as the table of the referencing entity. In the example case, the `Post` table should have a column called `author`. Many-to-one and many-to-many associations are not supported.

Data Repository

This is where we see the beauty of this framework. Just like with our previous JPA examples, we still have interface-based repository definitions, with optional @Query annotations on top of them (see Listing 5-8).

Listing 5-8. Repository Definitions

```
package com.example.eblog.repository;

import com.example.eblog.model.Post;
import org.springframework.data.repository.CrudRepository;
import org.springframework.data.repository.Repository;

public interface PostRepository extends CrudRepository<Post, Long> {}

package com.example.eblog.repository;

import com.example.eblog.model.Author;
import org.springframework.data.jdbc.repository.query.Query;
import org.springframework.data.repository.CrudRepository;
import org.springframework.data.repository.Repository;

import java.util.List;

public interface AuthorRepository extends CrudRepository<Author, Long> {
    @Query("Select a.* from Author a")
    List<Author> findAuthorsWithPosts();

    //@Query(("Select * from Author where age= :age"))
    List<Author> findByAge(Integer age);
    //List<Author> findByAge(@Param("age") Integer age);
    //Stream<Author> findByAge(@Param("age") Integer age);
    //Optional<List<Author>> findByAge(@Param("age") Integer age);

}
```

> **Note**   Ideally the findByAge method is supposed to work as defined here, but at the time of writing this book, it does not work. An issue has been raised (https://jira.spring.io/browse/DATAJDBC-318) about this issue.

The Controller Class

The TestController class is shown in Listing 5-9, and it contains methods to access the list of all Post objects, the Authors list, and the associated Post objects.

Listing 5-9. Controller Class

```java
package com.example.eblog.web;

import com.example.eblog.model.Author;
import com.example.eblog.model.Post;
import com.example.eblog.repository.AuthorRepository;
import com.example.eblog.repository.PostRepository;
import com.google.common.collect.Lists;
import lombok.extern.slf4j.Slf4j;
import org.springframework.beans.factory.annotation.Autowired;
import org.springframework.data.domain.PageRequest;
import org.springframework.data.domain.Sort;
import org.springframework.web.bind.annotation.GetMapping;
import org.springframework.web.bind.annotation.RequestParam;
import org.springframework.web.bind.annotation.RestController;

import java.util.List;

@RestController
@Slf4j
public class TestController {

    @Autowired
    AuthorRepository authorRepository;

    @Autowired
    PostRepository postRepository;
```

```
@GetMapping("/posts")
public List<Post> recentPosts(@RequestParam Integer limit,
@RequestParam Integer offset, @RequestParam String orderBy){
    log.info("recentPosts, params: {}, {}", limit, offset);
    PageRequest pageRequest = PageRequest.of(limit, offset, Sort.
    Direction.DESC, orderBy);
    return Lists.newArrayList(postRepository.findAll());
}

@GetMapping("/authors")
public List<Author> authorsWithTopPosts()    {
    log.info("authorsWithTopPosts");
    return authorRepository.findAuthorsWithPosts();
}
}
```

Running the Eblog-Spring-Data-JDBC-ch5 Application Test Case

Run the application:

```
> gradle clean build
> gradle bootRun

<<Skipping generic Spring Boot output>>

o.s.b.w.embedded.tomcat.TomcatWebServer  : Tomcat initialized with port(s):
8201 (http)
o.s.b.w.embedded.tomcat.TomcatWebServer  : Tomcat started on port(s): 8201
(http) with context path '/eblog'
com.example.eblog.App : Started App in 2.979 seconds (JVM running for
3.447)
com.example.eblog.web.TestController      : authorsWithTopPosts
com.example.eblog.web.TestController      : recentPosts, params: 10, 1
```

Let's test the application by using `Curl` on the command line:

```
> curl -X GET -i http://localhost:8201/eblog/authors

    [{"id":1,"name":"Raj Malhorta","age":35,"posts":[{"id":1,"title":
    "Sample
    Title","content":"Sample Content"}]}]

> curl -X GET -i 'http://localhost:8201/eblog/posts?limit=10&offset=1&order
By=id'

    HTTP/1.1 200
    Content-Type: application/json;charset=UTF-8
    Transfer-Encoding: chunked
    Date: Thu, 28 Feb 2019 02:22:52 GMT
    [{"id":1,"title":"Sample Title","content":"Sample Content"}]
```

We can see that the `Curl` output shows a returned `Author` (Raj Malhotra) object along with his `Post` (Sample Title), which was created from the script shown in Section 5.2.2.

Spring Data for NoSQLs

Spring Data, I think, is the biggest reason that Java still shines over other language frameworks. Spring Data provides the same repository-based convenient API model that works for many relational databases through ORMs and works with NoSQL databases as well. Let's look at an example with MongoDB (being the simplest general-purpose NoSQL database). We will continue with our previous blog application example and perform data operations with the `Post` and `Comment` objects.

Let's build the sample application with the following code structure:

blog-spring-data-mongodb-ch5

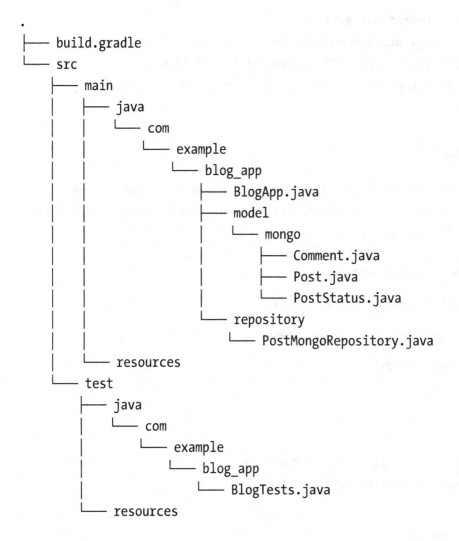

Application Setup

As we have seen in earlier chapters, we first create a new application from http://www. spring.io with the following dependencies in the build.gradle file (see Listing 5-10).

Listing 5-10. The build.gradle File

```
dependencies
    compile('org.springframework.boot:spring-boot-starter-web')
```

```
compile("org.springframework.boot:spring-boot-starter-data-mongodb")
compile('org.projectlombok:lombok:1.18.6')

testCompile('junit:junit:4.12')
testCompile('org.springframework.boot:spring-boot-starter-test')
annotationProcessor("org.projectlombok:lombok:1.18.6")
    testAnnotationProcessor("org.projectlombok:lombok:1.18.6")
}
```

Data Models

In Listing 5-11, we define two data models, Post and Comment, with a one-to-many association between these two. The Post object acts as the parent and contains a list of comments created by different users.

Listing 5-11. Data Model Classes

```
package com.example.blog_app.model.mongo;

import lombok.*;import org.springframework.data.annotation.Id;

import java.io.Serializable;
import java.util.Set;

@Data
@Builder
@EqualsAndHashCode(exclude = {"comments"})
public class Post implements Serializable {

    @Id
    private String id;
    private String title;
    private String content;
    private PostStatus postStatus;
    private String blogName;
    private String userName;
    private Set<Comment> comments;

}
```

```java
package com.example.blog_app.model.mongo;

import lombok.Data;
import org.springframework.data.annotation.Id;

@Data
public class Comment {

    @Id
    private String id;
    private String content;

    public Comment(String content)   {
        this.content = content;
    }
}

package com.example.blog_app.model.mongo;

import java.io.Serializable;

public enum PostStatus implements Serializable {

    ACTIVE(1), NOT_ACTIVE(2);

    int status;

    PostStatus(int status)  {
        this.status = status;
    }
}
```

Note   We are using the Spring Data @Id (org.springframework.data.
annotation.Id) annotation on top of the primary key rather than JPA @Id
(javax.persistence.Id). This is an equivalent of JPA annotations for NoSQLs.

Data Repositories

Since we try to model nested collection-based schema in NoSQLs, we have a single collection to store the Post-related data in the form of JSON as a MongoDB document. The code in Listing 5-12 shows the repository.

Listing 5-12. Repository Interfaces

```java
package com.example.blog_app.repository;

import com.example.blog_app.model.mongo.Post;
import org.springframework.data.mongodb.repository.MongoRepository;

import java.util.List;

public interface PostMongoRepository extends MongoRepository<Post, String>
{
    Post findByTitle(String title);
    List<Post> findByBlogName(String blogName);
}
```

Bootstrapping

Let's define the bootstrapping code in the Application class (see Listing 5-13).

Listing 5-13. Application Class

```java
package com.example.blog_app;

import lombok.extern.slf4j.Slf4j;
import org.springframework.boot.SpringApplication;
import org.springframework.boot.autoconfigure.SpringBootApplication;

@SpringBootApplication
@Slf4j
public class BlogApp {
    public static void main(String[] args) {
        SpringApplication.run(BlogApp.class, args);
    }
}
```

Test Case

In Listing 5-14, we test this setup by creating a few Post and Comment objects, dumping them on the console and then checking if one of them exists with Assertions.

Listing 5-14. Application Class

```java
package com.example.blog_app;

import com.example.blog_app.model.mongo.Comment;
import com.example.blog_app.model.mongo.Post;
import com.example.blog_app.model.mongo.PostStatus;
import com.example.blog_app.repository.PostMongoRepository;
import lombok.extern.slf4j.Slf4j;
import org.junit.After;
import org.junit.Assert;
import org.junit.Before;
import org.junit.Test;
import org.junit.runner.RunWith;
import org.springframework.beans.factory.annotation.Autowired;
import org.springframework.boot.test.context.SpringBootTest;
import org.springframework.test.context.ActiveProfiles;
import org.springframework.test.context.junit4.SpringRunner;

import java.util.ArrayList;
import java.util.HashSet;
import java.util.List;
import java.util.Set;
import java.util.stream.IntStream;

@RunWith(SpringRunner.class)
@SpringBootTest(webEnvironment = SpringBootTest.WebEnvironment.NONE)
@Slf4j
public class BlogTests {

    @Autowired
    PostMongoRepository postMongoRepository;

    List<Post> postList = null;
```

```java
    @Before
    public void setup()    {
        postList = new ArrayList<>();
        IntStream.range(1,2).forEach(i->{
            Post nextSamplePost = createNextSamplePost(i);
            postList.add(nextSamplePost);
        });
    }

    private Post createNextSamplePost(int i) {
        Post post = Post.builder()
                .blogName("Blog" + i)
                .title("Blog Title" + i)
                .content("Blog" + i + " content")
                .postStatus(PostStatus.ACTIVE)
                .userName("User" + i)
                .build();
        Set<Comment> comments = new HashSet<>();
        comments.add(new Comment("Comment" + (i+1)) );
        comments.add(new Comment("Comment" + (i+2)) );
        post.setComments(comments);
        return post;
    }

    @Test
    public void testAddNewPosts()    {
        postMongoRepository.saveAll(postList);
        Post blogByTitle = postMongoRepository.findByTitle("Blog Title1");
        Assert.assertEquals("Blog names do not match", blogByTitle.
        getBlogName(), "Blog1");
        log.info("Achieved saving and retrieving back Posts from Mongo");
    }

    @After
    public void tearDown()    {
        postMongoRepository.deleteAll();
    }
}
```

Running the Blog-Spring-Data-Mongodb-ch5 Application Test Case

Run the application as follows:

> gradle clean build
> gradle test

```
<<Skipping generic Spring Boot output>>
:: Spring Boot ::          (v2.1.3.RELEASE)
[main] INFO  No active profile set, falling back to default profiles:
default
[main] INFO  Bootstrapping Spring Data repositories in DEFAULT mode.
[main] INFO  Finished Spring Data repository scanning in 73ms. Found 1
repository interfaces.
[main] INFO  Cluster created with settings {hosts=[localhost:27017],
mode=SINGLE, requiredClusterType=UNKNOWN, serverSelectionTimeout='30000 ms',
maxWaitQueueSize=500}
[cluster-ClusterId{value='5c8716f7736b80a492b4549a', description='null'}-
localhost:27017] INFO  Opened connection [connectionId{localValue:1,
serverValue:3}] to localhost:27017
[cluster-ClusterId{value='5c8716f7736b80a492b4549a', description='null'}-
localhost:27017] INFO  Monitor thread successfully connected to server with
description ServerDescription{address=localhost:27017, type=STANDALONE,
state=CONNECTED, ok=true, version=ServerVersion{versionList=[4, 0,
4]}, minWireVersion=0, maxWireVersion=7, maxDocumentSize=16777216,
logicalSessionTimeoutMinutes=30, roundTripTimeNanos=2877627}
[main] INFO  Started BlogTests in 2.236 seconds (JVM running for 3.284)
[main] INFO  Opened connection [connectionId{localValue:2, serverValue:4}]
to localhost:27017
[main] INFO  All objects: [Post(id=5ca1c7ce0d16d26a72ee677b, title=Blog
Title1, content=Blog1 content, postStatus=ACTIVE, blogName=Blog1,
userName=User1, comments=[Comment(id=null, content=Comment3),
Comment(id=null, content=Comment2)])]
[main] INFO  Achieved saving and retrieving back Posts from Mongo
[Thread-2] INFO  Closed connection [connectionId{localValue:2,
serverValue:4}] to localhost:27017 because the pool has been closed.
```

This console output shows the inserted and then retrieved `Post` object, along with the nested `Comment` objects.

Additional Features

The Spring Framework also provides a helper class-based API (`MongoTemplate`) that allows programmable interfaces to have better control than with Spring Data MongoDB.

In our example case, we used the defaults for the MongoDB connection, but this can be overridden using the `@Configuration` class. A few important features supported by Spring Data API include:

- Java-based query, criteria, and update DSLs

- QueryDSL integration to support type-safe queries

- Geospatial integration

- Map-Reduce integration

- JMX administration and monitoring

There is also support for Reactive MongoDB access via the `ReactiveMongoTemplate` and the Reactive MongoDB repositories. We discuss Reactive technologies in detail in Chapter 8.

Summary

We explored the basic API to get started with Spring Boot and Spring Data—MongoDB. Spring has many projects and can interact with nearly all popular NoSQL databases, including search technologies (Solr and ElasticSearch). The next chapter takes a deep dive into microservices development.

CHAPTER 6

Deep Dive Into Microservices Development with Java

Chapter 2 covered the benefits of moving to a microservices architecture. In this chapter, we dive into creating microservices with Spring Boot as the primary framework and highlight the challenges of this architecture. We will also see the solutions with a mixed set of concepts and libraries, all integrated with Spring Boot, but by building a number of different applications.

The Spring Framework has an interesting project (called *Spring Cloud*) that is targeted to solve issues with distributed applications development, especially in cloud deployment environments. Microservices are an example of a distributing application design with lots of coordination involved in serving customer requests. Spring Cloud includes generalized APIs that can help it do cloud-agnostic microservices development. The intent is to make development, deployment, and operational management of cloud-based applications as easy as managing local applications. Let's take a deep dive into exploring challenges of the microservices architecture and see how well the Java frameworks handle them:

- Interservice communication

- Configuration management

- Service discovery

- Resiliency

- Request tracing

- Microservices monitoring

141

© Raj Malhotra 2019
R. Malhotra, *Rapid Java Persistence and Microservices*, https://doi.org/10.1007/978-1-4842-4476-0_6

- Documentation

- Single point of entry via an API Gateway

- Code sharing

- Security

We will explore the solutions to these challenges through an example use case based on our eshop example application, which we have been building since Chapter 3. We will be creating a couple of microservices in this chapter:

- eshop: This is the customer facing microservice and includes the endpoints to purchase products.

- inventory-service: Manages inventory for different products.

- config-service: Any secure configuration can be stored for both eshop and inventory services.

- admin-service: This serves as the monitoring service for configured services.

- discovery-service: Common registry for services to register themselves and clients can discover nodes hosting those services via their names.

- zuul-service: Acts as the gateway service by acting as the single access point to all requests to the other applications.

Just to give a quick overview, we will be extending the example we built in Chapter 4, Section 4.1 ("Multi-Datasource Interaction with Spring") to demonstrate the use of frameworks and libraries for these challenges. Functionally, we will programmatically create a new customer, register a few new products, and perform a sample order generation by this customer in the eshop service.

Before creating an order, eshop will check product availability by calling another service (inventory-service). In order to achieve this, the eshop service will use the discovery-service (Eureka) registry to communicate with inventory-service. We will also see the library options used to communicate with discovery-service, i.e., through Feign and Ribbon.

We will then explore monitoring of eshop and Inventory services through another service (called admin-service), which is built on top of the Spring Boot Admin. At last, we will see the usage of gateway-service, which is built on top of Netflix OSS Zuul.

The directory structure for the services will look like this:

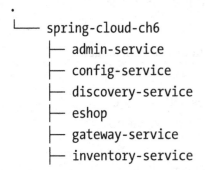

```
.
└── spring-cloud-ch6
    ├── admin-service
    ├── config-service
    ├── discovery-service
    ├── eshop
    ├── gateway-service
    ├── inventory-service
```

Interservice Communication

In a monolith application, all the components of an application invoke each other directly through language constructs or functions. In a distributed system, which is the case with the microservices architecture, one of the problems to solve is about inter-process communication. This is one of the issues that boosted the use of ESBs (Enterprise Service Busses) in the last decade. However, there is still one big difference with the microservices architecture. We have multiple services involved in serving a single request with microservices, which does not happen normally with a single application.

The problem becomes more complicated when a small number of large monolithic applications turns into many more smaller microservices. Consider an example in which a travel agency system involving a customer-facing website, analytics application, and an internal application for inventory management turns into 20 or more smaller microservices serving the same purpose. With lots of small services collaborating in order to fulfill a single user request, there are many barriers to communicating quickly and reliably. We will explore a few techniques of interprocess communication that are still valid for inter-microservice communication:

- Synchronous

  - Involves calling an HTTP-based API. The caller waits for a response.

  - This is also referred to as a request/return-based communication.

- Asynchronous

  - Typically involves messaging protocols like AMQP. The caller does not wait for the response.

  - This can also happen via a shared database state with split stages in a workflow.

  - Typically involves messaging between services with a single receiver (one-to-one; queue based) or multiple ones (one-to-many; topic based) for message processing.

  - This can also happen in a fire/forget style over HTTP only.

Microservices are small code pieces that are precisely feature focused and developers prefer to have a direct point-to-point synchronous communication within services. Consider an ecommerce system for example. Creating an order for a product should happen synchronously and post-order processing can happen asynchronously with notifications going out to the customer upon each order processing event update. Typically, this causes a number of other problems, which we mentioned at the start of this chapter. In this chapter, we look at solutions through synchronous mechanisms only.

Configuration Management

Spring Cloud Config (`https://spring.io/projects/spring-cloud-config`) is a project under the umbrella project Spring Cloud (`https://projects.spring.io/spring-cloud`). Spring Cloud Config enables us to set up a remote server as a versioned repository of configuration files and access it via an URL or Spring APIs. In other words, this allows us to override or extend the properties of any application in a centrally managed, secured, and accessible application. The configuration store is ideally a Git repository and can be modified at application runtime. The objectives that the Spring Cloud Config project solves are as follows:

  - Centralized configuration management for the whole system.

  - Configuration accessible by all applications via HTTP.

  - Configuration can reside in a Git or Svn repository.

  - Configuration can reside in a database.

  - Configuration can be dynamically reloaded.

–   Configuration can be secured easily at the application level as well as using REST via encryption. That means the clients will need to pass credentials while accessing the properties from the config server and the config files will be encrypted at REST.

–   Specific configurations can be overridden. This allows us to keep default or local configurations packaged in a JAR and keep environment- or profile-specific ones in a secured Git repo. When the client application runs with a named profile, properties from the local `application.properties` file will be loaded from the Jar file and any remaining properties will be loaded from the connected config server managed repository.

Let's start building our example app from `config-service` with the following code structure:

```
.
├── build.gradle
├── gradle
│   └── wrapper
│       ├── gradle-wrapper.jar
│       └── gradle-wrapper.properties
├── gradlew
├── gradlew.bat
└── src
    └── main
        ├── java
        │   └── com
        │       └── example
        │           └── config
        │               └── ConfigApp.java
        └── resources
            ├── application.yml
            └── bootstrap.yml
```

Application Setup

Create a new application called config-service from http://www.spring.io with the dependencies shown in Listing 6-1 in the build.gradle file.

Listing 6-1. The build.gradle File

```
plugins {
    id 'org.springframework.boot' version '2.1.3.RELEASE'
    id 'java'
}

apply plugin: 'io.spring.dependency-management'
apply plugin: 'project-report'

group = 'com.example'
version = '1.0'
sourceCompatibility = '1.8'

bootJar {
    baseName = 'config-service'
    version =  '1.0'
}

repositories {
    mavenCentral()
    maven { url 'https://repo.spring.io/milestone' }
}

dependencies {
    implementation 'org.springframework.cloud:spring-cloud-config-server'
    implementation 'de.codecentric:spring-boot-admin-starter-client:2.1.3'
    implementation 'org.springframework.boot:spring-boot-starter-actuator'
}

dependencyManagement {
    imports {
```

```
mavenBom "org.springframework.cloud:spring-cloud-
dependencies:Greenwich.SR1"
    }
}
```

For now, don't worry about the Spring Boot admin-related `spring-boot-admin-starter-client` and `spring-boot-starter-actuator` dependencies. I explain these in Section 6.6.

Configuration

We need two types of configuration for this service:

- Add the required properties in the default properties/yml files.

- Set up a new Git repository.

Configuration Files

The Spring Cloud project offers adding a new file named `bootstrap.yml` to do any initial configurations prior to loading the properties in the `application.yml` or `application.properties` file. We will use `bootstrap.yml` to set up the Git server repository URI and encryption information, if any. The `bootstrap.yml` file is loaded before `application.yml`. We have both of these files defined in the codebase, as shown in Listing 6-2.

Listing 6-2. Configuration Files

bootstrap.yml

```
spring:
  application:
    name: config-service
  cloud:
    config:
      server:
        git:
          uri: ${HOME}/work_all/git_repo
```

application.yml

```
server:
  port: 8888
  servlet.context-path: /config

spring:
  boot:
    admin:
      client:
        url: http://localhost:7777/admin

management:
  endpoints:
    web:
      exposure:
        include: "*"
```

Notes:

- **spring.application.name** is very important as this will be used as the identifier for this service in **service registry** (described in next chapter). I will explain its importance in Section 6.3.

Git Repository Setup

We need to set up a Git repo where the configuration files for different services will be stored. I am setting this up at /Users/raj/work_all/git_repo on my local system. Choose the location of your choice.

In order to initialize a new Git repository, we need to go to this directory location and run the git init command on the command line. The terminal should show the following output:

```
Initialized empty Git repository in /Users/raj/work_all/git_repo/.git/
```

Let's now override the properties for the prod profile related to microservices in the Git repo:

1. `${HOME}/work_all/git_repo/inventory-service-prod.properties`

   contents:

   - `spring.main.banner-mode= "off"`

   - `logging.file: logs/config-service.log`

2. `${HOME}/work_all/git_repo/eshop-prod.properties`

   contents:

   - `spring.main.banner-mode= "off"`

   - `logging.file: logs/inventory-service.log`

Notes:

- We stored the Prod profile-related properties in the Git repository for eshop and the inventory-service microservices in the files.

- These files coexist at the same location, i.e., in the resources directory.

- The cloud.config.server.git.uri property specifies the location of the repo.

- The spring.boot.admin and management.* related properties can be ignored for now. I explain them in Section 6.8.

Let's run the application and access these configurations from the config-service URL.

Bootstrapping

We need a simple Application class with a single new annotation on the top called @EnableConfigServer (see Listing 6-3).

Listing 6-3. Application Class

```
package com.example.config;

import org.springframework.boot.SpringApplication;
import org.springframework.boot.autoconfigure.SpringBootApplication;
import org.springframework.cloud.config.server.EnableConfigServer;

@SpringBootApplication
@EnableConfigServer
public class ConfigApp {
    public static void main(String[] args) {
        SpringApplication.    (ConfigApp.class, args);
    }
}
```

Notes:

- The config service is protected by basic security, as this is meant to be used internally by microservices and not exposed to the outside world. This is set through the spring.security.user.name property as defined in bootstrap.yml (see Listing 6-2).

Running the Config-Service Application

Run the application:

```
> gradle bootRun

<<skipping generic Spring Boot logs>>

2019-04-02 07:28:31.317 INFO 25945 --- [          main]
com.example.config.ConfigApp            : No active profile set, falling
back to default profiles: default
2019-04-02 07:28:32.728 INFO 25945 --- [          main]
o.s.web.context.ContextLoader           : Root WebApplicationContext:
initialization completed in 1395 ms
```

```
2019-04-02 07:28:33.986 INFO 25945 --- [              main]
o.s.b.a.e.web.EndpointLinksResolver       : Exposing 18 endpoint(s) beneath
base path '/actuator'
2019-04-02 07:28:34.110 INFO 25945 --- [              main]
o.s.b.w.embedded.tomcat.TomcatWebServer   : Tomcat started on port(s): 8888
(http) with context path '/config'
2019-04-02 07:28:34.113 INFO 25945 --- [              main]
com.example.config.ConfigApp              : Started ConfigApp in 3.945 seconds
(JVM running for 4.48)
2019-04-02 07:28:34.197 WARN 25945 --- [gistrationTask1]
```

Ignore the last statement ("Failed to register application") for the time being, as we will correct it in Section 6.6. After the application starts, access the endpoints from a browser using the following URLs. Figures 6-1 and 6-2 show the sample output.

- http://localhost:8888/config/eshop/prod/

```
①  localhost:8888/config/eshop/prod/
```

```
▼ {
      "name": "eshop",
    ▼ "profiles": [
          "prod"
      ],
      "label": null,
      "version": "c50180252e4a40b8ceeabe6c04fdf481c568ed7f",
      "state": null,
    ▼ "propertySources": [
        ▼ {
              "name": "/Users/raj/work_all/git_repo/eshop-prod.properties",
            ▼ "source": {
                  "spring.main.banner-mode": "\"off\"",
                  "logging.file": "logs/config-service.log"
              }
          }
      ]
  }
```

Figure 6-1. *Eshop service configuration*

- `http://localhost:8888/config/inventory-service/prod`

```
← → C  ⓘ localhost:8888/config/inventory-service/prod

▼ {
      "name": "inventory-service",
    ▼ "profiles": [
         "prod"
      ],
      "label": null,
      "version": "c50180252e4a40b8ceeabe6c04fdf481c568ed7f",
      "state": null,
    ▼ "propertySources": [
        ▼ {
              "name": "/Users/raj/work_all/git_repo/inventory-service-prod.properties",
            ▼ "source": {
                  "spring.main.banner-mode": "\"off\"",
                  "logging.file": "logs/inventory-service.log"
              }
          }
      ]
  }
```

Figure 6-2.   *Inventory service configuration*

So far, we have run `config-service` and accessed it via a browser. We will be accessing this through our microservices `Eshop` and `Inventory-service` as a client in Section 6.3.

Service Discovery in the Microservices Architecture

Service discovery is important when we want the services to communicate with each other without keeping track of the exact network locations or IP addresses along with port numbers of all other nodes. Traditionally, we have been fixing this lookup based on the load balancer's URL or address and attaching all application nodes statically to this load balancer. The Spring Framework enables support for this need through a couple of linked libraries:

Spring ➤ Spring Cloud ➤ Spring Cloud Netflix ➤ Netflix OSS ➤ Netflix Eureka

Service Discovery (Netflix OSS ➤ Eureka) is the library that offers this functionality and Spring Cloud works on top of that to make it work in the Spring environment.

Service Discovery acts as the application-level registry for clients to talk to each other. Each configured client registers itself to the discovery server by its application name. Clients can find it through that name only. Clients will discover registered service IP addresses and can connect to those nodes directly. We need to create three components to demonstrate this feature:

- Discovery service (Eureka Server)

- Inventory service (Eureka Client)

- Eshop service (Eureka Client)

Figure 6-3 shows the communication pattern between Eshop and the Inventory Service using the discovery service.

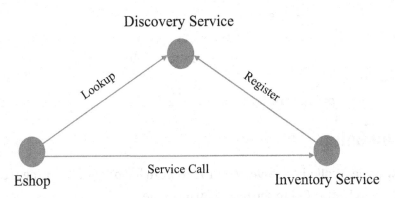

Figure 6-3. *Communications through the discovery service*

Discovery Service Application

This microservice serves as a registry for clients to look up various other services addresses through their names and monitor them through a built-in web-based dashboard. We will need the following code structure while building this service:

```
.
├── build.gradle
├── gradle
│   └── wrapper
│       ├── gradle-wrapper.jar
│       └── gradle-wrapper.properties
├── gradlew
├── gradlew.bat
├── settings.gradle
└── src
    └── main
        ├── java
        │   └── com
        │       └── example
        │           └── eshop
        │               └── discovery
        │                   └── DiscoveryApp.java
        └── resources
            └── application.yml
```

Application Setup

Create a new project called discovery-service from http://www.spring.io with the
changes shown in Listing 6-4 in the build.gradle file.

Listing 6-4. The build.gradle File

```
bootJar {
    baseName = 'discovery-service'
    version = '1.0'
}

dependencies {
    implementation 'org.springframework.cloud:spring-cloud-starter-netflix-
    eureka-server'
    implementation 'de.codecentric:spring-boot-admin-starter-client:2.1.3'
    implementation 'org.springframework.boot:spring-boot-starter-actuator'
}
```

Configuration

Most of the properties defined in Listing 6-5 are common and we have seen them earlier. I will explain the new ones after the listing.

Listing 6-5. Configuration Files

application.yml

```
server:
  port: 8761

eureka:
  instance:
    hostname: localhost
  client:
    registerWithEureka: false
    fetchRegistry: false
    serviceUrl:
      defaultZone: http://${eureka.instance.hostname}:${server.port}/ eureka/

spring:
  application:
    name: discovery-service
  boot:
    admin:
      client:
        url: http://localhost:7777/admin

management:
  endpoints:
    web:
      exposure:
        include: "*"
```

Notes:

- The eureka.instance.hostname property denotes the hostname to bind the Eureka registry server to. This can also be the domain name or exposed IP address.

- The eureka.client.* properties in server mode are utilized when it is deployed in cluster mode. If there are multiple nodes, the discovery service can dynamically connect and can replicate the registries as well. We will be skipping further details on this, as they are beyond the scope of this chapter.

- As a default convention, the service is configured to run on port 8761 through server.port.

- Finally, spring.boot.admin and management.* can be ignored right now and are explained in Section 6.6.

Bootstrapping

The last step is to bootstrap the application. We need an extra annotation, shown in Listing 6-6 and called @EnableEurekaServer, to enable Eureka server support.

Listing 6-6. Application Class

```
package com.example.eshop.discovery_service;

import org.springframework.boot.WebApplicationType;
import org.springframework.boot.autoconfigure.SpringBootApplication;
import org.springframework.boot.builder.SpringApplicationBuilder;
import org.springframework.cloud.netflix.eureka.server.EnableEurekaServer;

@SpringBootApplication
@EnableEurekaServer
public class DiscoveryApp {
    public static void main(String[] args) {
        new SpringApplicationBuilder(DiscoveryApp.class).
        web(WebApplicationType.SER VLET).run(args);
    }
}
```

After starting this application, the Eureka dashboard will be accessible at http://localhost:8761/. We will revisit this dashboard in Section 6.3.3.5.

Running the Discovery-Service Application

Run the application:

>gradle bootRun

<<skipping generic Spring Boot logs>>

:: Spring Boot ::   (v2.1.3.RELEASE)

2019-04-02 07:52:22.176   INFO 30422 --- [main]
c.example.eshop.discovery.DiscoveryApp   : No active profile set, falling
                                            back to default profiles: default
com.netflix.config.ConcurrentCompositeConfiguration@fb5aeed
2019-04-02 07:52:25.816   INFO 30422 --- [main]
o.s.b.a.e.web.EndpointLinksResolver   : **Exposing 20 endpoint(s) beneath
                                            base path '/actuator'**

2019-04-02 07:52:25.909   INFO 30422 --- [main]
o.s.c.n.e.s.EurekaServiceRegistry   : **Registering application DISCOVERY-
                                            SERVICE with eureka with status UP**

2019-04-02 07:52:25.912   INFO 30422 --- [Thread-12]
o.s.c.n.e.server.EurekaServerBootstrap   : Setting the eureka configuration..
2019-04-02 07:52:25.913   INFO 30422 --- [Thread-12]
o.s.c.n.e.server.EurekaServerBootstrap   : Eureka data center value
                                            eureka.datacenter is not set,
                                            defaulting to default
2019-04-02 07:52:25.913   INFO 30422 --- [Thread-12]
o.s.c.n.e.server.EurekaServerBootstrap   : Eureka environment value
                                            eureka.environment is not set,
                                            defaulting to test
2019-04-02 07:52:26.015   INFO 30422 --- [main]
o.s.b.w.embedded.tomcat.TomcatWebServer   : Tomcat started on port(s): **8761**
                                            (http) with context path"
2019-04-02 07:52:26.016   INFO 30422 ---
[main] .s.c.n.e.s.EurekaAutoServiceRegistration : Updating port to 8761
2019-04-02 07:52:26.021   INFO 30422 --- [main]
c.example.eshop.discovery.DiscoveryApp   : **Started DiscoveryApp in 4.934
                                            seconds (JVM running for 5.675)**

Inventory Service Application

We will create an in-memory database (H2) based app that is going to manage quantity and pricing for the products registered. We'll also expose an endpoint to check current quantity for a product which can be used by the clients. We will need the following code structure to build this service:

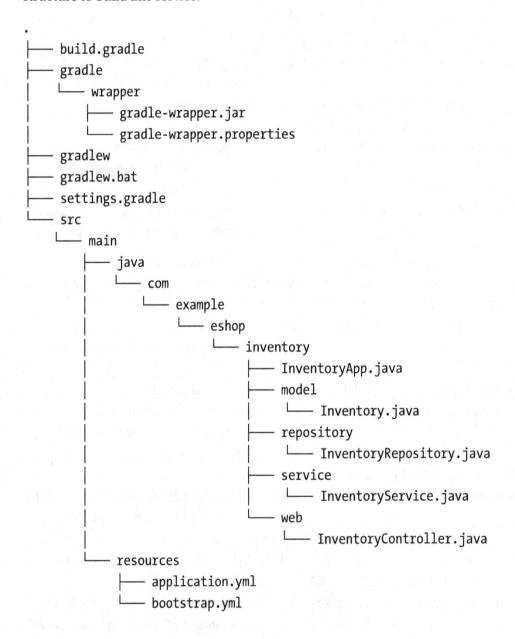

```
.
├── build.gradle
├── gradle
│   └── wrapper
│       ├── gradle-wrapper.jar
│       └── gradle-wrapper.properties
├── gradlew
├── gradlew.bat
├── settings.gradle
└── src
    └── main
        ├── java
        │   └── com
        │       └── example
        │           └── eshop
        │               └── inventory
        │                   ├── InventoryApp.java
        │                   ├── model
        │                   │   └── Inventory.java
        │                   ├── repository
        │                   │   └── InventoryRepository.java
        │                   ├── service
        │                   │   └── InventoryService.java
        │                   └── web
        │                       └── InventoryController.java
        └── resources
            ├── application.yml
            └── bootstrap.yml
```

Application Setup

Create a new application called inventory-service from http://www.spring.io with the changes in the build.gradle file, as shown in Listing 6-7.

Listing 6-7. The build.gradle File

```
bootJar  {
    baseName = 'inventory-service'
    version =  '1.0'
}
dependencies {

    compile ([
            "org.springframework.boot:spring-boot-starter-web",
            "org.springframework.boot:spring-boot-starter-data-jpa",
            "org.springframework.boot:spring-boot-starter-test",
            "org.projectlombok:lombok:1.18.6",
            "org.springframework.cloud:spring-cloud-starter-netflix-eureka-
            client",
            "org.springframework.cloud:spring-cloud-starter-config"
    ])

    compile("org.springframework.cloud:spring-cloud-starter-sleuth")
    compile("de.codecentric:spring-boot-admin-starter-client:2.1.3")
    compile("org.springframework.boot:spring-boot-starter-actuator")

    runtime("com.h2database:h2")
    testCompile("junit:junit")
}
```

Configuration

We have the config-service-related configuration properties in the bootstrap.yml file and the rest in application.yml (see Listing 6-8).

Listing 6-8. Configuration Files

bootstrap.yml

```yaml
spring:
  application:
    name: inventory-service
  profiles:
    active: dev
  cloud:
    config:
      uri: http://localhost:8888/config
```

application.yml

```yaml
server:
  servlet:
    contextPath: /inventory
  port: 8082

spring:
  jpa:
    hibernate.ddl-auto: create
    show-sql: true
    generate-ddl: true
  datasource:
    name: inventorydb
  boot:
    admin:
      client:
        url: http://localhost:7777/admin

management:
  endpoints:
    web:
      exposure:
        include: "*"
```

```yaml
eureka:
  client:
    serviceUrl:
      defaultZone: ${EUREKA_URI:http://localhost:8761/eureka}
  instance:
    preferIpAddress: false

spring.main.allow-bean-definition-overriding: true
```

Notes:

- In the `bootstrap.yml` file, we define Spring Cloud Config-related properties to connect to `config-service` at `http://localhost:8888/config`.

- In the `application.yml` file, we defined the `contentPath`, port, and JPA related properties to connect to H2 in the memory database.

- We also have Spring Boot admin-related properties, denoted by `spring.boot.*` and `management.*`, which can be ignored for the time being and are explained later.

- Further, we have the Eureka client-related properties (`eureka.client.*`), which will register this service to a discovery service. The inventory service should be able to connect to the `discovery-service` at `http://localhost:8761/eureka`. The location is defined as a key:value pair, such as `defaultZone: ${EUREKA_URI:http://localhost:8761/eureka}`.

- We have a new property called `spring.main.allow-bean-definition-overriding`. This is need post-Spring Boot 2.1.0 release to override any bean property. We are using this, as we are overriding the JPA and Eureka client-related properties.

Full Application Code

We will need the `Inventory` class as a data model and an `InventoryService` class to manage the CRUD operations for it (Listings 6-9 and 6-10). Along with these two, we also need a REST controller to access CRUD operations by other services (see Listing 6-12).

Listing 6-9. Model Class

```java
package com.example.eshop.inventory.model;

import lombok.Builder;
import lombok.Data;

import javax.persistence.Entity;
import javax.persistence.GeneratedValue;
import javax.persistence.Id;
import javax.persistence.Table;

@Entity
@Data
@Builder
@Table(name = "Inventory")
public class Inventory {

    @Id
    @GeneratedValue
    private Long inventoryId;

    Long productId;
    Integer price;
    Integer quantity;

}
```

Listing 6-10. Service Class with Business Logic

```java
package com.example.eshop.inventory.service;

import com.example.eshop.inventory.model.Inventory;
import com.example.eshop.inventory.repository.InventoryRepository;
import lombok.extern.slf4j.Slf4j;
import org.springframework.beans.factory.annotation.Autowired;
import org.springframework.stereotype.Service;

import java.util.Optional;
```

```java
@Service
@Slf4j
public class InventoryService {

    @Autowired
    InventoryRepository inventoryRepository;

    public Inventory getInventory(Long productId) {
        log.info("Inventory lookup request for productId: {}",
        productId);
        Optional<Inventory> inventory = inventoryRepository.
        findById(productId);
        return inventory.orElse(Inventory.builder()
                .inventoryId(1l)
                .productId(productId)
                .price(200)
                .quantity(2)
                .build());
    }
}
```

In this code, we query the database and either receive a product or build one using Optional. This way, we may optionally need to insert the entry in the database manually for the sample run. We have just returned a single product with quantity set to 2 and price at $200. Optionally, we can define InventoryRepository to connect to the H2 database, as shown in Listing 6-11. If data is inserted into the H2 tables, InventoryService in Listing 6-10 will return the data from the database.

Listing 6-11. Data Repository

```java
package com.example.eshop.inventory.repository;

import com.example.eshop.inventory.model.Inventory;
import org.springframework.data.jpa.repository.JpaRepository;

public interface InventoryRepository extends JpaRepository<Inventory,
Long> { }
```

Listing 6-12 contains the REST controller class needed to access CRUD operations via HTTP. We have a GET API that receives productId and returns the inventory details for this productId.

Listing 6-12. The REST Controller Class

```java
package com.example.eshop.inventory.web;

import com.example.eshop.inventory.model.Inventory;
import com.example.eshop.inventory.service.InventoryService;
import lombok.extern.slf4j.Slf4j;
import org.springframework.beans.factory.annotation.Autowired;
import org.springframework.web.bind.annotation.GetMapping;
import org.springframework.web.bind.annotation.PathVariable;
import org.springframework.web.bind.annotation.RestController;

@RestController
@Slf4j
public class InventoryController {

    @Autowired
    InventoryService inventoryService;

    @GetMapping("/api/inventory/{productId}")
    public Inventory getInventoryForProduct(@PathVariable("productId")
    Long productId) {
        log.info("Inventory request for product: {}", productId);
        Inventory inventory = inventoryService.getInventory(productId);
        log.info("inventory : {}", inventory);

        return inventory;
    }
}

package com.example.eshop.inventory;

import org.springframework.boot.SpringApplication;
import org.springframework.boot.autoconfigure.SpringBootApplication;
```

```
@SpringBootApplication
public class InventoryApp {

    public static void main(String[] args) {
        SpringApplication.run(InventoryApp.class, args);
    }

}
```

Notes:

- InventoryController exposes an endpoint with the URI set to /api/
  inventory/{productId}. The Inventory data model has a price and
  quantity that can be stored in H2 in the memory database through JPA.

- The InventoryController class acts as the RESTful web resource
  and has a GET verb method to get current available inventory for a
  product.

- There are different opinions as to using or avoiding autowiring in
  Spring through annotations. I feel that, unless the application is
  monolithic or big enough, it's not a problem. This used to create a
  problem when apps were very big and field injections were not done
  carefully, thus resulting in a God object (too big of a class instance).

Running the Inventory-Service Application

Let's run the service with profile set to Prod through the IDE. We will need to pass a VM
argument while running this Dspring.profiles.active=prod.

```
> gradle bootRun

<<skipping generic Spring Boot logs>>

:: Spring Boot ::          (v2.1.3.RELEASE)
2019-04-02 08:11:37.331    INFO [inventory-service,,,] 34042 ---
[          main]
c.c.c.ConfigServicePropertySourceLocator : Fetching config from server at :
                                           http:// localhost:8888/config/
2019-04-02 08:11:38.412    INFO [inventory-service,,,] 34042 ---
[          main]
```

c.c.c.ConfigServicePropertySourceLocator : **Located environment:
                                             name=inventory- service,
                                             profiles=[prod], label=null,**
version=70e66d9b8852ee1ba8511dbfcf4c6a245b87cbcc, state=null
2019-04-02 08:11:38.412   INFO [inventory-service,,,] 34042 ---
[main]
c.example.eshop.inventory.InventoryApp   : The following profiles are
active: prod
2019-04-02 08:11:39.774   INFO [inventory-service,,,] 34042 --- 2019-04-02
08:11:41.457   INFO [inventory-service,,,] 34042 --- [main]
o.s.b.w.embedded.tomcat.TomcatWebServer   : **Tomcat initialized with
                                            port(s): 8082** (http)
2019-04-02 08:11:41.499   INFO [inventory-service,,,] 34042 ---
[main]
o.apache.catalina.core.StandardService   : Starting service [Tomcat]
o.s.b.a.e.web.EndpointLinksResolver   : **Exposing 21 endpoint(s) beneath
                                            base path '/actuator'**
2019-04-02 08:11:47.334   INFO [inventory-service,,,] 34042 ---
[main]
com.netflix.discovery.DiscoveryClient   : Getting all instance registry
info from the eureka server
2019-04-02 08:11:48.161   INFO [inventory-service,,,] 34042 ---
[main]
com.netflix.discovery.DiscoveryClient   : The response status is 200
2019-04-02 08:11:48.164 INFO [inventory-service,,,] 34042 ---
[main]
com.netflix.discovery.DiscoveryClient   : Starting heartbeat executor:
renew interval is: 30
2019-04-02 08:11:48.167   INFO [inventory-service,,,] 34042 ---
[main]
**DiscoveryClient_INVENTORY-SERVICE/192.168.1.3:inventory-service:8082:
registering service...**

```
2019-04-02 08:11:48.235   INFO [inventory-service,,,] 34042 ---
[nfoReplicator-0]
com.netflix.discovery.DiscoveryClient    : DiscoveryClient_INVENTORY-SERVICE/
192.168.1.3:inventory-service:8082 - registration status: 204
2019-04-02 08:11:48.290   INFO [inventory-service,,,] 34042 ---
[          main]
o.s.b.w.embedded.tomcat.TomcatWebServer   : Tomcat started on port(s): 8082
                                            (http) with context path '/
                                            inventory'
```

Note the lines shown in bold in the output; they validate the connection to the config and discovery services. We can also visit the Inventory Service URL from a browser to see the response (http://localhost:8082/inventory/api/inventory/1) or use the CURL command on the console:

```
> curl http://localhost:8082/inventory/api/inventory/1

    {"inventoryId": 1,"productId": 1,"price": 200,"quantity": 2}
```

Eshop Application

This microservice has endpoints that allow customers to see the products list and place orders. Ideally in a enterprise setup, you should have different services for customer management, product catalogues, and order management. We will define a TestController to show the sample order flow here with the help of a few business services.

Most important of these services is OrderService, which is going to communicate to another microservice (Inventory Service) and then decide based on the response which products are available. If a product is not available, OrderService performs the transaction and returns the order object along with its location in the header. CustomerService and ProductService contain the methods to create the sample customer and product.

For the purpose of communicating to the inventory service, Eshop can take a number of approaches:

– Netflix OSS – Eureka Client with a REST Template

The Eureka client library offers a lookup via configured property called eureka.client.serviceUrl.defaultZone. This provides a list to all instances, which can used to connect to one of them.

    –   Netflix OSS – Ribbon with a REST Template

Ribbon also offers configuration, lookup, and connection management to Eureka server(s). Ribbon differs from Eureka Client in a way and offers auto load balancing based on a couple of algorithms rather than manually selecting one from a list.

    –   Netflix OSS – Feign

This is an interface-based client that has a target URI annotated over it as a declaration. Feign internally uses Ribbon APIs only.

    –   Spring Cloud API abstraction offers a simple solution to both the EurekaClient and Ribbon-based approaches through the `@LoadBalanced` annotation as well as through a `DiscoveryClient` class. EurekaClient internally uses Jerysey APIs and Spring Cloud `org.springframework.cloud.client.discovery.DiscoveryClient` can be utilized for Spring-preferred HTTP communication APIs.

We discuss the simple options from the Spring Cloud `@LoadBalanced` annotation and Feign in the services section. We need the following code structure to build this application:

```
.
├── build.gradle
├── gradle
│   └── wrapper
│       ├── gradle-wrapper.jar
│       └── gradle-wrapper.properties
├── gradlew
├── gradlew.bat
└── src
    └── main
        ├── java
        │   └── com
        │       └── example
```

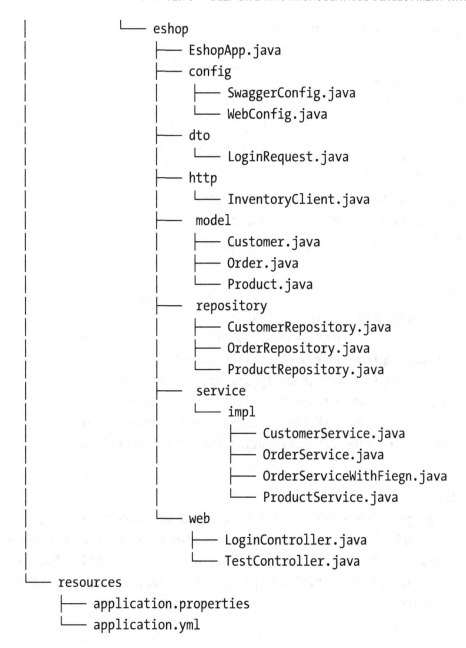

```
└── eshop
    ├── EshopApp.java
    ├── config
    │   ├── SwaggerConfig.java
    │   └── WebConfig.java
    ├── dto
    │   └── LoginRequest.java
    ├── http
    │   └── InventoryClient.java
    ├── model
    │   ├── Customer.java
    │   ├── Order.java
    │   └── Product.java
    ├── repository
    │   ├── CustomerRepository.java
    │   ├── OrderRepository.java
    │   └── ProductRepository.java
    ├── service
    │   └── impl
    │       ├── CustomerService.java
    │       ├── OrderService.java
    │       ├── OrderServiceWithFiegn.java
    │       └── ProductService.java
    └── web
        ├── LoginController.java
        └── TestController.java
└── resources
    ├── application.properties
    └── application.yml
```

Application Setup

Create a new application called eshop from http://www.spring.io with the changes shown in Listing 6-13 in the build.gradle file.

Listing 6-13. The build.gradle File

```
bootJar {
  baseName = 'eshop'
  version = '1.0'
}

dependencies {
  compile ([
      "javax.xml.bind:jaxb-api:2.3.1",
      "org.glassfish.jaxb:jaxb-runtime:2.3.2",
      "javax.activation:javax.activation-api:1.2.0"
  ])

  compile ([
      "org.projectlombok:lombok:1.18.6",
      "mysql:mysql-connector-java:8.0.15",
      "org.springframework.boot:spring-boot-starter-web",
      "org.springframework.boot:spring-boot-starter-data-jpa",
      "org.springframework.boot:spring-boot-starter-test",
      "org.springframework.cloud:spring-cloud-starter-sleuth",
      "org.springframework.boot:spring-boot-starter-actuator"
  ])

  compile ([
      "org.springframework.cloud:spring-cloud-starter-openfeign",
      "org.springframework.cloud:spring-cloud-starter-netflix-eureka-client",
      "org.springframework.cloud:spring-cloud-starter-netflix-hystrix",
      "org.springframework.cloud:spring-cloud-starter-netflix-hystrix-
      dashboard"
  ])

  compile ([
      "de.codecentric:spring-boot-admin-starter-client:2.1.3",
      "io.springfox:springfox-swagger2:2.9.2",
      "io.springfox:springfox-swagger-ui:2.9.2"
  ])
```

```
testCompile("junit:junit")
}
```

Configuration

Most of the properties in this configuration file are similar to what we previous defined in inventory-service. Listing 6-14 shows this file.

Listing 6-14. Configuration File

application.yml

```
server:
  servlet:
    context-path: /eshop
  #port: 0
  port: 8081

spring:
  application:
    name: eshop
  datasource:
    url: jdbc:mysql://localhost:3306/db1
    username: root
    password: mysql
    driver-class-name: com.mysql.jdbc.Driver
  jpa:
    hibernate.ddl-auto: update
    show-sql: true
    generate-ddl: true
  boot:
    admin:
      client:
        url: http://localhost:7777/admin

spring.jpa.hibernate.ddl-auto: update
```

```yaml
eureka:
  client:
    serviceUrl:
      defaultZone: ${EUREKA_URI:http://localhost:8761/eureka}
  instance:
    preferIpAddress: false

management:
  endpoints:
    web:
      exposure:
        include: "*"
```

Data Model, Repository and Controller Class

In this step, we define three components:

- Model (Listing 6-15)

- Repositories (Listing 6-16)

- Controller (Listing 6-17)

Let's start with the domain model, shown in Listing 6-15.

Listing 6-15. Domain Model Classes

```java
package com.example.eshop.model;

import lombok.Data;

import javax.persistence.Entity;
import javax.persistence.GeneratedValue;
import javax.persistence.GenerationType;
import javax.persistence.Id;
import java.io.Serializable;

@Data
@Entity
public class Customer implements Serializable {
```

```java
    @Id
    @GeneratedValue(strategy=GenerationType.IDENTITY)
    private Long customerId;
    private String name, email, password;
}

package com.example.eshop.model;

import lombok.Data;

import javax.persistence.Entity;
import javax.persistence.GeneratedValue;
import javax.persistence.GenerationType;
import javax.persistence.Id;
import java.io.Serializable;

@Data
@Entity
public class Product implements Serializable {

    @Id
    @GeneratedValue(strategy=GenerationType.IDENTITY)
    private Long productId;

    private String name;
    private Integer price, quantity;

}

package com.example.eshop.model;

import java.io.Serializable;
import javax.persistence.Entity;
import javax.persistence.GeneratedValue;
import javax.persistence.GenerationType;
import javax.persistence.Id;
import javax.persistence.Table;

import lombok.*;
```

```java
@Data
@Entity
@Table(name="`Order`")
public class Order implements Serializable {

    @Id
    @GeneratedValue(strategy=GenerationType.IDENTITY)
    private Long orderId;
    private Long productId, customerId;
    private int quantity, price;

}
```

We have a minimal set of fields in these models. The order object has to be enclosed in ` ` ` ` characters in the @Table annotation because Order is a keyword in MySQL. The repository interface definitions are shown in Listing 6-16.

Listing 6-16. Repository Interfaces

```java
package com.example.eshop.repository;

public interface CustomerRepository extends JpaRepository<Customer, Long>{ }

public interface ProductRepository extends JpaRepository<Product, Long> { }

public interface OrderRepository extends JpaRepository<Order, Long>{ }
```

We do not need any custom queries, thus the repositories in Listing 6-16 are defined as blank. We define the Controller class as shown in Listing 6-17.

Listing 6-17. Controller Class

```java
package com.example.eshop.web;

import com.example.eshop.model.Order;
import com.example.eshop.service.impl.CustomerService;
import com.example.eshop.service.impl.OrderService;
import com.example.eshop.service.impl.ProductService;
import lombok.extern.slf4j.Slf4j;
import org.springframework.http.ResponseEntity;
import org.springframework.web.bind.annotation.PostMapping;
```

```java
import org.springframework.web.bind.annotation.RestController;
import org.springframework.web.servlet.support.ServletUriComponentsBuilder;

import java.net.URI;
import java.util.Objects;

@RestController
@Slf4j
public class TestController {

    @Autowired
    private OrderService orderService;

    @Autowired
    private ProductService productService;

    @Autowired
    private CustomerService customerService;

    @PostMapping(value = "/api/orders", produces = "application/json")
    public ResponseEntity<?> purchaseSampleProduct()  throws Exception {

        customerService.registerNewCustomers();
        productService.registerNewProducts();

        Order order = orderService.orderProduct();
        log.info("Order status: {}", Objects.isNull(order));

        URI uri = ServletUriComponentsBuilder.fromCurrentRequest().path("/{id}")
                .buildAndExpand(order.getOrderId()).toUri();

        return ResponseEntity.created(uri).build();
    }
}
```

Notes:

- We have an endpoint with the URI path set to /api/orders.

- The purchaseSampleProduct() method in the TestController class delegates control to customer and product services to create a few sample objects.

- At last we call `OrderService` to create an order and send back the success response with the HTTP code set to 201. Ideally we should be sending back the URL of the order object as well, but we skip it here to keep things simple.

Service Classes

We will start by defining the `CustomerService` and `ProductService` classes, which just have the simple self-explanatory methods to create sample `Customer` and `Product` objects. See Listing 6-18.

Listing 6-18. Service Classes

```java
package com.example.eshop.service.impl;

import com.example.eshop.model.Customer;
import com.example.eshop.repository.CustomerRepository;
import lombok.extern.slf4j.Slf4j;
import org.springframework.beans.factory.annotation.Autowired;
import org.springframework.stereotype.Service;
import org.springframework.transaction.annotation.Isolation;
import org.springframework.transaction.annotation.Propagation;
import org.springframework.transaction.annotation.Transactional;

@Service
@Slf4j
public class CustomerService {

    @Autowired
    CustomerRepository customerRepository;

    @Transactional(propagation=Propagation.REQUIRED,
    isolation=Isolation.DEFAULT)
    public void registerNewCustomers() {
        Customer customer = new Customer();
        customer.setName("Raj Malhotra");
        customer.setEmail("raj.malhotra@example.com");
        customer.setPassword("password");
        customerRepository.saveAndFlush(customer);
```

```java
        }
    }

package com.example.eshop.service.impl;

import com.example.eshop.model.Product;
import com.example.eshop.repository.ProductRepository;
import lombok.extern.slf4j.Slf4j;
import org.springframework.beans.factory.annotation.Autowired;
import org.springframework.stereotype.Service;

@Service
@Slf4j
public class ProductService {

    @Autowired
    ProductRepository productRepository;

    public void registerNewProducts() {
        Product product = new Product();
        product.setName("Superb Java");
        product.setPrice(400);
        product.setQuantity(3);
        productRepository.save(product);
    }
}
```

Order Service Implementation Using the Eureka Client

We need three more additions to the code to enable the Netflix Eureka client:

- Configuration to declare load balanced REST template

- Define the OrderService class

- The @EnableDiscoveryClients annotation on top of the Application class

We just need a single bean definition to declare the REST template along with a @LoadBalanced annotation on the top. This code is shown in Listing 6-19.

Listing 6-19. Web Configuration for Load-Balanced REST Template

```
package com.example.eshop.config;

import org.springframework.cloud.client.loadbalancer.LoadBalanced;
import org.springframework.context.annotation.Bean;
import org.springframework.context.annotation.Configuration;
import org.springframework.web.client.RestTemplate;

@Configuration
public class WebConfig {

    @Bean
    @LoadBalanced
    public RestTemplate restTemplate() {
        return new RestTemplate();
    }
}
```

Spring has multiple options to connect to EurekaServer:

- Native EurekaClient (com.netflix.discovery.EurekaClient)

- DiscoveryClient (org.springframework.cloud.client.discovery. DiscoveryClient)

- RestTemplate

The easiest option is to use the RestTemplate, which is integrated with the EurekaClient and Ribbon (load balancing) APIs.

Let's now define OrderService and look at using the Eureka Client (see Listing 6-20).

Listing 6-20. OrderService Using Eureka Client

```
package com.example.eshop.service.impl;

import com.example.eshop.http.InventoryClient;
import com.example.eshop.model.Order;
import com.example.eshop.repository.OrderRepository;
import com.fasterxml.jackson.databind.ObjectMapper;
```

```java
import com.netflix.hystrix.contrib.javanica.annotation.HystrixCommand;
import lombok.extern.slf4j.Slf4j;
import org.springframework.beans.factory.annotation.Autowired;
import org.springframework.stereotype.Service;
import org.springframework.web.client.RestTemplate;

import java.util.Map;

@Service
@Slf4j
public class OrderService {

    @Autowired
    ProductService productService;

    @Autowired
    OrderRepository orderRepository;

    @Autowired
    @LoadBalanced
    RestTemplate restTemplate;

    @Autowired
    InventoryClient inventoryClient;

    public Order orderProduct()    {

        Order order = null;

        Map<String, Integer> map = null;
        ObjectMapper mapper = new ObjectMapper();

        String resultJson =
                this.restTemplate
                .getForObject("http://INVENTORY-SERVICE/
                        inventory/api/inventory/" + 1, String.class);
        try {
            map = mapper.readValue(resultJson.getBytes(),
                                                HashMap.class);
            log.info("Result from inventory service: {}", map);
```

```java
        }catch(Exception e) {
            log.error("Error while reading back json value: {}", map);
            return null;
        }

        Integer qty = map.get("quantity");
        if(qty >=2)
            order = createOrder(1l, 1l, 2, 400);

        log.info("Orders {}", orderRepository.findAll());

        return order;
    }

    public Order createOrder(Long productId, Long customerId, int
    quantity, int price) {
        Order order = new Order();
        order.setCustomerId(customerId);
        order.setProductId(productId);
        order.setPrice(price);
        order.setQuantity(quantity);
        order = orderRepository.save(order);
        return order;
    }

    private Order handleInventoryFailure() {
        log.error("Cannot connect to inventory service with 20%
requests failing in 10 seconds interval");
        return null;
    }
}
```

Notes:

- We have the RestTemplate code to communicate to the inventory service through its service name (INVENTORY-SERVICE) registered in the discovery service (Eureka Server).

- After receiving the response from the inventory service, we use
  Jackson's Object mapper to convert the returned JSON string to an
  object of java.util.Map.

- There are more methods in the RestTemplate to retrieve an Object
  return type directly. We have used this approach for simplicity.

At last, we need to annotate the Application class with @EnableDiscoveryClient
(see Listing 6-21) to enable the Eureka Client feature in the application.

Listing 6-21. Application Class

```
package com.example.eshop;

import lombok.extern.slf4j.Slf4j;
import org.springframework.boot.CommandLineRunner;
import org.springframework.boot.SpringApplication;
import org.springframework.boot.autoconfigure.SpringBootApplication;
import org.springframework.cloud.client.circuitbreaker.
EnableCircuitBreaker;
import org.springframework.cloud.client.discovery.EnableDiscoveryClient;
import org.springframework.cloud.openfeign.EnableFeignClients;

@SpringBootApplication
@EnableDiscoveryClient
@Slf4j
public class EshopApp {

    public static void main(String[] args) throws Exception {
        SpringApplication.run(EshopApp.class, args);
    }
}
```

Running the Eshop Application

Run the application:

```
> gradle bootRun
```

```
<<skipping generic Spring Boot logs>>
```

```
:: Spring Boot ::          (v2.1.3.RELEASE)
2019-04-02 08:42:32.698   INFO [eshop,,,] 39989 --- [          main]
com.example.eshop.EshopApp               : No active profile set, falling
                                           back to default profiles: default

2019-04-02 08:42:40.095   INFO [eshop,,,] 39989 --- [          main]
o.s.b.a.e.web.EndpointLinksResolver      : Exposing 21 endpoint(s) beneath
                                           base path '/actuator'

2019-04-02 08:42:41.768   INFO [eshop,,,] 39989 --- [          main]
com.netflix.discovery.DiscoveryClient    : Initializing Eureka in region
                                           us-east-1

o.s.c.n.e.s.EurekaServiceRegistry        : Registering application ESHOP
                                           with eureka with status UP

2019-04-02 08:42:42.612   INFO [eshop,,,] 39989 --- [          main]
com.netflix.discovery.DiscoveryClient    : Saw local status change event
StatusChangeEvent [timestamp=1554174762612, current=UP, previous=STARTING]
2019-04-02 08:42:42.877   INFO [eshop,,,] 39989 --- [          main]
o.s.b.w.embedded.tomcat.TomcatWebServer  : Tomcat started on port(s): 8081
                                           (http) with context path '/eshop'
```

We have successfully started the eshop service on port 8081. We also have the other three services running in standalone mode—config-service, discovery-service, and inventory-service. We can now visit the eshop service order-creation API using CURL from a terminal:

```
> curl -H "Content-Type: application/json" -X POST -i http://localhost:8081/
eshop/api/orders
```

```
    HTTP/1.1 201
    Location: http://localhost:8081/eshop/api/orders/1
    Content-Length: 0
    Date: Tue, 02 Apr 2019 03:28:35 GMT
```

This output shows a successful response from the eshop service. The request makes an implicit hit to inventory-service as well and the following log statement is printed on the console of inventory-service.

```
c.e.e.i.service.InventoryService    : Inventory lookup request for productId: 1
c.e.e.inventory.web.InventoryController   : inventory :
Inventory(inventoryId=1, productId=1, price=200, quantity=2)
```

By looking at the output of these two services, we can confirm calls between eshop and inventory-service. The log statement "Inventory lookup request for productId: 1" in the console of inventory-service confirms this.

Discovery Service Dashboard

Let's also look at the dashboard, as mentioned in Section 6.3.1, provided by the Eureka Server (discovery-service) in a browser. The location bar should read http:// localhost:8761/.

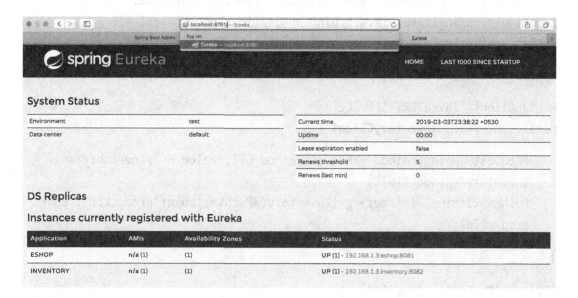

Figure 6-4. *Eureka Server dashboard*

From the output in Figure 6-4, we can see that eshop and inventory-service have been registered successfully and appear in green on the discovery-service web dashboard. If any service or even one of the nodes with a service goes down, this will be reflected on this dashboard in red.

Order Service Implementation Using Feign

As mentioned at the start of Section 6.3.3, let's build the same `OrderService` again with Feign-based implementation. We will need three more additions to enable this, as mentioned in Listing 6-22:

- A new interface to declare remote URI for Feign client

- An `@EnableFeignClients` annotation on top of the `Application` class

- The `OrderServiceWithFeign` class

Listing 6-22. Service API Code

Feign Interface:

```
package com.example.eshop.http;

import org.springframework.cloud.openfeign.FeignClient;
import org.springframework.web.bind.annotation.PathVariable;
import org.springframework.web.bind.annotation.RequestMapping;
import org.springframework.web.bind.annotation.RequestMethod;

import java.util.HashMap;

@FeignClient("INVENTORY-SERVICE")
public interface InventoryClient {

    @RequestMapping(method = RequestMethod.GET, value = "/inventory/api/
    inventory/{productId}")
    HashMap<String, Integer> getInventory(@PathVariable("productId") Long
    productId);

}
```

Application class changes :

```
package com.example.eshop;

import lombok.extern.slf4j.Slf4j;
import org.springframework.boot.CommandLineRunner;
import org.springframework.boot.SpringApplication;
import org.springframework.boot.autoconfigure.SpringBootApplication;
```

```java
import org.springframework.cloud.client.discovery.EnableDiscoveryClient;
import org.springframework.cloud.openfeign.EnableFeignClients;

@SpringBootApplication
@EnableFeignClients
@EnableDiscoveryClient
@Slf4j
public class EshopApp {

    public static void main(String[] args) throws Exception {
        SpringApplication.run(EshopApp.class, args);
    }
}
```

New OrderService changes :

```java
package com.example.eshop.service.impl;

import com.example.eshop.http.InventoryClient;
import com.example.eshop.model.Order;
import com.example.eshop.repository.OrderRepository;
import lombok.extern.slf4j.Slf4j;
import org.springframework.beans.factory.annotation.Autowired;
import org.springframework.stereotype.Service;

import java.util.Map;

@Service
@Slf4j
public class OrderServiceWithFiegn {

        @Autowired
        OrderRepository orderRepository;

        @Autowired
        InventoryClient inventoryClient;

        public Order orderProduct()     {

            Order order = null;
```

```
    Map<String, Integer> map = inventoryClient.getInventory(1l);
    log.info("Result from inventory service through feign: {}", map);

    Integer qty = map.get("quantity");
    if(qty >=2)
        order = createOrder(1l, 1l, 2, 400);

    log.info("Orders {}", orderRepository.findAll());

    return order;
    }
}
```

Notes:

- In InventoryClient, we declared the Feign annotation (@FeignClient("INVENTORY- SERVICE")) and mentioned the exact service name of the target registered service in the Eureka Server (discovery-service).

- We have added the annotation (@EnableFeignClients) on top of the Application class.

- Next, we injected the InventoryClient in the service class via autowiring.

- This is all we need. The rest of the code is nearly the same as with OrderService from the previous section.

- The clear difference we can see is the reduced and clean code due to the declarative REST client.

Resiliency in the Microservices Architecture

The microservices architecture helps break down problems into pieces and therefore a single request may flow through a couple of requests for a single use case. This poses a new risk of system failure to end clients due to any single service failing in the request flow. Netflix OSS Hystrix helps by handling such failures gracefully. This is based on a well known circuit- breaker pattern. Let's see this example through the Eshop service, which we created in Section 6.3.3. Hystrix also provides a web-based dashboard for monitoring applications.

As a recap, we created `TestController` in the eshop service and it calls the `OrderService` class. `OrderService` further calls the `inventory-service` to check inventory for the given `productId`.

Now let's say that `inventory-service` stops responding due to a system crash or it starts throwing errors due to the database not responding. In both these cases, `TestController` will keep sending all requests to the same failing `inventory-service` forever. With Hystrix in place, we can configure the calling service to detect continuous failures in calls and add a fallback method to be called in such situations. Let's see a code example.

We will need a dependency addition in `build.gradle` in the eshop service:

```
compile("org.springframework.cloud:spring-cloud-starter-netflix-hystrix")
```

We also need to make the changes to the `OrderService` and `Application` classes shown in Listing 6-23.

Listing 6-23. Service Class

```
public class OrderService {

    @HystrixCommand(
            fallbackMethod = "handleInventoryFailure",
            commandProperties = {
        @HystrixProperty(name =
            "execution.isolation.thread.timeoutInMilliseconds", value =
            "3000"),
        @HystrixProperty(name = "circuitBreaker.requestVolumeThreshold",
        value ="2")
    })
    public Order orderProduct()   {
            String resultJson = this.restTemplate.getForObject("http://
            INVENTORY-SERVICE/inventory/api/inventory/" + 1, String.
            class);
                // skipping repeating rest of the code

    }
```

```java
        private Order handleInventoryFailure() {
                log.error("Inventory Service is responding very slow");
                return null;
        }
}

@SpringBootApplication
@EnableFeignClients
@EnableDiscoveryClient
@Slf4j
@EnableCircuitBreaker
@EnableHystrixDashboard
public class EshopApp {
  public static void main(String[] args) throws Exception {
    SpringApplication.run(EshopApp.class, args);
  }
}
```

Notes:

- If the orderProduct() method starts taking too long due to the inventory-service being slow, the Hystrix library is going to call the alternative method (handleInventoryFailure()) as a fallback.

- By default, this TimeOut interval is 10 seconds and can be changed by setting the Hystrix property, as we have done in the code (changed it to 3000 milliseconds or 3 seconds).

- We added an annotation on top of the Application class called @EnableCircuitBreaker to enable this feature in the application.

Checking Hystrix

We need to restart the eshop and inventory-service applications to apply these changes.

```
> gradle bootRun

<<skipping generic Spring Boot logs>>
:: Spring Boot ::          (v2.1.3.RELEASE)
```

```
70051 --- [           main] com.example.eshop.EshopApp
:No active
profile set, falling back to default profiles: default
70051 --- [           main] o.s.boot.actuate.endpoint.EndpointId
: Endpoint ID
'service-registry' contains invalid characters, please migrate to a valid
format.
70051 --- [           main] o.s.b.w.embedded.tomcat.TomcatWebServer
: Tomcat initialized with port(s): 8081 (http)
70051 --- [           main] o.s.b.a.e.web.ServletEndpointRegistrar
: Registered '/actuator/hystrix.stream' to hystrix.stream-actuator-endpoint
70051 --- [           main] o.s.c.n.e.s.EurekaServiceRegistry
: Registering application ESHOP with eureka with status UP
70051 --- [           main] o.s.b.w.embedded.tomcat.TomcatWebServer
: Tomcat started on port(s): 8081 (http) with context path '/eshop'
```

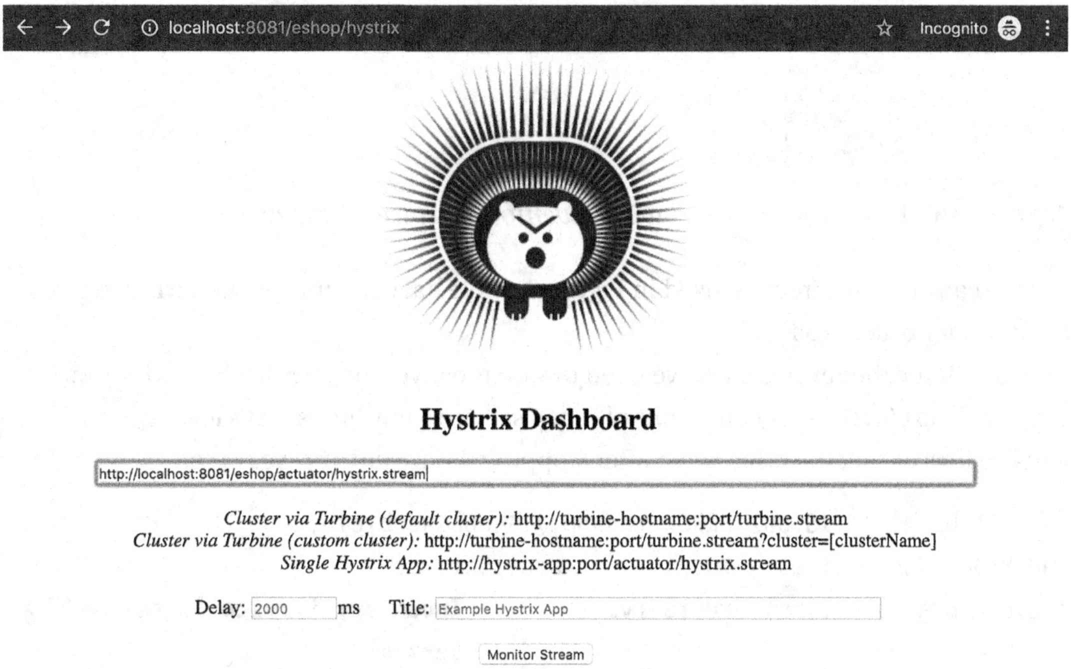
localhost:8081/eshop/hystrix
Incognito
Hystrix Dashboard
http://localhost:8081/eshop/actuator/hystrix.stream
Cluster via Turbine (default cluster): http://turbine-hostname:port/turbine.stream
Cluster via Turbine (custom cluster): http://turbine-hostname:port/turbine.stream?cluster=[clusterName]
Single Hystrix App: http://hystrix-app:port/actuator/hystrix.stream
Delay: 2000 ms
Title: Example Hystrix App
Monitor Stream

Figure 6-5. *Hystrix dashboard*

Hystrix also implicitly creates a default endpoint at "http://localhost:8081/eshop/hystrix.

Under the hood, Hystrix generates a stream of metrics data, available at http://localhost: 8081/eshop/actuator/hystrix.stream. We need to enter this Hystrix stream URL in the input box of the Hystrix dashboard screen, as shown in Figure 6-5. Additionally we need to visit the /api/orders API endpoint of eshop service again, as we did in Section 6.3.3.6. The dashboard will look like Figure 6-6.

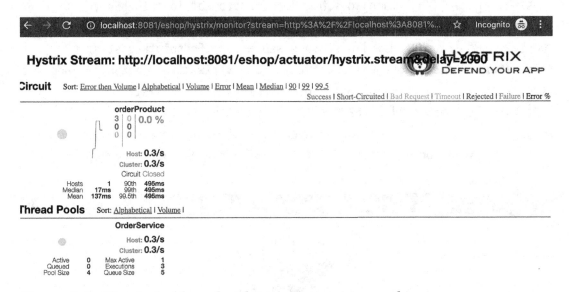

Figure 6-6. *Hystrix dashboard with inventory-service working*

We can see the Circuit Closed in Figure 6-6. We have a number appearing in green as "3" under orderProduct.

To validate the reverse case, we need to stop the inventory service for a while and visit the / api/orders API endpoint of eshop service a few times. Let's look at the console logs of eshop service again after stopping the inventory-service:

2019-04-02 22:13:18.002 ERROR [**eshop**,7155a8b13c0b7e1b,
2a018f069c73c5b7,false] 70051 --- [-OrderService-2]
c.e.eshop.service.impl.OrderService   : **Inventory Service is responding
                                           very slow**

2019-04-02 22:13:18.003 ERROR [**eshop**,7155a8b13c0b7e1b,
7155a8b13c0b7e1b,false] 70051 --- [nio-8081-exec-6]
com.example.eshop.web.TestController   : **Transactions are failing, please
                                            check after some time**

These log statements were added to the `OrderService.handleInventoryFailure()` method in the `eshop` service. This validates that the fallback method is getting called, in case of timeout from an inventory service. In other words, the circuit has opened and the fallback mechanism is working fine. We can now observe the same effect in the Hystrix dashboard, as shown in Figure 6-7.

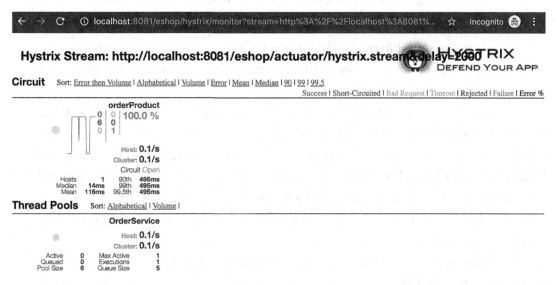

Figure 6-7. *Hystrix dashboard when inventory-service is not working*

We can see from Figure 6-7 that there are six requests that short-circuited. This means there are six requests that have been caught by Hystrix because target service (`inventory-service`) was not working.

Request Tracing in the Microservices Architecture

Another common challenge in distributed systems programming is that post production deployment, it becomes difficult to trace the request flow across services. This concern creates two problems to solve—centralized logs and request tracing.

For central logging, we need to merge all logs generated on multiple servers to a central point where we can do searching, troubleshooting, and analytics. This is not a new problem. The industry standard solutions collect and allow searching on logs from multiple nodes in a cluster. Examples include ELK, Fluentd, Graylog, Splunk, and more. They all support two modes of log collection:

- On the basis of an agent doing tail on the log files and sending the most recently collected ones incrementally to the server.

- Sending logs directly using their API SDKs from the application to the server.

Request tracing is a different problem to solve and becomes bigger with the increasing number of microservices. This is required when we want to trace a request or a transaction spanning multiple services.

Spring Cloud offers a solution for this need through Spring Cloud Sleuth. Let's say we want to trace a single failing (with some error code) request or even do log analysis based on some common attribute for any request across services. This library can be helpful in embedding a TraceId for each new request in logs. TraceId is a unique UUID for every single new request, generated by Spring Sleuth. If the request goes through multiple services, Spring Sleuth will track this ID and keep it the same in the second service logs as well.

There are four such attributes generated with two such IDs. The full syntax of this generated data looks like this:

```
[APPLICATION_NAME, TRACE_ID, SPAN_ID, EXPORT_LOGS_OR_NOT]
```

- APPLICATION_NAME: The name of the service

- TRACE_ID: The unique ID for the request

- SPAN_ID: The unique ID for each span of work. In our example, SPAN_ID will be different for the Eshop and Inventory services for the same request.

- EXPORT_LOGS_OR_NOT: Whether or not logs should be exported to some other tool.

There are tools also available today that can help you visualize the logs utilizing the generated attributes and trace the services. Two such examples are Google's Dapper and Zipkin. We will not discuss them in detail, as they are not in the scope of this book. In order to implement distributed tracing logs in an application, there are four steps:

1. Add the new dependencies to the eshop and inventory-service microservices in the build.gradle file and restart them:

   ```
   compile("org.springframework.cloud:spring-cloud-starter-sleuth")
   compile("org.springframework.cloud:spring-cloud-starter-zipkin")
   ```

2. Download and start the Zipkin Jar file as a service from zipkin.io:

   ```
   java -jar ./zipkin-server-2.12.7-exec.jar
   ```

3. Add a property to the application.yml file of eshop and inventory-service and restart them both:

   ```
   spring.zipkin.base-url: http://localhost:9411/
   ```

4. Visit the /api/orders API of the eshop service a couple of times again.

   ```
   > curl -H "Content-Type: application/json" -X POST -i
   http://localhost:8081/eshop/ api/orders
   ```

Once you have made these changes, Spring Cloud Sleuth will start adding the following attributes to each log statement.

```
/eshop/src/main/resources/application.yml
INFO [eshop,6e0abc792dc25b96,e49bf80a97204e7e,false] 67023 ---
[-OrderService-1]
c.e.eshop.service.impl.OrderService      : Result from inventory service:
{quantity=2, productId=1, price=200, inventoryId=1}

/inventory-service/src/main/resources/application.yml
INFO [inventory-service,3d3af1edbfa15240,50f818143fd68f39,false] 19246 ---
[nio-8082-exec-1] c.e.e.inventory.web.InventoryResource    : Inventory
request for product: 1
```

These logs can help trace the same request going across Eshop as well as inventory-services. Figure 6-8 shows this same correlation through Zipkin's UI.

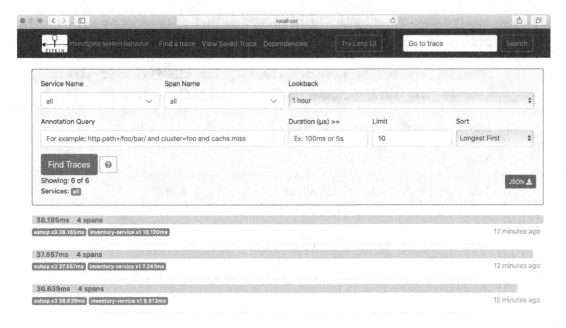

Figure 6-8. *Zipkin UI*

Figure 6-9 shows another second-level view when we click on the service names shown in green in Figure 6-8.

Figure 6-9. *Zipkin UI, second-level view*

Monitoring in the Microservices Architecture

Management and monitoring of the production applications is a vast topic and we will only discuss the easy options available in frameworks to support our continued example so far. We have an open source web-based application called Spring Boot Admin (SBA) for basic monitoring of Spring Boot applications. The information it provides through its UI is quite extensive.

The magic actually happens at first through another project, called the Spring Boot *Actuator*. The Actuator contains the services that keep collection metrics data from JVM and other system components. The Actuator also exposes the RESTful endpoints through which the same collected information can be directly viewed. The SBA application has been built as a UI on top of these Actuator endpoints. Table 6-1 shows a list of endpoints in the Actuator.

Table 6-1. *The Actuator Endpoints*

Endpoint ID	Description
auditevents	Exposes audit events (e.g. `auth_success`, `order_failed`) for your application.
info	Displays information about your application.
health	Displays your application's health status.
metrics	Shows various metrics information of your application.
loggers	Displays and modifies the configured loggers.
logfile	Returns the contents of the log file (if `logging.file` or `logging.pathproperties` are set).
httptrace	Displays HTTP trace info for the last 100 HTTP requests/responses.
env	Displays current environment properties.
flyway	Shows details of Flyway database migrations.
liquidbase	Shows details of Liquibase database migrations.
shutdown	Lets you shut down the application gracefully.
mappings	Displays a list of all `@RequestMapping` paths.
scheduledtasks	Displays the scheduled tasks in your application.
threaddump	Performs a thread dump.
heapdump	Returns a GZip-compressed JVM heap dump.

By default, the Actuator endpoints are exposed over the path {/contextPath}/actuator/*. **SBA** has two APIs to enable this feature in applications—Server and Client. The SBA client API keeps gathering and sending the monitoring metrics data collected from the Actuator endpoints to configured SBA Server continuously. Because of this, we need to enable the Actuator in all the applications that we want to monitor with SBA. In our example case, we need the following two steps:

1. Create a new service called `admin-service`.

2. Configure the existing `eshop` and `inventory-service` applications as `admin-service` clients.

The `admin-service` client we will create in this section is probably the smallest of all services we have built so far in this chapter. The code structure for this application is as follows:

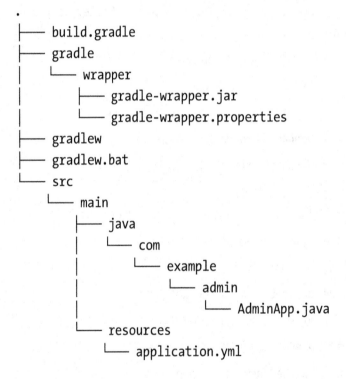

```
.
├── build.gradle
├── gradle
│   └── wrapper
│       ├── gradle-wrapper.jar
│       └── gradle-wrapper.properties
├── gradlew
├── gradlew.bat
└── src
    └── main
        ├── java
        │   └── com
        │       └── example
        │           └── admin
        │               └── AdminApp.java
        └── resources
            └── application.yml
```

Application Setup

Create a new app called `admin-service` from `http://www.spring.io` with the changes shown in Listing 6-24 in the `build.gradle` file.

Listing 6-24. The build.gradle File

```
bootJar {
    baseName = 'admin-service'
    version  = '1.0'
}

dependencies {
    compile("org.springframework.boot:spring-boot-starter-web")
    compile("de.codecentric:spring-boot-admin-server:2.1.3")
    compile("de.codecentric:spring-boot-admin-server-ui:2.1.3")
    compile("org.projectlombok:lombok:1.18.6")
}
```

As we see the dependencies, this is not a Spring project but another open source project under the Apache 2 license (https://github.com/codecentric/spring-boot-admin).

Configuration

Apart from common settings, we need to enable the basic security through Spring to secure access to its UI, as per Listing 6-25.

Listing 6-25. Application.yml

```
server:
  port: 7777

spring:
  application:
    name: admin-service
  boot:
    admin:
      context-path: /admin
      client:
        username: user
        password: secret
```

Application Class

We need to enable the admin server functionality by adding the @EnableAdminServer annotation to the top of the Application class, which we do in Listing 6-26.

Listing 6-26. Application Class

```
package com.example.admin;

import de.codecentric.boot.admin.server.config.EnableAdminServer;
import org.springframework.boot.SpringApplication;
import org.springframework.boot.autoconfigure.EnableAutoConfiguration;
import org.springframework.context.annotation.Configuration;

@Configuration
@EnableAutoConfiguration
@EnableAdminServer
public class AdminApp {
    public static void main(String[] args) {
        SpringApplication.run(AdminApp.class, args);
    }
}
```

Admin Service Client

We need to add the Spring Boot Admin client configuration settings in the application. yml file of all the other microservices that we need to monitor via this service. In our example case, let's add the properties in eshop, inventory-service, config-service, and discovery-service, as shown in Listing 6-27.

Listing 6-27. Application.yml

```
spring:
  boot:
    admin:
      client:
        url: http://localhost:7777/admin

management:
  endpoints:
```

```
web:
  exposure:
    include: "*"
```

Notes:

–   The management.endpoints.web.exposure.* properties are from the
    library Spring Boot Actuator. We can specify a comma-separated list
    of the endpoint names from Table 6-1 in Section 6.6. Specifying *
    means we are exposing all the endpoint data over HTTP.

–   The spring.boot.admin.client.* properties are related to the SBA
    client, which keeps sending data collected from these exposed
    Actuator endpoints on a regular interval to the configured admin
    server URL (note the client.url property).

Testing the Admin Service

To see this in action, start admin-service and then restart config-service, discovery-service, eshop, and inventory-service in sequence.

```
> gradle bootRun
:: Spring Boot ::              (v2.1.3.RELEASE)
2019-04-04 23:39:32.030    INFO 93382 --- [          main]
com.example.admin.AdminApp          : No active profile set, falling
                                      back to default profiles: default
2019-04-04 23:39:33.515    WARN 93382 --- [          main]
ion$DefaultTemplateResolverConfiguration  : Cannot find template location:
classpath:/templates/ (please add some templates or check your Thymeleaf
configuration)
2019-04-04 23:39:34.004    INFO 93382 --- [          main]
o.s.b.a.e.web.EndpointLinksResolver       : Exposing 2 endpoint(s) beneath
                                      base path '/actuator'
2019-04-04 23:39:34.706    INFO 93382 --- [          main]
o.s.b.web.embedded.netty.NettyWebServer    : Netty started on port(s): 7777
2019-04-04 23:39:34.715    INFO 93382 --- [          main]
com.example.admin.AdminApp          : Started AdminApp in 3.19
                                      seconds (JVM running for 3.682)
```

Once all these services are started, we can see the `admin-service` UI in the browser at `http:// localhost:7777/admin#/applications`. Figure 6-10 shows that all the services are getting monitored in the `admin-service`. If we click on the hyperlinks of any of these service names, all the metrics are shown, as shown in Figure 6-10 and Figure 6-11.

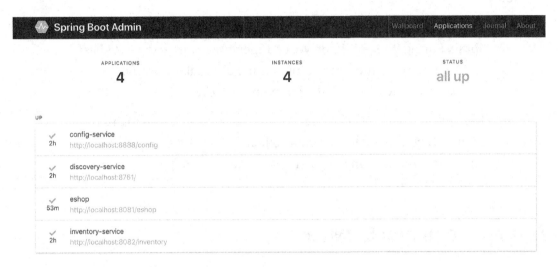

Figure 6-10. *Spring Boot Admin web console*

Figure 6-11. *eshop service details*

Rapid-Fire Documentation

There are quite a few options to describe REST API with Java. We will look at the OpenAPI Specification (OAS), a project within the OpenAPI Initiative. OpenAPI is a Linux Foundation Collaborative Project with over 20 members, including Adobe, IBM, Google, Microsoft, and Salesforce. The OpenAPI Specification (OAS) is aimed to define a standard, programming language-agnostic interface description for REST APIs.

This specification ends the search comparisons between feature sets of different frameworks, such as Json Schema, WADL, RAML, and Swagger. We will now have different implementations, just like JDBC drivers for this specification. The specification is so far fully implemented by a couple of clients for different languages. We will look at Swagger in this chapter, which is written in Java (https://github.com/swagger-api). Swagger provides a list of tools for authoring (Swagger Editor), viewing (Swagger UI), and generating code (Swagger Codegen):

- **Swagger Editor**: The browser-based editor where you can write OpenAPI specs.

- **Swagger UI**: renders OpenAPI specs as interactive API documentation.

- **Swagger Codegen**: generates server stubs and client libraries from an OpenAPI spec.

We can either create a YAML file and generate projects from that or we can embed Swagger specs related properties through its annotations within a Spring Boot application. We will cover the Spring Boot integration example in this section to enabling Swagger API through our microservices example. We need to include two dependencies in the eshop service to see a working example:

```
compile("io.springfox:springfox-swagger2:2.9.2")
compile("io.springfox:springfox-swagger-ui:2.9.2")
```

Java Configuration

We need to define Swagger-related configuration first and then define the annotations for RESTful resources in the controller classes. Listing 6-28 shows the basic Java configuration for Swagger.

Listing 6-28. Java Configuration for Swagger

```
package com.example.eshop.config;

import org.springframework.context.annotation.Bean;
import org.springframework.context.annotation.Configuration;
import springfox.documentation.builders.RequestHandlerSelectors;
import springfox.documentation.spi.DocumentationType;
import springfox.documentation.spring.web.plugins.Docket;
import springfox.documentation.swagger2.annotations.EnableSwagger2;
import static springfox.documentation.builders.PathSelectors.regex;

@Configuration
@EnableSwagger2
public class SwaggerConfig {

    @Bean
    public Docket productApi() {
        return new Docket(DocumentationType.SWAGGER_2)
                .select()
                .apis(RequestHandlerSelectors.basePackage("com.example.
                eshop"))
                .paths(regex("/api.*"))
                .build();

    }
    private ApiInfo apiInfo() {
        return new ApiInfoBuilder().title("Eshop Service API")
                .description("Eshop API reference for developers")
                .termsOfServiceUrl("http://localhost:8201/eshop")
                .contact(new Contact("Raj Malhotra", "http://
    www.example.com", "mraj6046@gmail.com")).license("Example License
    Title")
                .licenseUrl("http://localhost:8201/eshop/
    license").version("1.0").build();
    }

}
```

Notes:

- The first method, called `productApi()`, provides a `Docket` bean, which is a builder intended to be the primary interface into the Springfox framework.

- `Docket` allows you to define the package where controller classes annotated with Swagger annotations can be found and the paths for all APIs.

- The second bean, called `ApiInfo`, allows you to define the general information, such as user/author contact details and license information.

Customizing Swagger

As the next step, we need to describe the `Controller` class methods with Swagger annotations to define their descriptions, input, and output variables along with error codes. Listing 6-29 shows the final annotations on top of the Spring Web `RestControllers`.

Listing 6-29. Controller Class

```
package com.example.eshop.web;

import com.example.eshop.model.Order;
import com.example.eshop.service.impl.CustomerService;
import com.example.eshop.service.impl.OrderService;
import com.example.eshop.service.impl.ProductService;
import com.netflix.discovery.EurekaClient;
import com.netflix.discovery.shared.Applications;
import io.swagger.annotations.ApiOperation;
import io.swagger.annotations.ApiResponse;
import io.swagger.annotations.ApiResponses;
import lombok.extern.slf4j.Slf4j;
import org.springframework.beans.factory.annotation.Autowired;
import org.springframework.cloud.client.ServiceInstance;
import org.springframework.cloud.client.discovery.DiscoveryClient;
import org.springframework.http.HttpStatus;
```

```java
import org.springframework.http.ResponseEntity;
import org.springframework.web.bind.annotation.GetMapping;
import org.springframework.web.bind.annotation.PostMapping;
import org.springframework.web.bind.annotation.RestController;
import org.springframework.web.servlet.support.ServletUriComponentsBuilder;

import java.net.URI;
import java.util.List;
import java.util.Objects;

@RestController
@Slf4j
public class TestController {

    private OrderService orderService;
    private ProductService productService;
    private CustomerService customerService;

    public TestController(CustomerService customerService,
ProductService productService, OrderService orderService) {
        this.customerService = customerService;
        this.productService = productService;
        this.orderService = orderService;
    }
    @ApiOperation(value = "Order a product", response = Boolean.class)
    @ApiResponses(value = {
            @ApiResponse(code = 201, message = "Order created
            successfully"),
            @ApiResponse(code = 404, message = "The resource you were
            trying to reach is not found")
    })
    @PostMapping(value = "/api/orders", produces = "application/json")
    public ResponseEntity<?> purchaseSampleProduct()    throws Exception
{

        customerService.registerNewCustomers();
        productService.registerNewProducts();
```

```java
        Order order = orderService.orderProduct();

        if(Objects.isNull(order)) {
            log.error("Transactions are failing, please check after some
            time");
            return new
ResponseEntity<>(HttpStatus.INTERNAL_SERVER_ERROR);
        }

        log.info("Order status: {}", Objects.isNull(order));

        URI uri =
ServletUriComponentsBuilder.fromCurrentRequest().path("/{id}")
                .buildAndExpand(order.getOrderId()).toUri();

        return ResponseEntity.created(uri).build();
    }
}
```

When we restart the eshop service, documentation for the only RESTful endpoint
(/api/ order) we created in the service is available at http://localhost:8081/eshop/
swagger-ui.html (see Figure 6-12).

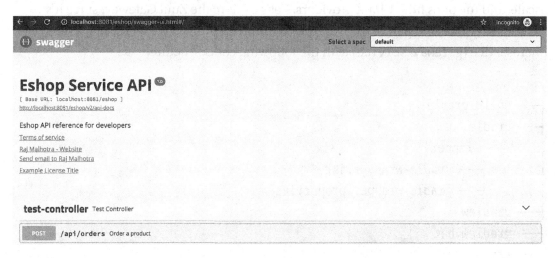

Figure 6-12. *Swagger UI*

API Gateway

API Gateway is a popular concept in the microservices architecture. If there are multiple microservices in any system, a central entry point for all incoming requests can be beneficial in a few essential cross-cutting ways:

- Routing

- Central authentication

- Authorization via Basic Auth, OAuth, JWT, API Key, etc.

- SSL termination

- Rate limiting

- Caching and monitoring

There are two popular API Gateways that are open source, written in Java, and easily integrated with Spring Frameworks:

- Netflix OS Zuul

- Spring Cloud Gateway

Additionally, there are more popular choices, such as Mashery, Apigee, Kong, WSO2, 3scale, and the ones from Cloud providers. Let's explore the Zuul Gateway, since it's a common choice and part of the Netflix OSS umbrella project. We will create a new microservice (`gateway-service`) with the following code structure:

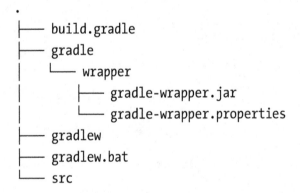

```
.
├── build.gradle
├── gradle
│   └── wrapper
│       ├── gradle-wrapper.jar
│       └── gradle-wrapper.properties
├── gradlew
├── gradlew.bat
└── src
```

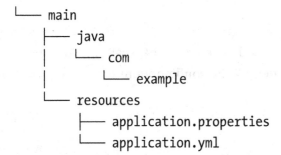

```
└── main
    ├── java
    │   └── com
    │       └── example
    └── resources
        ├── application.properties
        └── application.yml
```

We'll walk through the creation of the gateway in the following sections.

Application Setup

Create a new application called `gateway-service` from `http://www.spring.io` with the dependencies shown in Listing 6-30 in the `build.gradle` file.

Listing 6-30. The build.gradle File

```
bootJar {
    baseName = 'admin-service'
    version =  '1.0'
}

dependencies {
    compile("org.springframework.boot:spring-boot-starter-web")
    compile('org.springframework.cloud:spring-cloud-starter-netflix-zuul:
    2.1.1.RELEASE')
    compile("org.projectlombok:lombok:1.18.6")
}

dependencyManagement {
    imports {
        mavenBom "org.springframework.cloud:spring-cloud-
        dependencies:Greenwich.SR1"
    }
}
```

Configuration

Ideally, gateway-service should run on a load balancer so that scale and failover concerns can be addressed. Listing 6-31 defines the configurations for this service along with the explanation in notes.

Listing 6-31. Application.yml

application.yml

```
spring:
  application:
    name: zuul
  boot:
    admin:
      client:
        url: http://localhost:7777/admin

server:
  port: 9999

management:
  endpoints:
    web:
      exposure:
        include: "*"

zuul:
  ignoredServices: '*'
  routes:
    config:
      path: /config/**
      url: http://localhost:8888/config/
    eshop:
      path: /eshop/**
      url: http://localhost:8081/eshop/
    inventory:
      path: /inventory/**
```

```
    url: http://localhost:8082/inventory/
  admin:
    path: /admin/**
    url: http://localhost:7777/admin/
```

Notes:

- We have seen the most common use for this service to route requests
  to different domain URLs.

- The `zuul.routes.config.*` properties point to the URLs based on
  the context path.

Bootstrapping

We need to add another annotation called `@EnableZuulProxy` on top of the `Application`
class to enable Zuul functionality (see Listing 6-32).

Listing 6-32. Application Class

```
package com.example.eshop.gateway;

import org.springframework.boot.SpringApplication;
import org.springframework.boot.autoconfigure.SpringBootApplication;
import org.springframework.cloud.netflix.zuul.EnableZuulProxy;

@SpringBootApplication
@EnableZuulProxy
public class ZuulApp {
    public static void main(String[] args) {
        SpringApplication.run(ZuulApp.class, args);
    }
}
```

Filters

Filters are the mechanism by which we can customize Zuul behavior. These are custom
classes where we can implement any functionality and alter the routing. Typical use
cases for these is to perform authorization and logging at a central point, before the
request hits a functional microservice. Listing 6-33 provides an example of this.

Listing 6-33. Zuul Filter Implementation

```java
package com.example.eshop.gateway.filters;

import com.netflix.zuul.ZuulFilter;
import lombok.extern.slf4j.Slf4j;
import org.springframework.stereotype.Component;

@Component
@Slf4j
public class AuthPreFilter extends ZuulFilter {

    @Override
    public String filterType() {
        return "pre";
    }

    @Override
    public int filterOrder() {
        return 0;
    }

    @Override
    public boolean shouldFilter() {
        return true;
}

    @Override
    public Object run() {
        //Check JWT headers and check Authorization tokens validity
        // log requests
         return null;
    }

}
```

Notes:

- The `filterType()` method is used to classify a filter by type. Standard types in Zuul are pre for pre-routing filtering, route for routing to an origin, post for post-routing filters, and error for error handling.

- The filterOrder() method is used to define the ordering of filters.
  This ordering does not have to be sequential.

- The shouldFilter() method contains the logic that determines
  when to execute this filter.

- Finally, the run() method can be overridden to add custom
  functionality.

Running the Application

Run the application:

```
> gradle bootRun

<<skipping generic Spring Boot logs>>

:: Spring Boot ::        (v2.1.3.RELEASE)
2019-04-06 12:46:01.386   INFO 69797 --- [           main]
com.example.eshop.gateway.ZuulApp        : No active profile set, falling
                                           back to default profiles: default
2019-04-06 12:46:03.170   INFO 69797 --- [           main]
o.s.web.context.ContextLoader            : Root WebApplicationContext:
                                           initialization completed in
                                           1759 ms
2019-04-06 12:46:04.975   INFO 69797 --- [           main]
o.s.b.a.e.web.EndpointLinksResolver      : Exposing 21 endpoint(s) beneath
                                           base path '/actuator'
2019-04-06 12:46:05.142   INFO 69797 --- [           main]
o.s.b.w.embedded.tomcat.TomcatWebServer  : Tomcat started on port(s): 9999
                                           (http) with context path "
2019-04-06 12:46:05.146   INFO 69797 --- [           main]
com.example.eshop.gateway.ZuulApp        : Started ZuulApp in 5.164
                                           seconds (JVM running for 4.412)
```

Once the gateway-service is up and running, we can access the eshop, config-service, inventory-service, and admin-service endpoints through just the gateway-service base URL instead of keeping separate URLs for each of them in client applications. As an example:

- To access the Config service, the URL now will be
  `http://localhost:8888/config/`

- To access the Admin service, the URL now will be
  `http://localhost:7777/admin/`

- To access the Eshop service, the URL now will be
  `http://localhost:8081/eshop/`

- To access the Inventory service, the URL now will be
  `http://localhost:8082/inventory/`

Code Reuse Across Services

This is very often discussed as a practical case as to whether we should reuse code created across microservices or not. This is generally required to share the common DTO between different functional services, which makes the services interdependent. We use microservices to create separate of concerns between loosely coupled independent applications, but we are doing the opposite now.

This also brings up a concern as to when different services are implemented in different languages, which means the same code cannot be used. I have also seen situations in which decision makers said that they were building services in Java three years back, are still using Java, and will be using Java in next three years as well, so they should not be worried about this issue. I shall leave the decision to the reader and discuss how code reuse can happen in various ways in Java:

- Using a multi-module project based on Maven or Gradle.

  - Very often again we see open source projects using this technique. The Spring Framework itself is an example. If you look at the Spring content module Grade file (`spring-content.gradle`) in the GitHub repository (`https://github.com/spring-projects/spring-framework/blob/master/spring-context/spring-context.gradle`), it depends on other modules such as `spring-core` and `spring-eans`. We will not discuss multi-module build setups here, as they are out of scope for this book.

- Using a build artifact repository manager solution like Archiva (open source), JFrog, or Sonatype Nexus. In other languages, these solutions are referred to as package managers.

  - This can be achieved using the `uploadArchives` configuration property in Gradle. With every new build, a new version of the Jar file can be uploaded to the internal repository of the organization. For example, if we have `common-models` as the module, all versions of this can be uploaded to the internal repository and then used as a dependency in other services.

- Copying the common code in all services again.

  - This is the worst method because all common data models can be copied again and again in different services. As an example, if the `product-catalog` and `inventory` services need a `Product` object, they can be copied.

- Carefully creating different consumer versions of shared domain classes.

  - This is often the preferred approach, as described by many experts. Taking the same example as before, let's say that the `product-catalog` service owns the `Product` data model. If `inventory-service` also needs this object, should we create a `ProductView` class so that a focused subview of the actual object can be created in this service? This could contain a few lesser attributes as well as different ones. Even if the actual `Product` class changes in `product-service`, `ProductView` can remain the same. This approach also supports polyglot microservices very well, as there is no code sharing.

Microservices Security

Securing a distributed system with microservices brings multiple new challenges over a monolith having user registration, logins, and authorization in a single application. There are still a lot of common concerns in both cases, such as different modes of authentication, authorization at the methods level within code, OWASP, and more.

We may need to have OAuth-based authentication with a monolith because there might be multiple monolith applications in your enterprise.

In an enterprise, you may need to design a SSO (Single Sign On) with a corporate LDAP system. OAuth, SAML, SSO, and JWTs are still the same however with microservices, so we may want to keep the authentication and token validation at the API Gateway level. Let's try to explore this idea by enabling JWT (Json Web Tokens)-based token authentication in gateway-service and token creation in the eshop service.

Eshop Service Changes

W we need to have login in the front-end facing microservice, which is eshop for us. We will need to create a LoginController class to handle authentication and create a JWT token based on a predefined user with the email raj@example.com. Additionally we need a dependency addition in the build.gradle file:

```
compile group: 'io.jsonwebtoken', name: 'jjwt', version: '0.9.1'
```

Let's now look at the controller class.

Login Controller

We will create a LoginRequest DTO to hold the username/password from the user and the controller class. See Listing 6-34.

Listing 6-34. Controller and DTO Classes

DTO

```
package com.example.eshop.dto;
import lombok.Data;

@Data
public class LoginRequest {
    private String email;
    private String password;
}
```

<u>Controller</u>

```java
package com.example.eshop.web;

import com.example.eshop.dto.LoginRequest;
import io.jsonwebtoken.Jwts;
import io.jsonwebtoken.SignatureAlgorithm;
import org.springframework.security.crypto.bcrypt.BCryptPasswordEncoder;
import org.springframework.web.bind.annotation.RequestBody;
import org.springframework.web.bind.annotation.RequestMapping;
import org.springframework.web.bind.annotation.RequestMethod;
import org.springframework.web.bind.annotation.RestController;

import javax.servlet.ServletException;
import java.util.Date;
import lombok.*;

@RestController
public class LoginController {

    String DEFAULT_EMAIL = "raj@example.com";
    String DEFAULT_PASSWORD = "password";

    @RequestMapping(value = "/login", method = RequestMethod.POST)
    public String login(@RequestBody LoginRequest loginRequest) throws
ServletException {

        var jwtToken = "";

        val email = loginRequest.getEmail();
        val password = loginRequest.getPassword();

        if(!(DEFAULT_PASSWORD.equals(password))
                || (DEFAULT_EMAIL.equals(email)))  {
            // throw error
        }

        jwtToken = Jwts.builder().setSubject(email)
                    .claim("roles", "admin")
                    .signWith(SignatureAlgorithm.HS256, "secretkey")
```

```
                    .setIssuedAt(new Date())
                    .compact();

        return jwtToken;
    }
}
```

Notes:

- We have a rest API at /login that accepts the plain username and password in the LoginRequest bean. Ideally, the password should be sent over an SSL-protected connection and be in digest form. We are using the basic example with plain text for credentials through API, just for simplicity.

- The Jwts class is a lightweight API that creates and validates JSON web tokens.

- We are also using a plain symmetric key as secretkey, but I suggest you use asymmetric keys for this purpose.

- We set the role as an attribute as a claim. We can use claims to add any custom attributes and create a token with user profile information. The token can be validated and then passed to other downstream services, which can decode and perform authorization based on the user profile information.

Testing Token Generation

After restarting the eshop service, run the following command on the console using CURL:

```
> curl -H "Content-Type: application/json" -d '{"email":"raj@example.com",
"password":"password"}' -X POST
http://localhost:8081/eshop/login
```

eyJhbGciOiJIUzI1NiJ9.eyJzdWIiOiJyYWpAZXhhbXBsZS5jb20iLCJyb2xlcyI6ImFkbWluIi
wiaWF0Ijox NTUONjA3NTIzfQ.p4FzUPRKUi2NT0OOrWQxWv760i4eB2LKO_fcWexlDos

This response shows the auth token, marked in bold. We will utilize this token in the next step to validate and allow services access.

Gateway-Service Changes

In this service, we validate the token passed by a remote client in every request. If the Authorization header is invalid or corrupt, we will send an HTTP 401 with an error description. We just need to change the AuthPreFilter class in gateway-service (see Listing 6-35).

Listing 6-35. Zuul PreFilter Class

```
package com.example.eshop.gateway.filters;

import com.netflix.zuul.ZuulFilter;
import com.netflix.zuul.context.RequestContext;
import io.jsonwebtoken.Claims;
import io.jsonwebtoken.Jwts;
import io.jsonwebtoken.SignatureException;
import lombok.extern.slf4j.Slf4j;
import org.springframework.stereotype.Component;

import javax.servlet.http.HttpServletRequest;

@Component
@Slf4j
public class AuthPreFilter extends ZuulFilter {

    //Check JWT headers and all OAUTH service if required
    @Override
    public Object run() {

        RequestContext context = RequestContext.getCurrentContext();
        HttpServletRequest request = context.getRequest();

        final String token = request.getHeader("Authorization");

        if (token == null) {
            context.setSendZuulResponse(false);
            context.setResponseStatusCode(401);
            context.setResponseBody("Authorization header is missing");
            return null;
        }
```

```java
        try {
            final Claims claims = Jwts.parser().setSigningKey("secretkey").
            parseClaimsJws(token).getBody();
            log.info("Claims: {}", claims);
            context.addZuulRequestHeader("Authorization", "Basic " + token);

        } catch (final SignatureException e) {
            context.setSendZuulResponse(false);
            context.setResponseStatusCode(401);
            context.setResponseBody("API key is not valid");
        }
        return null;
    }

    @Override
    public String filterType() {
        return "pre";
    }

    @Override
    public int filterOrder() {
        return 0;
    }

    @Override
    public boolean shouldFilter() {
        return true;
    }
}
```

Notes:

- We have already seen the ZuulFilter in Section 6.8.4. Additionally we added the code to decode and extract the token with the same signed symmetric key.

- If the key is tempered, we cannot decode it again and hence the authentication will get broken at the gateway level.

- Once we have validated the token, we send it back as a header in request.

Testing Gateway Authentication

After restarting the gateway-service, run the following commands through CURL for validating as well as accessing the /api/orders API of the eshop service.

```
curl -H "Authorization:
eyJhbGciOiJIUzI1NiJ9.eyJzdWIiOiJyYWpAZXhhbXBsZS5jb20iLCJyb2xlcyI6ImFkb
WluNTIzfQ.p4FzUPRKUi2NTOOOrWQxWv76Oi4eB2LKO_fcWexlDos" -i -X POST
http://localhost:9999/eshop/ api/orders
```

```
HTTP/1.1 201
Location: http://localhost:8081/eshop/api/orders/2
Date: Sun, 07 Apr 2019 03:47:24 GMT
Transfer-Encoding: chunked
```

These results have been collected after the sample run and show that the token we received in Section 6.10.1.2 has been successfully validated. This also shows that the eshop service API has responded. Let's also look at how the gateway-service behaves if an invalid token is sent in request.

```
curl -H "Authorization: WRONG_TOKEN" -i -X POST http://localhost:9999/
eshop/api/ orders
```

```
HTTP/1.1 401
Transfer-Encoding: chunked
Date: Sun, 07 Apr 2019 03:56:28 GMT
API key is not valid
```

We will receive this message if the token sent in request is invalid.

Summary

We covered the essential concepts—with problems and solutions—to help you get started with Java and Spring Cloud as microservices stacks. There are more frameworks as well to handle the concerns we discussed in this chapter. I suggest you explore Netflix OSS in more detail as well. In the next part of this book, we look at the technologies and concepts related to scaling Java.

PART III

Making HTTP Faster

CHAPTER 7

Java GraphQL Development

GraphQL is a query language for APIs and a runtime for fulfilling those queries with your existing data. GraphQL was developed by Facebook in 2012 and then publicly released in 2015. There has been lot of development recently around GraphQL, especially since tools like AWS Cloud AppSync and frameworks like Prisma came about. GraphQL's primary purpose is to handle issues with RESTful API design and make HTTP communication faster.

Instead of having multiple URL-based conventions, GraphQL works on the basis of a single endpoint accepting all requests through POST in a graph-like data structure that looks similar to JSON. GraphQL has its own Schema Definition Language (SDL) that defines data models with standard types, validations, and actions to retrieve and update those models. GraphQL follows the CQRS (Command Query Responsibility Segregation) design pattern, which states that it is better to separate code related to reading data from code that updates that data. This keeps the responsibilities clear. The domain objects for reading and writing can also be different from the ones for updating datastores.

Important Concepts

For developers coming from REST API design, there are a couple of interesting new concepts in GraphQL that simplify the development process:

- Single **endpoint**: GraphQL application works on a single /GraphQL endpoint and various requests are routed to registered resolver classes.

- POST-based requests: All requests are POST-based and have to be sent in an SDL complaint format, which can be quite descriptive, lengthy, and nested.

© Raj Malhotra 2019
R. Malhotra, *Rapid Java Persistence and Microservices*, https://doi.org/10.1007/978-1-4842-4476-0_7

- **Schema based:** GraphQL allows you to define a JSON-like schema for API clients through SDL. The schema or contract-first mode helps ensure better coordination between the UI and the backend teams.

- Query: All GET requests that do not intend to create or update any resources are called query.

- **Mutations:** All POST, PUT, and DELETE requests are mutations in GraphQL.

- **Resolvers:** All custom registered functions that the GraphQL Engine or framework can call are called resolvers.

- **Schema stitching:** This is the technique of creating a single unified schema from multiple schemas. This is useful when different microservices have their own schemas and a front service can provide a combined view for all of them. This way, the front microservice can act as a gateway. This feature does not exist in Java APIs, but is expected to be added soon.

- **Subscriptions:** This feature allows Websockets programming to provide near real-time responses to the clients in push and pull models.

How It Works

We are looking at the simplified step-by-step process of creating a GraphQL service:

1. Start by creating a JSON schema (the schema-first approach). Otherwise, the schema can be generated from the objects (code-first approach) later.

2. Create a series of *resolvers* (implementation classes) based on the schema that's defined when implementing queries and mutations.

3. Run and test the application by using its built-in web-based client or explorer (GraphiQL with Java).

4. Connect to the GraphQL REST endpoint as a client.

5. Combine, if required, multiple GraphQL endpoint-based microservices into one through the schema stitching process and then connect to it as usual.

Advantages Over REST

GraphQL focuses primarily on the client side problems of accessing hundreds of different RESTful API URLs, thus wasting lots of bandwidth. GraphQL solves a number of problems:

- Fetch exactly what you need.

- Declarative and no over fetching.

- Get multiple resources in a single request.

- Schema-based API that acts as a contract between the client and the service.

- Single API endpoint, thus there is no hassle of keeping too many URLs in the client code.

- No more API versions hassle. The deprecated fields can be marked as @deprecated in the schema with a description. The tools can start showing it deprecated and clients can also start ignoring it.

- Nice ready-made documentation on-the-go. The built-in editor tools provide excellent documentation on-the-fly.

- Ready-made tool for rapid-fire testing. The built-in tools provide good support for testing as well.

- An easy solution for multiple microservices through schema stitching.

- Overall communication is more efficient than REST.

- Built-in semantics for pagination.

- Built-in support for near real-time messaging through subscriptions (more precisely, Websockets).

The Graph data structure is actually quite powerful and it can easily represent the connected and nested resources very well. We have already seen and enjoyed its power through graph databases. With GraphQL, REST API clients start requesting the object graph in the nested form and can fetch the related, nested, and connected resources. Let's look at the preceding advantages in detail:

- Fetch exactly what you need:

  In GraphQL, you request the exact attributes you need in the response. In REST, however, you can only visit an URL and will always receive a fixed response.

  Example:

  ```
  query: allPosts {
      id
      author
      title
      content
  }
  }
  ```

- Declarative and no over fetching:

  Think of the REST API design, where clients may end up fetching all attributes instead of just the required ones. The GraphQL Engine by default does this at the HTTP layer only. That means even if your resolvers are querying full tables, the engine will return the attributes that are asked by the client in the request. This behavior can be useful when a field has been deprecated and the clients can simply start ignoring that field in the request. This does provide the capability to query and respond back dynamically based on the request structure.

- Get many resources in a single request:

  GraphQL allows you to query multiple resources in a single request. While REST APIs focus on URLs first, GraphQL focuses on the data as well. This ultimately gives you the advantage of faster communication over slower network connections.

Example:

```
query: {
        allPosts {
            id
            title
        }
        allUsers {
            id
            name
        }
}
```

- Schema-based API:

  Remember the long discussions around SOAP versus REST over contract first versus implementation first? Finally, GraphQL allows you to define its SDL-based schema first in a RESTful world.

  Example:

```
type Query {
  user(id: ID!): User!
}

type User {
  id: ID!
  email: String!
  name: String!
}
```

- Single API endpoint:

  REST-based client apps have to manage and connect to multiple URLs and keep changing the HTTP verbs. With GraphQL, clients have to connect to a single endpoint and through just the POST HTTP verb. The GraphQL Engine has to wire the classes (resolvers) against the query and mutation types in the schema along with supporting error-handling. As mentioned, by convention, all fetch (GET)-based requests should be handled by functions defined in the query type and PUT, and POST, DELETE operations are handled by functions defined in the mutations type.

- No more API versions hassle:

Since the GraphQL application works on a single endpoint and a schema, the only thing left is to mark fields in the schema as deprecated for a single URL. These deprecated fields can be tracked and hidden by client tools.

- Ready-made documentation on the go:

Nearly all GraphQL specification implementations provide a visual tool to access its schema and run sample queries. Within the Java space, this tool is called GraphiQL. This tool provides visual access to whole schemas along with comments, defined in the actual file being shown as the field description.

- Ready-made tool for rapid-fire testing:

GraphiQL can be used to do random testing for various schema types and resolvers. This can simply be enabled by including a dependency in the built-in file and defining the context path.

- Provides an easy solution for microservices through schema stitching:

GraphQL has a built-in system of binding different applications or services through the concept of schema stitching.

- Overall communication is more efficient than REST:

Since multiple requests can be combined and the client can specify which attributes it wants back, communication becomes easier and faster.

- Built-in semantics for pagination:

The GraphQL schema definition provides semantics for defining pagination attributes in a request.

Example:

```
query: allPosts(first: 2, skip: 2) {
    id
    author
    title
    content
  }
}
```

- Subscriptions:

    GraphQL provides built-in support for real-time client server communication via Websockets. In GraphQL terms, this is handled through subscriptions.

Risks and Disadvantages

GraphQL has a few risks to be cautious about while choosing it for certain applications:

- Caching

- Security concerns

- N+1 problem

- Error handling by responding with HTTP status codes

- Overall complexity in a big application

Let's explore these issues in detail:

- Caching:

    REST responses can easily be cached based on different URLs. Since GraphQL is based on dynamic, lengthy JSON graphs, it becomes difficult to cache them at the network layer. Frameworks like Apollo provide client-side caching support, but that may not always be enough.

- Security concerns:

  Since GraphQL allows nested queries, the depth of nested resources can cause severe load on the server and this can become cyclic as well.

- N+1 problem:

  The N+1 problem means that the server executes multiple unnecessary round trips to datastores for nested data. Say that a client app has requested to fetch list of all authors along with the top 10 posts written by them. If the GraphQL resolvers are not optimized, this can end up being one query that fetches all the authors and then N number of queries for the list of top posts from all those authors.

- HTTP status codes in responses:

  As with RESTful services, we have a single POST-based endpoint here. We do not have a clear list of different endpoints, each having their own HTTP error handling, like Controller classes in REST. We can do generic error handling but the problem comes when we want to return different HTTP status codes for different requests. This can make the code more readable at times.

- Complexity:

  Although this removes a lot of burden from the client, it does make the server side a bit more complex. Since this is based on the graph structure, highly nested requests can become quite complex to handle, as they require resolution to the N+1 problem as well.

GraphQL Java Example

We will focus on GraphQL development with SpringBoot using a schema-first approach. Let's build an example with the following steps:

1. Build a new Gradle project from spring.io.

2. Create a schema.

3. Create JPA entity models and repositories.

4. Create input DTOs.

5. Create the Query and Mutation resolver classes.

6. Define the application config and do a sample run.

Let's build an application called "" with the following code structure:

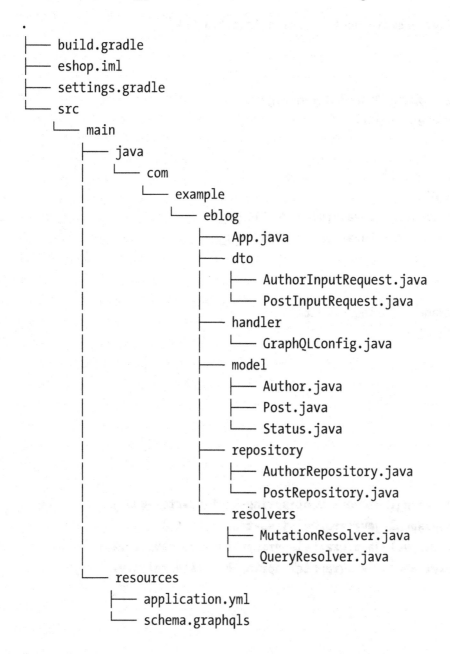

```
.
├── build.gradle
├── eshop.iml
├── settings.gradle
└── src
    └── main
        ├── java
        │   └── com
        │       └── example
        │           └── eblog
        │               ├── App.java
        │               ├── dto
        │               │   ├── AuthorInputRequest.java
        │               │   └── PostInputRequest.java
        │               ├── handler
        │               │   └── GraphQLConfig.java
        │               ├── model
        │               │   ├── Author.java
        │               │   ├── Post.java
        │               │   └── Status.java
        │               ├── repository
        │               │   ├── AuthorRepository.java
        │               │   └── PostRepository.java
        │               └── resolvers
        │                   ├── MutationResolver.java
        │                   └── QueryResolver.java
        └── resources
            ├── application.yml
            └── schema.graphqls
```

Application Setup

Start by building a new application called eblog-graphql-ch7 from http://start. spring.io/ with the following dependencies in the build.gradle file (see Listing 7-1).

Listing 7-1. Th'e Build File

```
plugins {
    id 'org.springframework.boot' version '2.1.3.RELEASE'
    id 'java'
}

apply plugin: 'io.spring.dependency-management'
apply plugin: 'project-report'

java {
    group = 'com.example'
    version = '1.0'
    sourceCompatibility = JavaVersion.VERSION_1_8
    targetCompatibility = JavaVersion.VERSION_1_8
}

bootJar {
    archieveBaseName = 'eblog-service'
    version =   '1.0'
}

repositories {
    mavenCentral()
}

dependencies {

    compile('org.springframework.boot:spring-boot-starter-web')
    compile('com.graphql-java:graphql-java-tools:5.2.4')
    compile('com.graphql-java:graphql-spring-boot-starter:5.0.2')
    compile('com.graphql-java:graphiql-spring-boot-starter:5.0.2')
```

```
compile('org.springframework.boot:spring-boot-starter-data-jpa')
compile('mysql:mysql-connector-java:8.0.15')
compile('org.projectlombok:lombok:1.18.6')
testCompile('junit:junit:4.12')
}
```

Schema File: Resources/Schema.Graphqls

GraphQL has its own schema definition language (SDL) that describes the types used in a service and defines how those types can be queried. Listing 7-2 shows the schema for this example.

Listing 7-2. resources/schema.graphqls

```
type Post {
    id: ID!
    title: String!
    content: String!
    status: Status!
    author: Author!
}

type Author {
    id: ID!
    name: String!
    age: Int
    posts: [Post]!
    status: Status!
}

enum Status {
    ACTIVE
    NON_ACTIVE
}

input PostInputRequest {
    title: String!
    content: String!
```

```
    authorId: Int!
}

input AuthorInputRequest {
    name: String!
    age: Int
}

type Mutation {
    newPost(input: PostInputRequest): Post!
    newAuthor(input: AuthorInputRequest): Author!
}

type Query {
    recentPosts(limit: Int, offset: Int, orderBy: String): [Post]
    authorsWithTopPosts: [Author]
}
```

Notes:

- We have two data models—Post and Author—with the respective fields, as mentioned in their type definition. We have all standard datatypes supported—Int, String, Boolean, Date, and Objects.

- The field definition is composed of field name on the left side and its type on the right side of the colon separator, such as {fieldname} : {fieldType}. The ! symbol signifies whether the field is mandatory. If we put the field in square brackets, it becomes a list like [Post] is a list of POST objects.

- Enums can also be declared and mentioned as the datatype of any field.

- Input types help define the input request objects (or DTOs in technical speak).

- There are two special types to be defined in the GraphQL schema—Query and Mutation. The Query definition is used for wiring any functions in code that perform fetch operations on these types.

Mutation is similar, but conventionally it is used only for operations that update these types in the system. These both can be referred to as *resolvers*, as they help resolve the fields to different user-defined functions at runtime.

Data Models and Repositories

In the code in Listing 7-3, we are simply declaring domain objects (JPA entities) and related Spring Data repositories.

Listing 7-3. Domain Objects

```
package com.example.eblog.model;

import com.fasterxml.jackson.annotation.JsonIgnore;
import lombok.*;

import javax.persistence.*;
import java.io.Serializable;
import java.util.Set;

@Data
@Entity
@NoArgsConstructor
@ToString(exclude = {"posts"})
@EqualsAndHashCode(exclude = {"posts"})
public class Author implements Serializable {

    @Id
    @GeneratedValue(strategy = GenerationType.IDENTITY)
    private Long id;
    private String name;
    private int age;
    private Status status = Status.NON_ACTIVE;

    @OneToMany(fetch = FetchType.LAZY, mappedBy = "author")
    @JsonIgnore
    private Set<Post> posts;
```

```java
    public Author(String name, Integer age)  {
        this.name = name;
        this.age = age;
    }
}

package com.example.eblog.model;

import com.fasterxml.jackson.annotation.JsonIgnore;
import lombok.*;

import javax.persistence.*;
import java.io.Serializable;

@Data
@Entity
@Builder
@NoArgsConstructor
@ToString(exclude = {"author"})
@EqualsAndHashCode(exclude = {"author"})
public class Post implements Serializable {

    @Id
    @GeneratedValue(strategy = GenerationType.IDENTITY)
    private Long id;

    private String title;
    private String content;
    private Status status;

    @ManyToOne(fetch = FetchType.LAZY)
    @JsonIgnore
    private Author author;

}

package com.example.eblog.model;
```

```java
public enum Status {

    ACTIVE, NON_ACTIVE;

    public Status fromValue(String value) {
        return valueOf(value.toUpperCase());
    }

    public String toValue(Status status) {
        return status.name().toLowerCase();
    }
}

package com.example.eblog.repository;

import com.example.eblog.model.Author;
import org.springframework.data.jpa.repository.JpaRepository;
import org.springframework.data.jpa.repository.Query;

import java.util.List;

public interface AuthorRepository extends JpaRepository<Author, Long> {

    @Query("Select distinct a from Author a left join fetch a.posts")
    List454149_1_En findAuthorsWithPosts();

}
package com.example.eblog.repository;

import com.example.eblog.model.Post;
import org.springframework.data.jpa.repository.JpaRepository;
import org.springframework.stereotype.Repository;

@Repository
public interface PostRepository extends JpaRepository<Post, Long> {}
```

Input DTOs

In Listing 7-4, we are declaring the POJOs for accepting input for creating the Author and
POST objects from the Mutation resolvers.

Listing 7-4.   DTOs for Input

```java
package com.example.eblog.dto;

import lombok.Data;

@Data
public class AuthorInputRequest {
    String name;
    Integer age;
}

package com.example.eblog.dto;

import lombok.Data;

@Data
public class PostInputRequest {
    String title;
    String content;
    Long authorId;
}
```

Query and Mutation Classes

The classes in Listing 7-5 provide the implementation to resolve different types and fields as defined in the schema, per the exact matching method signature. For example, we saw the newPost(input: PostInputRequest): Post! declaration in the schema. Spring will match and call the function among all Spring-annotated classes with the signature defined as public Post newPost(PostInputRequest postInputRequest).

Listing 7-5.   Query Classes

```java
package com.example.eblog.resolvers;

import com.coxautodev.graphql.tools.GraphQLQueryResolver;
import com.example.eblog.model.Author;
import com.example.eblog.model.Post;
import com.example.eblog.repository.AuthorRepository;
import com.example.eblog.repository.PostRepository;
```

```java
import lombok.extern.slf4j.Slf4j;
import org.springframework.beans.factory.annotation.Autowired;
import org.springframework.data.domain.PageRequest;
import org.springframework.data.domain.Sort;
import org.springframework.stereotype.Service;

import java.util.List;

@Service
@Slf4j
public class QueryResolver implements GraphQLQueryResolver {

    @Autowired
    AuthorRepository authorRepository;

    @Autowired
    PostRepository postRepository;

    public List<Post> recentPosts(Integer limit, Integer offset, String
    orderBy){
        log.info("recentPosts, params: {}, {}", limit, offset);
        PageRequest pageRequest = PageRequest.of(limit, offset, Sort.
        Direction.DESC, orderBy);
        return postRepository.findAll(pageRequest).getContent();
    }

    public List454149_1_En authorsWithTopPosts()    {
        log.info("authorsWithTopPosts");
        return authorRepository.findAuthorsWithPosts();
    }

}

package com.example.eblog.resolvers;

import com.coxautodev.graphql.tools.GraphQLMutationResolver;
import com.example.eblog.dto.AuthorInputRequest;
import com.example.eblog.dto.PostInputRequest;
import com.example.eblog.model.Author;
```

```java
import com.example.eblog.model.Post;
import com.example.eblog.model.Status;
import com.example.eblog.repository.AuthorRepository;
import com.example.eblog.repository.PostRepository;
import lombok.extern.slf4j.Slf4j;
import org.springframework.beans.factory.annotation.Autowired;
import org.springframework.stereotype.Service;

@Service
@Slf4j
public class MutationResolver implements GraphQLMutationResolver {

    @Autowired
    AuthorRepository authorRepository;

    @Autowired
    PostRepository postRepository;

    public Post newPost(PostInputRequest postInputRequest){

        Author author = authorRepository.findById(postInputRequest.
        getAuthorId())
                                        .orElse(new Author("Raj", 35));
        if(author.getId() == null)
            authorRepository.save(author);

        Post post = Post.builder()
                    .title(postInputRequest.getTitle())
                    .content(postInputRequest.getContent())
                    .author(author)
                    .status(Status.ACTIVE)
                    .build();

        post = postRepository.save(post);

        return post;
    }
```

```java
public Author newAuthor(AuthorInputRequest authorInputRequest)   {
    Author author = new Author(authorInputRequest.getName(),
    authorInputRequest.getAge());
    author = authorRepository.save(author);
    return author;
}
}
```

Notes:

- We implemented GraphQLQueryResolver and
  GraphQLMutationResolver as the marker interfaces.

- The code is pretty straightforward. In the QueryResolver class, the
  recentPosts() method provides paginated POST objects as the
  responses. In the authorWithTopPosts method, we are returning the
  object graph of the authors along with their recent top post. These are
  created as nested objects.

- In the MutationResolver class, we have two methods to create POST and
  Author objects from their corresponding input objects from the users.

- The GraphQL Engine validates the input object fields before delegat-
  ing control to the implementation methods.

- The error handling can be customized by declaring a Spring Bean of
  type GraphQLErrorHandler and customizing it. This is shown in
  Listing 7-6.

Listing 7-6. Error Handling Configuration

```java
package com.example.eblog.handler;

import graphql.ExceptionWhileDataFetching;
import graphql.GraphQLError;
import graphql.servlet.GraphQLErrorHandler;
import org.springframework.context.annotation.Bean;
import org.springframework.context.annotation.Configuration;

import java.util.List;
import java.util.stream.Collectors;
```

```java
@Configuration
public class GraphQLConfig  {

    @Bean
    public GraphQLErrorHandler errorHandler() {

        return new GraphQLErrorHandler() {

            @Override
            public List<GraphQLError> processErrors(List<GraphQLError>
                                                            errors) {

                List<GraphQLError> clientErrors = errors.stream()
                        .filter(this::isClientError)
                        .collect(Collectors.toList());

                // do something with the client side errors

                List<GraphQLError> serverErrors = errors.stream()
                        .filter(e -> !isClientError(e))
                        .collect(Collectors.toList());

                // do something with the server side errors

                return errors;
            }

            protected boolean isClientError(GraphQLError error) {
                return !(error instanceof ExceptionWhileDataFetching ||
                                        error instanceof
                                        Throwable);
            }
        };
    }
}
```

We get a handle to the errors in any request by the GraphQL Engine. We can log them or add more information to the errors list.

Configuration

We have access to the common properties needed to declare Hibernate connection properties and customize the context path. The GraphQL Java engine requires us to define the `graphql.servlet.mapping` property in order to declare the path for mapping its POST RESTful endpoint. GraphiQL is the built-in application from the `graphql-tools` project and requires similar self-explanatory properties to be declared. See Listing 7-7.

Listing 7-7. The application.yml File

```
server:
  port: 8201
  servlet:
    contextPath: /eblog

graphql:
  servlet:
    mapping: /graphql
    enabled: true
    corsEnabled: true

graphiql:
  mapping: /graphiql
  endpoint: /eblog/graphql
  enabled: true
  pageTitle: GraphiQL

spring:
  datasource:
    url: jdbc:mysql://localhost:3306/eblog?autoReconnect=true
    username: root
    password: mysql
    driver-class-name: com.mysql.jdbc.Driver
  jpa:
    hibernate.ddl-auto: create
    show-sql: true
  generate-ddl: true
```

Running the eblog-graphql-ch7 Application

```
> gradle bootRun
<<Skipping generic Spring Boot output>>

:: Spring Boot ::        (v2.1.3.RELEASE)
2019-03-24 09:24:10.622  INFO 77186 --- [          main] com.example.
eblog.App                      : Starting App on Rajs-MacBook-Pro.local with
PID 77186 (started by raj in /Users/raj/work_all/book_ code/rapid-java-
persistence-and-microservices/ch7/eshop-graphql-ch7)
2019-03-24 09:24:11.479  INFO 77186 --- [          main] .s.d.r.c.Reposit
oryConfigurationDelegate : Finished Spring Data o.hibernate.jpa.internal.
util.LogHelper  : HHH000204: Processing PersistenceUnitInfo [
        name: default
        ...]
2019-03-24 09:24:13.053  INFO 77186 --- [          main] org.hibernate.
Version                         2019-03-24 09:24:15.531  INFO 77186 --- [
main] o.s.b.w.embedded.tomcat.TomcatWebServer  : Tomcat started on port(s):
8201 (http) with context path '/eblog'
2019-03-24 09:24:15.533  INFO 77186 --- [          main] com.example.
eblog.App                      : Started App in 5.404 seconds (JVM running
for 5.872)
```

Notice that Hibernate is generating the following statements:

```
Hibernate: drop table if exists author
Hibernate: drop table if exists post
Hibernate: create table author (id bigint not null auto_increment, age
integer not null, name varchar(255), status integer, primary key (id))
engine=MySQL5InnoDBDialect
Hibernate: create table post (id bigint not null auto_increment, content
varchar(255), status integer, title varchar(255), author_id bigint, primary
key (id)) engine=MyISAM
Hibernate: alter table post add constraint FK5l759v7apba3lqguc7bp8h456
foreign key (author_id) references author (id)
```

Open a browser now and visit the http://localhost:8201/eblog/graphiql URL to launch the GraphiQL Editor (see Figure 7-1).

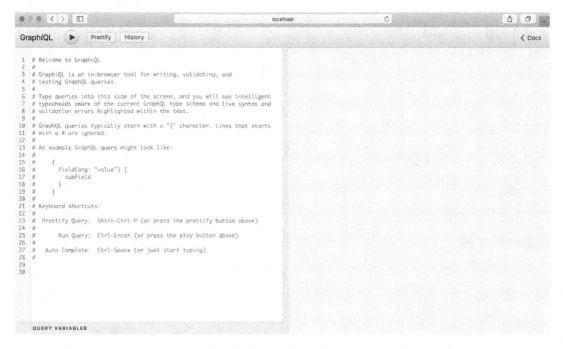

Figure 7-1. *GraphiQL Editor*

Note the following about the editor:

- The left pane accepts input.

- The right pane will show the output or errors.

- There is built-in support for Prettify, History, Docs (Documentation), and Query Variables.

- As mentioned, you can delete all contents and press Crtl+Space for all suggestions.

Let's look at the two predefined mutation and query inputs, along with the results (see Figures 7-2 and 7-3).

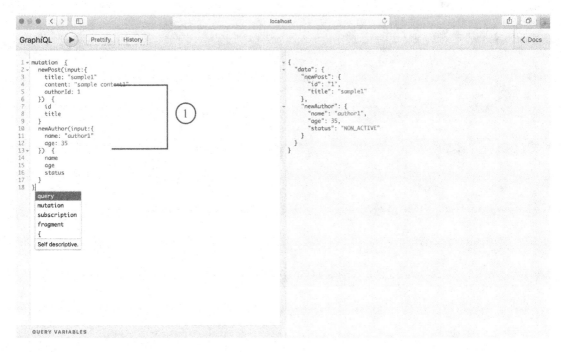

Figure 7-2. *GraphiQL mutations example*

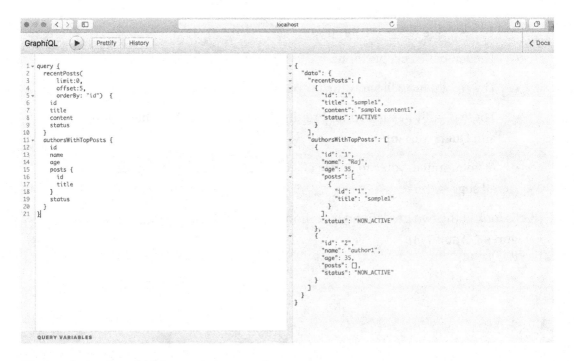

Figure 7-3. *GraphiQL queries example*

Points to note:

- We combined two data updates into a single mutation request as newPost and newAuthor.

- The request starts with mutation { and then actual multiple defined inputs start from there.

- In mutations, you can expect the returned object graph attributes. This is allowed only if the return type has been specified in the schema against that mutation.

- Just like mutations, queries are also combined into a single network request—recentPosts and authorsWithTopPosts.

- Notice that the recentPosts query also receives the pagination attributes called limit and offset. GraphQL also supports RelayJS like cursor-based pagination, which may come in handy.

- Notice that authorsWithTopPosts has a related posts collection. Clients can specify all attributes, of which all the resources are required in the output.

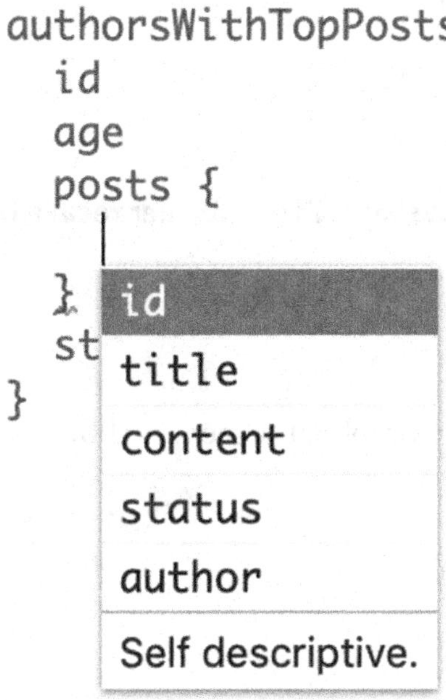

Figure 7-4. *GraphiQL Contextual help example*

There is also a provision to view the complete schema through this UI only, by clicking on the right-side Docs link. This will display the navigation sidebar, showing schema details along with any comments describing the purpose of any field (see Figure 7-5).

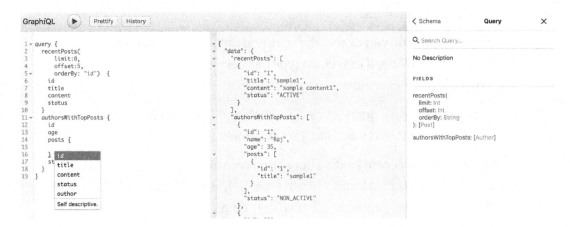

Figure 7-5. *GraphiQL documentation example*

If we have a deprecated field, let's say age in the Author object, we need to update the schema as follows:

```
type Author {
    id: ID!
    name: String!
    age: Int @deprecated(reason: "Field is deprecated!")
    posts: [Post]!
    status: Status!
}
```

This is going to reflect on the GraphiQL screen, as shown in Figure 7-6.

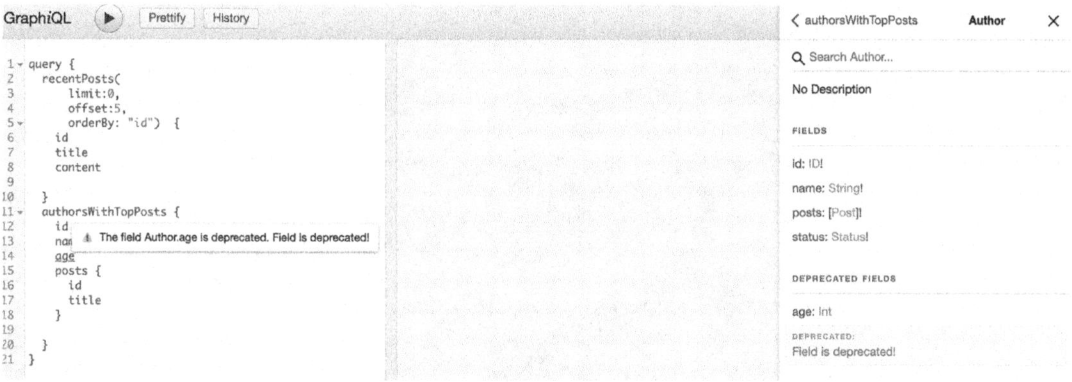

Figure 7-6. *GraphiQL*

This ends our example to explore the basic concepts and starting point with Spring Boot. Let's also look at a few projects that might be useful to explore GraphQL Java APIs:

- GraphQL SPQR (`https://github.com/leangen/GraphQL-SPQR`) can be helpful in writing GraphQL using the code-first approach.

- GraphQL JPA (`https://github.com/jcrygier/graphql-jpa`) can be useful to auto-generate a complete CRUD application from just the JPA entities using a code-first approach.

- GraphQL Java DateTime (`https://github.com/donbeave/graphql-java-datetime`) is another project that is helpful in mapping GraphQL Date Time datatypes to Java LocalDateTime and other `java.time` types.

Summary

This chapter outlined an example with the GraphQL Java libraries to help you get started. I suggest that you explore more of these examples, as this is a new expanding space of concepts. The next chapter explores another major paradigm in Java that is making HTTP communication faster and is improving scalability—Reactive frameworks.

CHAPTER 8

Java Reactive Development

There has been significant focus in recent years on network programming using event-driven asynchronous runtime environments and frameworks, such as Node.js in JavaScript and RxJava (ReactiveX in Java). The NIO (New IO) package is the foundation for Reactive programming in Java. Reactive programming is not new in application development. When it comes to huge volumes of data or concurrent hits, we often need asynchronous processing to make our systems fast and responsive. Along with being asynchronous, our systems must work on streams (continuous sequence of events) in non-blocking mode.

Data volumes and scale of operations are increasing every day, which means it's getting almost impossible to keep increasing hardware resources using traditional methods. We also want simpler hardware with reduced cost to handle loads when demand is down. I started getting interested in Reactive programming when Node.js showed how much time was wasted in an application simply waiting on I/O channels. I don't deeper into Node.js details because that is a different model and Java can do better, by using multiple CPU cores.

The Reactive Manifesto

The Reactive Manifesto includes basic goals and guidelines and is available at https://www.reactivemanifesto.org/. It's the result of contributions from various organizations to standardize Reactive development. The Reactive Manifesto describes how to design Reactive systems based on four principles:

- Responsive: The system responds in a timely manner if at all possible and stays responsive to all user commands. The system should detect problems quickly and deal with them effectively, by providing a consistent response even during problem times. Functional programming, based on smaller stateless functions responding to events through a background thread, is one of the ways we can design such systems.

© Raj Malhotra 2019

R. Malhotra, *Rapid Java Persistence and Microservices*, https://doi.org/10.1007/978-1-4842-4476-0_8

- Resilient: The system stays responsive in the face of failure. Failures do occur at times in systems. The intent is to avoid a chain reaction of various components of the system and handle the messaging to the users gracefully. Includes recovery or retry logic in case of a failure.

- Elastic: The system stays responsive under varying workloads. Reactive systems can react to changes to the input rate by increasing or decreasing the resources allocated to those inputs. Container-based deployment solutions like Docker and Kubernetes are examples of elasticity.

- Message-Driven: Reactive systems rely on asynchronous message-passing between components that ensures loose coupling, isolation, and location transparency, and provides the means to delegate errors as messages. Messages are supposed to be immutable and thus thread safe by design. Akka and Vert.x are the popular reactive Java platforms based on message passing.

Based on these principles, there are various APIs, frameworks, and libraries that have been developed. The NIO (New Input Output) package in core Java is a precise library that handles I/O operations reactively. Netty and Apache Mina have been around for years providing NIO-based networking options. For general development, we still need higher-level APIs that work with Java Streams.

The Reactive Streams Project

Reactive Streams is a specification that provides a standard for asynchronous stream processing with non-blocking back pressure. By specification, we mean that there are multiple implementations, just like with JDBC drivers. There are example implementations provided by the Reactive Streams community in multiple languages, which is available at `https://github.com/reactive-streams`. For Java, the API can be found at `https://github.com/reactive-streams/reactive-streams-jvm`. We have been implementing two basic concepts for years—the Observer and Publish/Subscribe patterns. Reactive Streams are based on these concepts, but with following components in the API:

- Publisher: A publisher is responsible for producing an unbounded number of sequenced elements (stream) and publishing them according to the demand received from its subscriber(s).

  Definition:

  ```
  public interface Publisher<T> {
      public void subscribe(Subscriber<? super T> s);
  }
  ```

- Subscriber: Just like the observer in the Observer pattern, the subscriber is responsible for observing the source stream and reacting when items are pushed by the producer.

  Definition:

  ```
  public interface Subscriber<T> {
      public void onSubscribe(Subscription s);
      public void onNext(T t);
      public void onError(Throwable t);
      public void onComplete();
  }
  ```

- Subscription: Every subscriber has to implement this interface. This model is passed to the subscriber on each event occurrence.

  Definition:

  ```
  public interface Subscription {
      public void request(long n);
      public void cancel();
  }
  ```

- Processor: This interface is responsible for the processing logic of received items by the publisher and delegated to the subscriber as a handler.

  Definition:

  ```
  public interface Processor<T, R> extends Subscriber<T>,
  Publisher<R> {}
  ```

253

There are two more concepts involved in Reactive Streams:

- Back Pressure: In a non-Reactive system, a producer might keep on producing the items even if the consumers can't consume with that speed, resulting in *back pressure* on the clients. Reactive Systems allow the clients to acknowledge to the producer their capacity issues and readiness to accept more items.

- Non-Blocking: From the core Java world, we have been working on non-blocking concurrent applications through atomic variables. Essentially in simple terms, Reactive systems allow the user thread to keep processing actions, putting all I/O operations in a queue. They can then pick processes and respond to the user thread through a callback. This is how the Node.js world works, by using event food for processing all background operations.

Since there are various APIs on building Reactive systems in Java, I introduce a few of them here and then explain one in particular as an example.

The RxJava (Reactive Extensions) Project

RxJava is another framework for Reactive development; it's based on ReactiveX implementation (`http://reactivex.io/`). ReactiveX is a combination of the best ideas from the Observer pattern, the Iterator pattern, and functional programming. In ReactiveX, an observer subscribes to an observable. the Observer then reacts to the stream of items emitted by the observable (just like the publisher in Reactive Streams). By using Java concurrent APIs and offloading the processing to the background threads, user actions can wait on future objects and lower-level concurrency and non-blocking I/O concerns are the responsibility of the framework. There have been two versions of this API so far and at present RxJava 2 is the one in use. ReactiveX is the umbrella project under which RxJava is the Java library. Some of these concepts come up in the JDK as well, thus we will be looking at the API from Java 9 in the next section.

Reactive APIs Within Core Java

Java 8 started with providing basic constructs for functional programming and streams. Java 9 introduced the Flow API and common interfaces for Reactive programming as per Reactive Streams, which get lots of benefit from the Java 8 improvements. The following APIs are in the Java 9 `java.util.concurrent.Flow` class:

- The `Flow.Publisher<T>` interface defines methods to produce items and control signals.

- The `Flow.Subscriber<T>` interface defines methods to receive those messages and signals.

- The `Flow.Subscription` interface defines the methods to link the publisher and subscriber.

- The `Flow.Processor<T,R>` interface defines methods to do some advanced operations, like chaining transformations of items from publishers to subscribers.

- The only class in this API, `SubmissionPublisher<T>`, uses the `Executor` supplied in its constructor for delivery to subscribers to handle back pressure.

We have been building producer- and consumer-based applications with multithreading from Java 1.3 onward, using `wait()` and `notify()`. With Java 5, we can do that easily using blocking queues, executors, and other concurrency APIs. In simplified form, with a distributed system, these tasks are implemented using messaging as publishers/subscribers. With Java 9, we can implement the same producer/consumer in the form of the publisher/subscriber based on those Reactive APIs. The APIs are interesting but we may not be able to build a complete real-world application with only those, so let's look at the Spring Reactive APIs in the next section.

Reactor and Spring Reactive

In this section, we dive deep into a concrete example, because I want to focus on creating a full-fledged web application (microservice) that involves HTTP requests as well as database connectivity. The Spring community started with a project named "Project Reactor" (`https://projectreactor.io/`) to create a fully non-blocking foundation. This API easily integrates with the Java functional API, CompletableFuture, and Stream API.

The Spring Framework has another web API (Web Flux) built on top of the Reactor APIs. This is an alternative to the Spring Web MVC API built on the Servlet APIs. As per the Spring docs, the reason for this API was a need for a non-blocking API to handle concurrency with a smaller number of threads and scale with fewer hardware resources. The Reactive API in Java evolved from previous version features, such as annotations, concurrency APIs, atomic classes, and the NIO package. Functional programming, the Streams API, and the CompletableFuture API in Java 8 also contributed to the success of Reactive Java.

In Spring WebFlux, we have the Mono and Flux APIs. They provide a rich set of functional operators to work on streams of (0 or 1) or (0 to N) data items. WebFlux API accepts a publisher as input, allows the operator to work on it, and finally returns Mono<T> or Flux<T> as the output. The Spring WebFlux supports two types of APIs for Reactive programming:

- Annotated Controllers: Spring MVC styled REST controllers supporting Mono and Flux return types.

- Functional Endpoints: Lambda-based, lightweight, and functional programming model.

In general, functional programming can be harder than imperative programming for some developers. Imperative programming maps naturally to how we think of a sequence of steps to perform a task. Further, in an enterprise application, we may need to work on many frameworks and libraries that have not yet moved to functional programming. For example, JPA and JDBC are first. Recently, the community started working on Reactive database drivers and Spring Data styled wrapper APIs.

The API is named R2DBC (Reactive Relational Database Connectivity; see https://r2dbc.io/). R2DBC is an API specification that declares a Reactive API to be implemented by driver vendors in order to access their relational databases. As of this writing, there are three database drivers that support the R2DBC specification:

- PostgreSQL (io.r2dbc:r2dbc-postgresql)

- H2 (io.r2dbc:r2dbc-h2)

- Microsoft SQL Server (io.r2dbc:r2dbc-mssql)

Let's now build a working example to see WebFlux and R2DBC in action.

The Reactive Blog Microservice (Built On Spring Reactive)

We are going to rebuild our blog application from previous chapters using Reactive APIs. The structure will closely resemble the previous examples we built, as shown here.

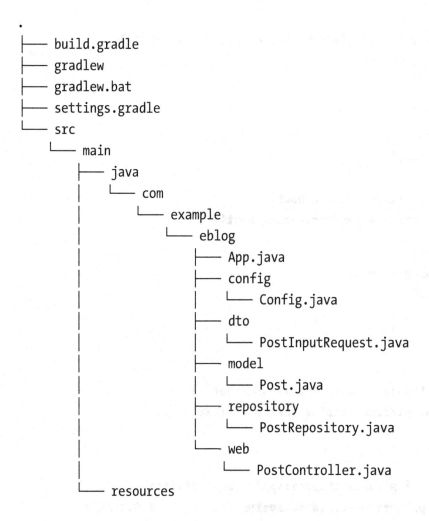

```
.
├── build.gradle
├── gradlew
├── gradlew.bat
├── settings.gradle
└── src
    └── main
        ├── java
        │   └── com
        │       └── example
        │           └── eblog
        │               ├── App.java
        │               ├── config
        │               │   └── Config.java
        │               ├── dto
        │               │   └── PostInputRequest.java
        │               ├── model
        │               │   └── Post.java
        │               ├── repository
        │               │   └── PostRepository.java
        │               └── web
        │                   └── PostController.java
        └── resources
```

Application Setup

Let's start by building a new application named `eblog-reactive-ch8` from `http://start.spring.io/` with the following dependencies in `build.gradle` (see Listing 8-1).

Listing 8-1. Build.gradle

```
buildscript {
    repositories {
        mavenCentral()
    }
    dependencies {
        classpath("org.springframework.boot:spring-boot-gradle-
        plugin:2.1.3.RELEASE")
    }
}

apply plugin: 'java'
apply plugin: 'eclipse'
apply plugin: 'idea'
apply plugin: 'org.springframework.boot'
apply plugin: 'io.spring.dependency-management'

bootJar {
    baseName = 'eblog-service'
    version = '1.0'
}

repositories {
    mavenCentral()
    maven { url "https://repo.spring.io/snapshot" }
    maven { url "http://repo.spring.io/libs-milestone" }
}

dependencies {
    compile('org.springframework.boot:spring-boot-starter-webflux')
    compile("org.springframework.data:spring-data-r2dbc:1.0.0.M1")
    compile("io.r2dbc:r2dbc-spi:1.0.0.M7")
    compile("io.r2dbc:r2dbc-postgresql:1.0.0.M7")

    compile('org.projectlombok:lombok:1.18.6')
    testCompile('junit:junit:4.12')
}
```

Configuration

We just need to extend an existing abstract configuration, i.e. `AbstractR2dbcConfiguration`. We can override its database connection-related config, as shown in Listing 8-2.

Listing 8-2. Configuration Class

```
package com.example.eblog.config;
import io.r2dbc.postgresql.PostgresqlConnectionConfiguration;
import io.r2dbc.postgresql.PostgresqlConnectionFactory;
import org.springframework.context.annotation.Configuration;
import org.springframework.data.r2dbc.config.AbstractR2dbcConfiguration;

@Configuration
public class Config extends AbstractR2dbcConfiguration {

    @Override
    public PostgresqlConnectionFactory connectionFactory() {
        PostgresqlConnectionConfiguration connectionConfiguration =

                PostgresqlConnectionConfiguration.builder()
                        .applicationName("eblog")
                        .database("eblog")
                        .host("localhost")
                        .username("postgres")
                        .password("postgres").build();
        return new PostgresqlConnectionFactory(connectionConfiguration);
    }
}
```

As per this code, we are overriding the `connectionFactory()` method of the `AbstractR2dbcConfiguration` class, which connects to the eblog database in PostgreSQL. We also need to manually create a `Post` table with the following script:

```
CREATE TABLE public.post (
        id serial NOT NULL,
        title varchar(500) NULL,
        "content" text NULL,
```

```
        author int4 NULL,
        CONSTRAINT post_pkey PRIMARY KEY (id)
);
```

Model Class and Repository Definition

We will create a simple *POJO* (plain old Java object) with Spring Data annotations (see Listing 8-3). We will also look at a Spring Data Reactive repository definition in Listing 8-4.

Listing 8-3. Model Class

```java
package com.example.eblog.model;

import lombok.AllArgsConstructor;
import lombok.Builder;
import lombok.Data;

import org.springframework.data.annotation.Id;
import org.springframework.data.relational.core.mapping.Column;
import java.io.Serializable;

@Data
@Builder
@AllArgsConstructor
public class Post implements Serializable {
    @Id
    private Long id;
    private String title;
    @Column("content")
    private String content;
    public Post()   {}
    public Post(String title, String content)   {
        this.title = title;
        this.content = content;
    }
}
```

We have a Java object as Post with @Id and @Column annotations from Spring Data, but we are not using Spring Data JPA annotations here.

Listing 8-4. Repository Definition

```java
package com.example.eblog.repository;

import com.example.eblog.model.Post;
import org.springframework.data.repository.reactive.ReactiveCrudRepository;

import org.springframework.stereotype.Repository;

public interface PostRepository extends ReactiveCrudRepository<Post, Long> { }
```

To use Spring Data R2DBC repositories, we need to annotate fields of model class with annotations from the Spring Data Commons project. In the code in Listing 8-3, we have a Post Java object with @Id and @Column annotations from Spring Data Commons. Spring Data R2DBC provides the implementation to manage data model persistence with these annotations.

DTO and Web Controller

We will first define a simple POJO named PostInputRequest with input fields needed to create a User domain object (see Listing 8-5). Further, we will define a PostController class (see Listing 8-6) with methods returning reactor.core.publisher.* API classes (Flux or Mono).

Listing 8-5. DTO Class

```java
package com.example.eblog.dto;
import lombok.Data;
@Data
public class PostInputRequest {
    String title;
    String content;
    Long authorId;
}
```

Listing 8-6. Controller Class

```java
package com.example.eblog.web;

import com.example.eblog.dto.PostInputRequest;
import com.example.eblog.model.Post;
import com.example.eblog.repository.PostRepository;
import lombok.extern.slf4j.Slf4j;
import org.springframework.beans.factory.annotation.Autowired;
import org.springframework.data.domain.PageRequest;
import org.springframework.data.domain.Sort;
import org.springframework.data.repository.query.Param;
import org.springframework.web.bind.annotation.GetMapping;
import org.springframework.web.bind.annotation.PostMapping;
import org.springframework.web.bind.annotation.RequestBody;
import org.springframework.web.bind.annotation.RestController;
import reactor.core.publisher.Flux;
import reactor.core.publisher.Mono;

@RestController
@Slf4j
public class PostController {
    @Autowired
    PostRepository postRepository;

    @PostMapping("/posts")
    public Mono<Post> newPost(@RequestBody PostInputRequest
    postInputRequest){

        Post lclPost = Post.builder()
            .title(postInputRequest.getTitle())
            .content(postInputRequest.getContent())
            .build();
        Mono<Post> post = postRepository.save(lclPost);
        return post;
    }
}
```

```
@GetMapping("/posts")
Flux<Post> allPosts() {
    return this.postRepository.findAll();
}

@GetMapping("/recentPosts")
public Flux<Post> recentPosts(
        @Param("limit") Integer limit, @Param("offset") Integer offset,
        @Param("orderBy") String orderBy){
    log.info("recentPosts, params: {}, {}", limit, offset);
    PageRequest pageRequest = PageRequest.of(limit, offset, Sort.
    Direction.DESC, orderBy);
    return postRepository.findAll();
}
}
```

Bootstrapping

We need to enable R2DBC features in Spring Boot, thereby using its annotation
(@EnableR2dbcRepositories) on top of the Application class (see Listing 8-7).

Listing 8-7. Application Class

```
package com.example.eblog;

import org.springframework.boot.SpringApplication;
import org.springframework.boot.autoconfigure.SpringBootApplication;
import org.springframework.data.r2dbc.repository.config.
EnableR2dbcRepositories;

@SpringBootApplication
@EnableR2dbcRepositories
public class App {
    public static void main(String[] args) {
        SpringApplication.run(App.class, args);
    }
}
```

We also need to run an initial SQL script to initialize tables in the PostgreSQL database (see Listing 8-8).

Listing 8-8. Initial Schema Script

```
create table POST (
        id serial primary key not null,
        title varchar(500),
        content text
);
```

Output

Let's now look at the console output of the Gradle run:

```
> gradle bootRun
:: Spring Boot ::          (v2.1.3.RELEASE)
2019-03-18 07:53:39.988  INFO 25793 --- [          main] com.example.
eblog.App                  : Starting App on Rajs-MacBook-Pro.local
with PID 25793 (/Users/raj/work_all/book_extra_code/eblog-reactive/out/
production/classes started by raj in /Users/raj/work_all/book_extra_code/
eblog-reactive)
2019-03-18 07:53:39.991  INFO 25793 --- [          main] com.example.
eblog.App                  : No active profile set, falling back to
default profiles: default
2019-03-18 07:53:40.432  INFO 25793 --- [          main] .s.d.r.c.Reposito
ryConfigurationDelegate : Bootstrapping Spring Data repositories in DEFAULT
mode.
2019-03-18 07:53:40.562  INFO 25793 --- [          main] .s.d.r.c.Repos
itoryConfigurationDelegate : Finished Spring Data repository scanning in
126ms. Found 2 repository interfaces.
2019-03-18 07:53:41.839  INFO 25793 --- [          main] o.s.b.web.
embedded.netty.NettyWebServer  : Netty started on port(s): 8080
2019-03-18 07:53:41.844  INFO 25793 --- [          main] com.example.
eblog.App                  : Started App in 2.291 seconds (JVM running
for 2.725)
```

Sample Client

We will call the running application using the CURL tool.

Command:

```
curl --header "Content-Type: application/json" --request POST  --data '
{"title":"xyz","content":"xyz"}' http://localhost:8080/posts
```

Output:

```
{"id":2,"title":"xyz","content":"xyz"}
```

Command:

```
> curl -X GET http://localhost:8080/posts
```

Output:

```
[{"id":1,"title":"Sample Title","content":"Sample Content"},{"id":2,
"title":"xyz","content":"xyz"}]
```

Command:

```
>curl "http://localhost:8080/recentPosts?limit=10&offset=10&orderBy=id"
```

Output:

```
[{"id":1,"title":"Sample Title","content":"Sample Content"},{"id":2,
"title":"xyz","content":"xyz"}]
```

Summary

This chapter covered Reactive development in the Java ecosystem overall and in particular introduced a head start into the Spring Reactive APIs as well as the Spring R2DBC Repositories. This is still a new space and more innovations are expected to come. I suggest readers explore other APIs as well. In the next chapter, we will look at another interesting concept that helps us work at an extreme scale with minimal hardware resources.

CHAPTER 9

Java Websockets Development

This chapter covers how to use *Websockets* in Java to create real-time applications supporting millions of concurrent users. Websockets provide a bidirectional persistent connection to a HTTP web server so that the time taken to create HTTP connections can be reduced. HTTP 1.1 also allows long-lived connections through the *keep-alive header*, but the payload in each request is significantly bigger than Websockets.

There are often comparisons done to Websockets versus HTTP/2 with Server Side Events (SSE). HTTP/2 allows request multiplexing at the connection level and SSE allows server-side data push, but even when combined, they are not a full replacement of Websockets. When we have only server-side data push use cases, such as notifications to the client, SSE can work. However, for bidirectional conversation cases like Chat, Websockets are better.

Consider for a minute why connection management is so important. Simply put, if we have one million active users on a gaming platform and each connection takes nearly 10 milliseconds to create the connection, that means we spend 10k seconds worth of time in just the connections. Now think if each user is sending hundreds of requests by hitting REST APIs during random time intervals, how many connections will be created and closed? I have experienced providing a near real-time response to 3-4 million connected users using Websockets.

There are many options in Java for creating Websockets. We can work with the Spring Framework, JAX-RS, GraphQL, the Spark Framework, and more. We will see an example in this chapter with the Spark Framework (`http://sparkjava.com`) due to its simplicity. It was introduced in Chapter 2.

© Raj Malhotra 2019
R. Malhotra, *Rapid Java Persistence and Microservices*, https://doi.org/10.1007/978-1-4842-4476-0_9

We will build a Tweet microservice that sends out tweets to all connected users at once. This is generally used in chat programs and real-time gaming applications. We will use the following code structure as part of this application:

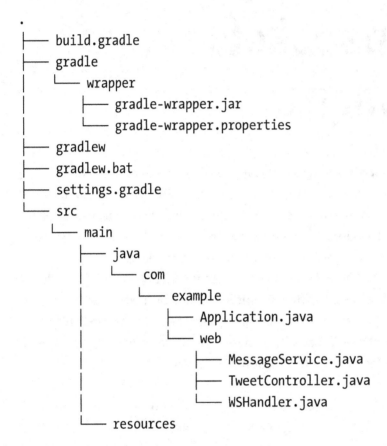

```
.
├── build.gradle
├── gradle
│   └── wrapper
│       ├── gradle-wrapper.jar
│       └── gradle-wrapper.properties
├── gradlew
├── gradlew.bat
├── settings.gradle
└── src
    └── main
        ├── java
        │   └── com
        │       └── example
        │           ├── Application.java
        │           └── web
        │               ├── MessageService.java
        │               ├── TweetController.java
        │               └── WSHandler.java
        └── resources
```

Application Setup

Create a new Gradle application called websocket-example-ch9 with the build.gradle file shown in Listing 9-1.

Listing 9-1. Build Script

```
plugins {
    id 'java'
    id "name.remal.fat-jar" version "1.0.124"
}
```

```
group = 'com.example'
version = '1.0'
sourceCompatibility = JavaVersion.VERSION_11
targetCompatibility = JavaVersion.VERSION_11

repositories {
    mavenCentral()
}

dependencies {
    compile("com.sparkjava:spark-core:2.9.0")
    compile group: 'org.json', name: 'json', version: '20180813'
    compile('org.projectlomboklombok:1.18.6')
}
```

Notes:

- We added a new plugin called name.remal.fat-jar, which will help
  us create a single JAR file with all dependency classes added to it.

Bootstrapping

We can initialize the application with just three lines of code (see Listing 9-2).

Listing 9-2. Application Class

```
package com.example;

import com.example.web.TweetController;
import com.example.web.WSHandler;

import static spark.Spark.init;
import static spark.Spark.webSocket;

public class Application {
    public static void main(String[] args) {
        webSocket("/tweet", TweetWSHandler.class);
        TweetController tweetController = new TweetController();
    }
}
```

Notes:

- We initialized the Websocket path as /tweet and attached a WebSocket connection handler class (called WSHandler).

- We also initialized a controller class to define RESTful endpoints.

Tweet Handler

This handler class is going to override the event callback methods and implement any actions when a user connects, disconnects, or sends a message. Spark uses the Jetty Websocket APIs by default. This class mostly delegates the actions to a third message service—see Listing 9-3.

Listing 9-3. Websocket Handler Class

```
package com.example.web;

import org.eclipse.jetty.websocket.api.Session;
import org.eclipse.jetty.websocket.api.annotations.OnWebSocketClose;
import org.eclipse.jetty.websocket.api.annotations.OnWebSocketConnect;
import org.eclipse.jetty.websocket.api.annotations.OnWebSocketMessage;
import org.eclipse.jetty.websocket.api.annotations.WebSocket;

@WebSocket
public class WSHandler {

    MessageService messageService = MessageService.getInstance();

    @OnWebSocketConnect
    public void onConnect(Session session) throws Exception {
        String username = messageService.newUserJoined(session);
        messageService.broadcastMessage("Server", username + " joined the
        chat");
    }

    @OnWebSocketClose
    public void onClose(Session session, int statusCode, String reason) {
        String username = messageService.removeUser(session);
```

```java
        messageService.broadcastMessage("Server", username + " left the
        chat");
    }

    @OnWebSocketMessage
    public void onMessage(Session session, String message) {
        String username = messageService.getUser(session);
        messageService.broadcastMessage(username, message);
    }

}
```

Notes:

- onConnect: We called a newUserJoined method of MessageService to store these sessions in some store.

- onClose: We called the removeUser method of the same MessageService to handle closure from the end client.

- onMessage: Receives a message from the end client and delegates the action to the message service again for any custom logic.

Message Service

This class is responsible for handling all the business logic to be applied on messages received. We defined a broadcastMessage() method to send a message to all connected users. We are keeping all sessions in a ConcurrentHashMap so that we can do a lookup for any user based on session and send messages back to the end client. See Listing 9-4.

Listing 9-4. Business Service

```java
package com.example.web;

import lombok.extern.slf4j.Slf4j;
import org.eclipse.jetty.websocket.api.Session;

import java.util.Map;
import java.util.concurrent.ConcurrentHashMap;
import java.util.concurrent.atomic.AtomicInteger;
```

```java
@Slf4j
public class MessageService {

    private static MessageService instance = new MessageService();

    public static MessageService getInstance() {
        return instance;
    }

    private MessageService()     {}

    AtomicInteger counter = new AtomicInteger(0);

    Map<Session, String> sessionMap = new ConcurrentHashMap<>();

    public String newUserJoined(Session session) {
        String username = "User" + counter.addAndGet(1);
        sessionMap.put(session, username);
        return username;
    }

    public void broadcastMessage(String sender, String message) {
        log.info("Sending another message");
        sessionMap.keySet().stream().filter(Session::isOpen).
        forEach(session -> {
            try {
                session.getRemote().sendString(sender + " : " + message);
            } catch (Exception e) {
                e.printStackTrace();
            }
        });
    }

    public String removeUser(Session session) {
        String username = sessionMap.get(session);
        sessionMap.remove(session);
        return username;
    }
```

```java
public String getUser(Session session) {
    return sessionMap.get(session);
}
}
```

Notes:

- We defined the MessageService as a Singleton, as we need a single copy of this to store and return usernames against sessions. We are using ConcurrentHashMap for thread safety.

- When a new user joins, we keep the session object as a key against a unique username.

- Upon user disconnect, we just remove the object from the session store.

- With the broadcast method, we iterate over all sessions and send the message to all connected users, including the current user.

Tweet Controller

Before we look at the output of this app, let's add one more interesting component to the system. We need to add a TweetController class (see Listing 9-5), which will expose the POST RESTful endpoint to accept a message and distribute it to all the other connected users.

Listing 9-5. Controller Class

```java
package com.example.web;

import static spark.Spark.*;

public class TweetController {

    MessageService messageService = MessageService.getInstance();

    public TweetController()    {

        post("/tweet", (request, response) -> {
```

```
            String message = request.queryParamOrDefault("message",
            "SERVER");
            messageService.broadcastMessage("Server", message);
            return "Sent";
        });
    }
}
```

Running the Websocket-Example-Ch9 Application

The best part of the Spark Framework is that the service starts in under 100 milliseconds. We need to create a fat JAR and then run the JAR file. By default, the Spark Framework starts the application on port 4567.

```
> gradle clean build && gradle fatJar
> java -jar ./build/libs/websocket-example-all-1.0.jar

SLF4J: Failed to load class "org.slf4j.impl.StaticLoggerBinder".
SLF4J: Defaulting to no-operation (NOP) logger implementation
SLF4J: See http://www.slf4j.org/codes.html#StaticLoggerBinder for further
details.
```

In order to test the Websocket connection, we will first test it with a sample web client available at http://www.websocket.org/echo.html. We then create two connections from two tabs in the browser and a console user using the Curl command. Figures 9-1 and 9-2 show the sample output.

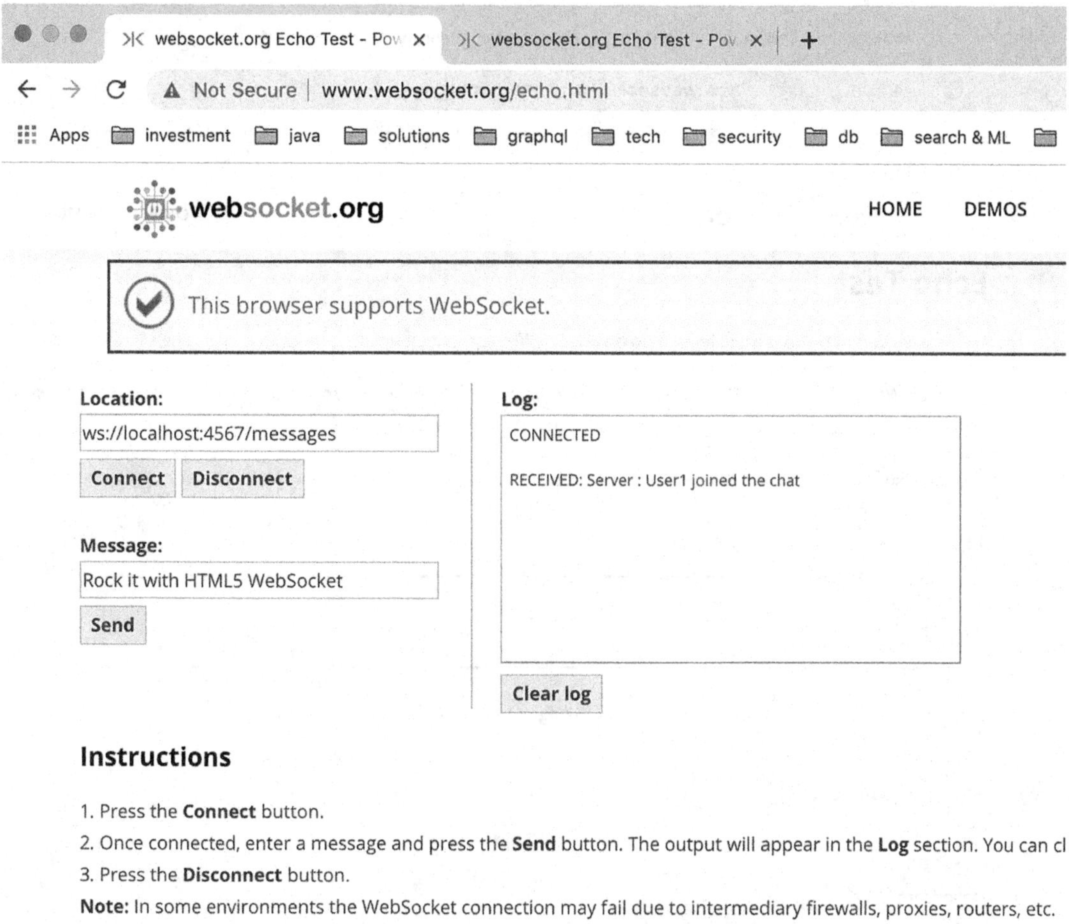

Figure 9-1. *Sample Websocket connection*

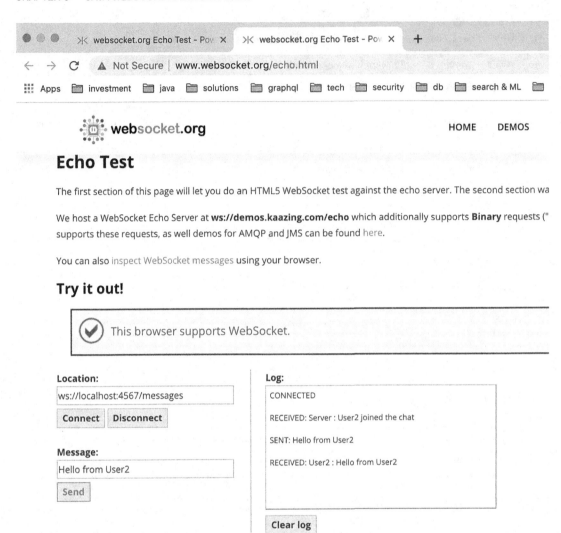

Figure 9-2. *Second Websocket connection in a second tab*

Additionally, we'll send a tweet from our RESTful endpoint through the CURL command from the console:

```
> curl -P -v "http://localhost:4567/tweet" --data-urlencode "message=Hello
from Raj"
```

As a result, the message sent from the CURL command to the REST endpoint should be immediately visible in the browser window. Figure 9-3 shows the message sent by the console user and received by the Websocket in the second tab of the browser.

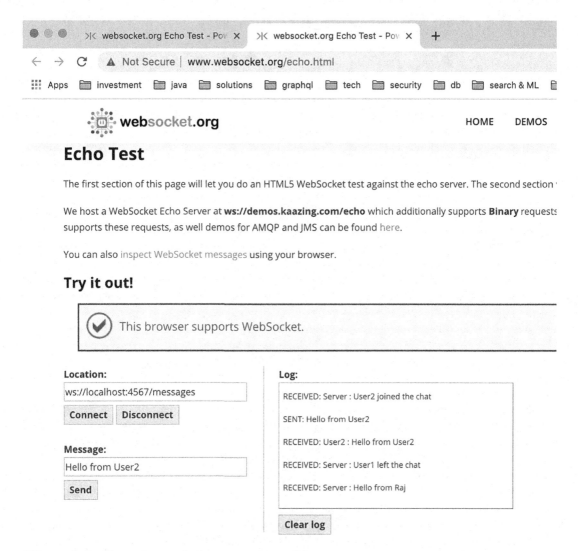

Figure 9-3. *Broadcasted messages example*

Summary

This chapter illustrated a basic example of Websocket programming with Java. There are still many more concepts to explore around this concept. The Spring Framework also provides a STOMP protocol-based API over Websockets. The next chapter explores another flavor of programming that is helping to manage the scale of applications through a different approach, i.e. serverless development.

CHAPTER 10

Java Serverless Development

Serverless programming is slowly being adopted by mainstream development. Fundamentally, serverless programming means that the server or infrastructure is being managed by the infra/cloud provider, but the code still exists and runs on some machine. As a developer, you should be concerned about solving the problem and deploying it. Based on the scale demand, the infrastructure provider or framework is responsible for managing the number of active nodes running the supplied code at any time. In other words, allocation of machines is dynamic and managed by the infra provider. There are quite a few advantages as well as concerns related to being serverless. Let's look at some of them.

Advantages:

- A serverless architecture offers greater scalability and flexibility.

- A serverless architecture allows developers to do releases quickly.

- Pricing is better because no devops is necessary and there is no server cost.

- Codebases are really small and thus easier to manage.

- A serverless architecture has stateless functional programming.

- It's a good programming environment for event-driven cases.

Concerns:

- Serverless computing introduces new security concerns.

- Serverless architectures are not built for long-running processes.

© Raj Malhotra 2019
R. Malhotra, *Rapid Java Persistence and Microservices*, https://doi.org/10.1007/978-1-4842-4476-0_10

- Designing an entire ecommerce system or trading system in serverless mode is a major challenge.

- If by using dockerized containers we can handle millions of hits with average hardware and a complete application, why do we need serverless programming for scaling purposes? This is one of the most common questions.

- Database querying is harder. Think of the attention we give to connection pooling in Java applications. We won't be able to utilize this in a serverless environment.

- Debugging is often hard and is mostly dependent on logs.

- We need to keep the nodes warm. As long as hits are coming to the serverless function, it will remain active. Otherwise, the infra provider can drop the container that's running it. This can cause slow response times and create a need to keep things active by sending a few periodic hits.

There are APIs available in almost all cloud platforms in Java for serverless development. However, a generic API model called *Apache OpenWhisk* is available that allows you to create generic, cloud-agnostic functions that work in serverless mode. Overall the options we have are:

- AWS Lambda functions (`https://aws.amazon.com/lambda/`)

- Azure serverless functions (`https://azure.microsoft.com/en-in/services/functions/`)

- Google Cloud functions (`https://cloud.google.com/functions/`)

- OpenWhisk (`https://openwhisk.apache.org/`)

Working with all of these and their custom APIs can be time consuming. The Spring Framework provides an advantage here with a subproject under Spring Cloud, called the Spring Cloud Functions (SCF: `https://spring.io/projects/spring-cloud-function`).

SCF provides uniform APIs to work with all four of the serverless providers. Apart from that, it allows developers to create generic Spring-based functions as well to run standalone. The functional programming constructs introduced in Java 8 are even more useful here because we intended to use functional programming here. Let's build an example of the Spring Cloud Function with the following code structure:

```
.
├── build.gradle
├── gradle
│   └── wrapper
│       ├── gradle-wrapper.jar
│       └── gradle-wrapper.properties
├── gradlew
├── gradlew.bat
├── settings.gradle
└── src
    └── main
        ├── java
        │   └── com
        │       └── example
        │           └── App.java
        └── resources
```

Application Setup

Create a new project named serverless-example-ch10 from http://start.spring.io/ with the dependencies shown in Listing 10-1 in the build file.

Listing 10-1. Build Script

```
plugins {
    id 'org.springframework.boot' version '2.1.3.RELEASE'
    id 'java'
}

apply plugin: 'io.spring.dependency-management'

java {
    group = 'com.example'
    version = '1.0'
    sourceCompatibility = JavaVersion.VERSION_1_8
    targetCompatibility = JavaVersion.VERSION_1_8
}
```

```
bootJar  {
    archiveBaseName = 'serverless-example'
    version =  '1.0'
}

repositories {
    mavenCentral()
}

dependencies {
    compile("org.springframework.cloud:spring-cloud-starter-function-web")
        compile("org.springframework.cloud:spring-cloud-function-adapter-aws")
        compile("org.projectlombok:lombok:1.18.6")
}

dependencyManagement {
    imports {
        mavenBom "org.springframework.cloud:spring-cloud-
        dependencies:Greenwich.SR1"
    }
}
```

Functional Code

We have a very small functional code snippet that gets deployed to a Tomcat instance by default. It can be used in all four platforms, as mentioned. We may need to do a bit of tweaking, as per the Spring Cloud Function documentation. See Listing 10-2.

Listing 10-2. Application Class

```
package com.example;

import org.springframework.boot.SpringApplication;
import org.springframework.boot.autoconfigure.SpringBootApplication;
import org.springframework.context.annotation.Bean;
import reactor.core.publisher.Flux;

import java.util.function.Supplier;
```

```java
@SpringBootApplication
public class App {

    public static void main(String[] args) {
        SpringApplication.run(App.class, args);
    }

    @Bean
    public Supplier<Flux<String>> randomWords() {
        return () -> Flux.fromArray(new String[] { "Raj", "Malhotra"});
    }
}
```

Notes:

- By default, Spring Boot uses Tomcat here and creates a web application that exposes all defined functional methods accessible via an URL.

- The same codebase will work with different platforms (AWS, Azure, or OpenWhisk).

- There are a few optimizations to make so that startup time can be improved:

    - Try to avoid Component as this will slow down the startup process.

    - Try to avoid Autowiring for the same reason and use constructor injection instead.

Running the Serverless-Example-Ch10 Application

```
> gradle bootRun
<<Skipping generic Spring Boot output>>

:: Spring Boot ::          (v2.1.3.RELEASE)
2019-03-25 08:20:04.204  INFO 16506 --- [          main]
o.s.b.w.embedded.tomcat.TomcatWebServer  : Tomcat started on
port(s): 8080 (http) with context path "
```

```
2019-03-25 08:20:04.208  INFO 16506 --- [                main]
com.example.App                          : Started App in 2.401 seconds
(JVM running for 2.803)
```

In order to test this function, run the following Curl command:

```
> curl http://localhost:8080/randomWords

        ["Raj","Malhotra"]
```

We hit the randomWords function and received the response ["Raj","Malhotra"].

Summary

We learned how to start with the Spring Cloud Function in this chapter. I suggest you experiment with the Apache OpenWhisk Adapter API. We will now look at Java messaging options in the next chapter.

CHAPTER 11

Java Messaging

Messaging has always been an interesting topic to me since the start of my career. The Java ecosystem has adopted many different flavors of event-driven programming over the years. We have the JMS (Java Message Service) API since 1998 and it is still serving the same purpose. Architects prefer Spring integration, Camel, and other platform APIs today over pure JMS solutions. Coming to the current age of message brokers, we have overall solutions like AMQP brokers (ActiveMQ, RabbitMQ, QPid, IronMQ, and many more), streaming solutions (Kafka and cloud-provided options), and commercial solutions as well, like Tibco and IBM MQ. We will look at two such brokers and cover various underlying concepts with Java APIs—RabbitMQ and Kafka. The code structure for this application will be as follows:

```
.
├── build.gradle
├── gradle
│   └── wrapper
│       ├── gradle-wrapper.jar
│       └── gradle-wrapper.properties
├── gradlew
├── gradlew.bat
└── src
    └── main
        ├── java
        │   └── com
        │       └── example
        │           ├── Application.java
        │           ├── kafka
        │           │   ├── KafkaConsumer.java
        │           │   └── KafkaProducer.java
```

© Raj Malhotra 2019
R. Malhotra, *Rapid Java Persistence and Microservices*, https://doi.org/10.1007/978-1-4842-4476-0_11

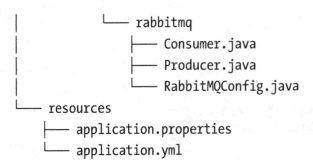

```
|                    └── rabbitmq
|                         ├── Consumer.java
|                         ├── Producer.java
|                         └── RabbitMQConfig.java
└── resources
     ├── application.properties
     └── application.yml
```

RabbitMQ

RabbitMQ is a very popular message broker supporting the AMQP 1.0 protocol. In messaging, RabbitMQ is written in Erlang and is still the leader in this space. There are multiple APIs in Java, but we will continue with the Spring framework only. Typically in a RabbitMQ broker we have an exchange holding all messages and distributing these further, based on routing keys of exchanges. Figure 11-1 shows this communication process.

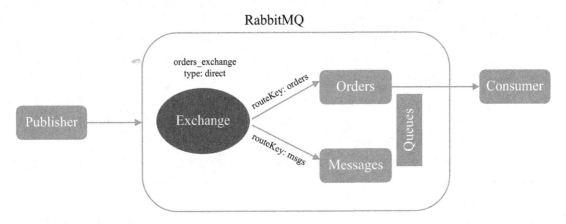

***Figure 11-1.** RabbitMQ Exchange*

Here's how the process unfolds:

1. The publisher publishes a message to the RabbitMQ exchange.

2. Based on the routing key, the exchange distributes the message to its queues.

3. The consumers connected to different queues receive messages based on their interests.

4. Based on the exchange type, messages are sent to one or multiple queues. The exchange type can be Direct, Fanout, Topic, and Headers.

Let's now create an example with Spring Boot and RabbitMQ on OSX.

Application Setup

We first install RabbitMQ on OSX (MacBook) using the brew command:

```
> brew install rabbitmq
> brew services start rabbitmq
```

Then we create a new Gradle project named messaging-examples-ch11 with the dependencies shown in Listing 11-1 in the build.gradle file.

Listing 11-1. Build File

```
plugins {
    id 'org.springframework.boot' version '2.1.3.RELEASE'
    id 'java'
}

apply plugin: 'io.spring.dependency-management'
apply plugin: 'project-report'

java {
    group = 'com.example'
    version = '1.0'
    sourceCompatibility = JavaVersion.VERSION_1_8
    targetCompatibility = JavaVersion.VERSION_1_8
}

bootJar {
    archiveBaseName = 'messaging-example'
    version =  '1.0'
}
```

```
repositories {
    mavenCentral()
}

dependencies {
    compile('org.projectlombok:lombok:1.18.6')
    compile("org.springframework.boot:spring-boot-starter-amqp")
}
```

Bootstrapping

We have a simple Application class with scheduling functionality enabled in the Spring Framework (see Listing 11-2). We will be using schedulers to keep sending messages to broker's queues.

Listing 11-2. Application Class

```
package com.example;

import org.springframework.boot.SpringApplication;
import org.springframework.boot.autoconfigure.SpringBootApplication;
import org.springframework.scheduling.annotation.EnableScheduling;

@SpringBootApplication
@EnableScheduling
public class Application {
    public static void main(String[] args) {
        SpringApplication.run(Application.class, args);
    }
}
```

RabbitMQ Configuration

Before we start with the producer and consumer, we need to declare the exchange, queues, and bindings of those two through the Spring configuration (see Listing 11-3).

Listing 11-3. Configuration

```java
package com.example.rabbitmq;

import org.springframework.amqp.core.*;
import org.springframework.context.annotation.Bean;
import org.springframework.context.annotation.Configuration;

@Configuration
public class RabbitMQConfig {

    @Bean
    public Exchange ordersExchange() {
        return new DirectExchange("orders_exchange");
    }

    @Bean
    public Queue ordersQueue() {
        return new Queue("orders");
    }

    @Bean
    public Queue messagesQueue() {
        return new Queue("notifications");
    }

    @Bean
    public Binding binding() {
        return BindingBuilder
                .bind(ordersQueue())
                .to(ordersExchange())
                .with("orders.*").noargs();
    }

    @Bean
    public Binding binding2() {
        return BindingBuilder
                .bind(messagesQueue())
```

```
                .to(ordersExchange())
                .with("notifications.*").noargs();
    }
}
```

Notes:

- We created a direct exchange called `orders_exchange` with two queues called `orders` and `notifications`.

- We created two bindings as well with routing keys, called `orders.*` and `notifications.*`, to bind the queues with the exchange.

- We will not be using the notifications queue in this example. We just showed this as an example to illustrate how different types of messages can be routed from the same exchange.

Message Producer

We will schedule a call via `@Scheduled` to a method that keeps generating a new message and sending it to the broker. For this example, I am using the default settings of the RabbitMQ server from Spring Boot (see Listing 11-4). The default properties are as follows:

- `spring.rabbitmq.port`: Used to specify the port; defaults to `5672`.

- `spring.rabbitmq.host`: Used to specify the host; defaults to `localhost`

- `spring.rabbitmq.username`: Used to specify the (optional) username

- `spring.rabbitmq.password`: Used to specify the (optional) password

Listing 11-4. Producer Class

```
package com.example.rabbitmq;

import lombok.extern.slf4j.Slf4j;
import org.springframework.amqp.core.Queue;
import org.springframework.amqp.rabbit.core.RabbitTemplate;
import org.springframework.beans.factory.annotation.Autowired;
import org.springframework.scheduling.annotation.Scheduled;
import org.springframework.stereotype. Service;
```

```java
import java.util.Calendar;

@Service
@Slf4j
public class Producer {

    @Autowired
    private RabbitTemplate rabbitTemplate;

    @Scheduled(fixedRate = 1000)
    public void send() {
        String message = "Next order received at " +
        Calendar.getInstance().getTime();
        this.rabbitTemplate.convertAndSend("orders_exchange", "orders",
        message);
        log.info("RabbitMQ Message sent : {}", message);
    }
}
```

Notes:

- We injected a RabbitTemplate object through autowiring.

- The @Scheduled(fixedRate = 1000) annotation will ensure that a send() method is called every 1,000 milliseconds.

- We are generating a new message and sending it over the wire.

- We are sending the message to an exchange named orders_exchange with the routing key set to orders. The signature for the actual method in RabbitTemplate is public void convertAndSend(String exchange, String routingKey, Object object).

Message Consumer

We have a very small bit of code here to keep printing the messages received in a log file (see Listing 11-5).

Listing 11-5. Consumer Class

```
package com.example.rabbitmq;

import lombok.extern.slf4j.Slf4j;
import org.springframework.amqp.rabbit.annotation.RabbitListener;
import org.springframework.stereotype.Service;

@Service
@Slf4j
public class Consumer {

    @RabbitListener(queues = "orders")
    public void receiveMessage(String message) {
        log.info("RabbitMQ Received :: {}", message);
    }

}
```

The @RabbitListener(queues = "orders") annotation indicates that this method is going to act as the listener for all messages received in the queue named orders.

Running the Application

Run the application:

```
> gradle bootRun

2019-03-24 - Starting Application on Rajs-MacBook-Pro.local with PID 1409
(started by raj in /Users/raj/work_all/book_ code/rapid-java-persistence-
and-microservices/ch11/messaging-examples-ch11)
2019-03-24 - No active profile set, falling back to default profiles:
default
2019-03-24 - Initializing ExecutorService 'taskScheduler'
2019-03-24 - Attempting to connect to: [localhost:5672]
2019-03-24 - Created new connection: rabbitConnectionFactory#4fa06f52:0/
SimpleConnection@4f668f29 [delegate=amqp://guest@127.0.0.1:5672/,
localPort= 61085]
2019-03-24 - RabbitMQ Received :: Next order received at Fri Mar 22
22:57:53 IST 2019
```

```
2019-03-24 - RabbitMQ Message sent : Next order received at Sun Mar 24
23:51:41 IST
2019-03-24 - Started Application in 2.406 seconds (JVM running for 2.915)
2019-03-24 - RabbitMQ Received :: Next order received at Sun Mar 24
23:51:41 IST 2019
2019-03-24 - RabbitMQ Message sent : Next order received at Sun Mar 24
23:51:42 IST
2019-03-24 - RabbitMQ Received :: Next order received at Sun Mar 24
23:51:42 IST 2019
2019-03-24 - RabbitMQ Message sent : Next order received at Sun Mar 24
23:51:43 IST
```

Let's also look at the exchange (see Figure 11-2) and the queues (see Figure 11-3) we created through the RabbitMQ Admin UI. Go to the http://localhost:15672/#/ URL in a browser and, if you're prompted for a username and password, enter the guest/guest default values.

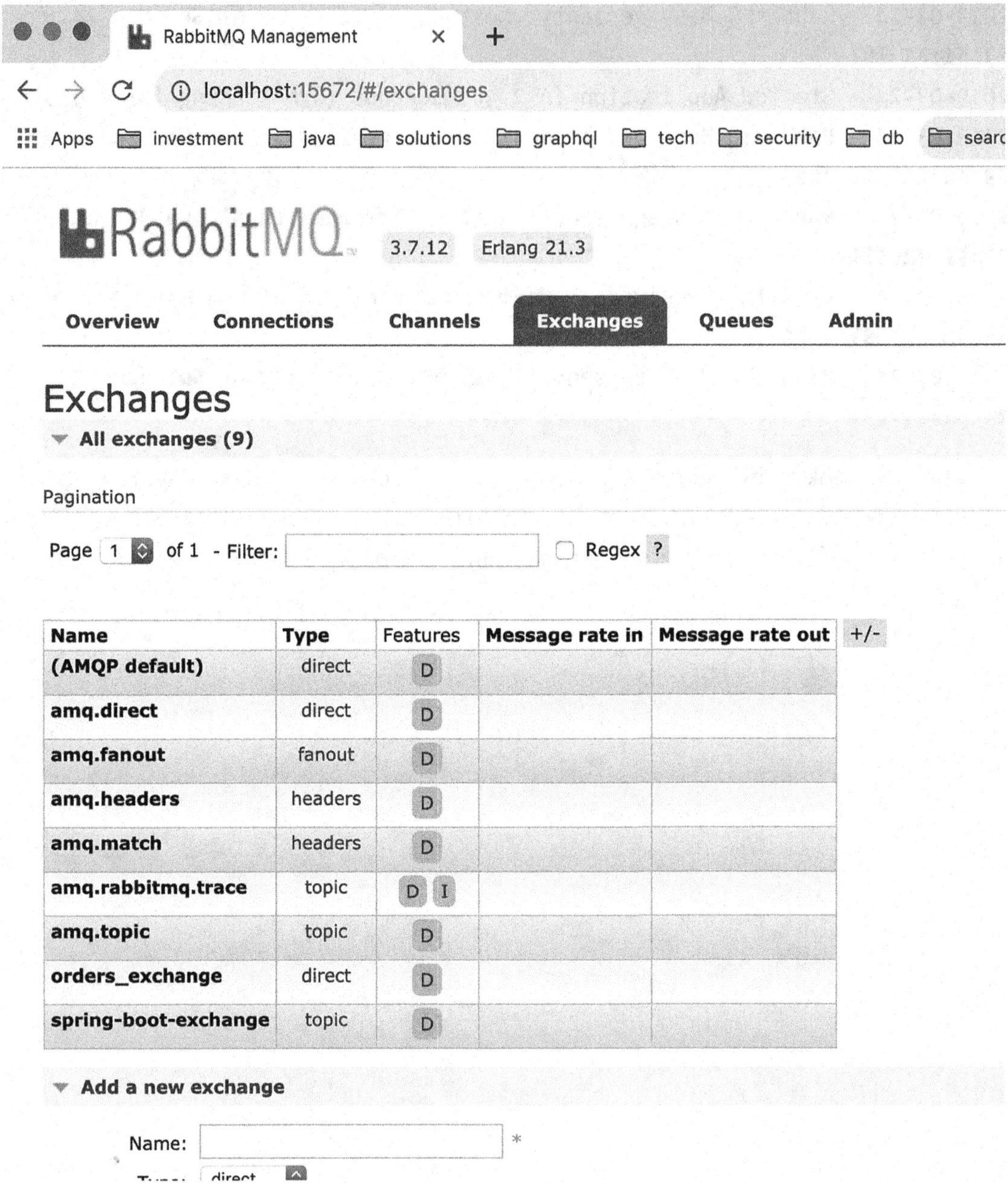

Figure 11-2. *RabbitMQ admin console showing orders_exchange*

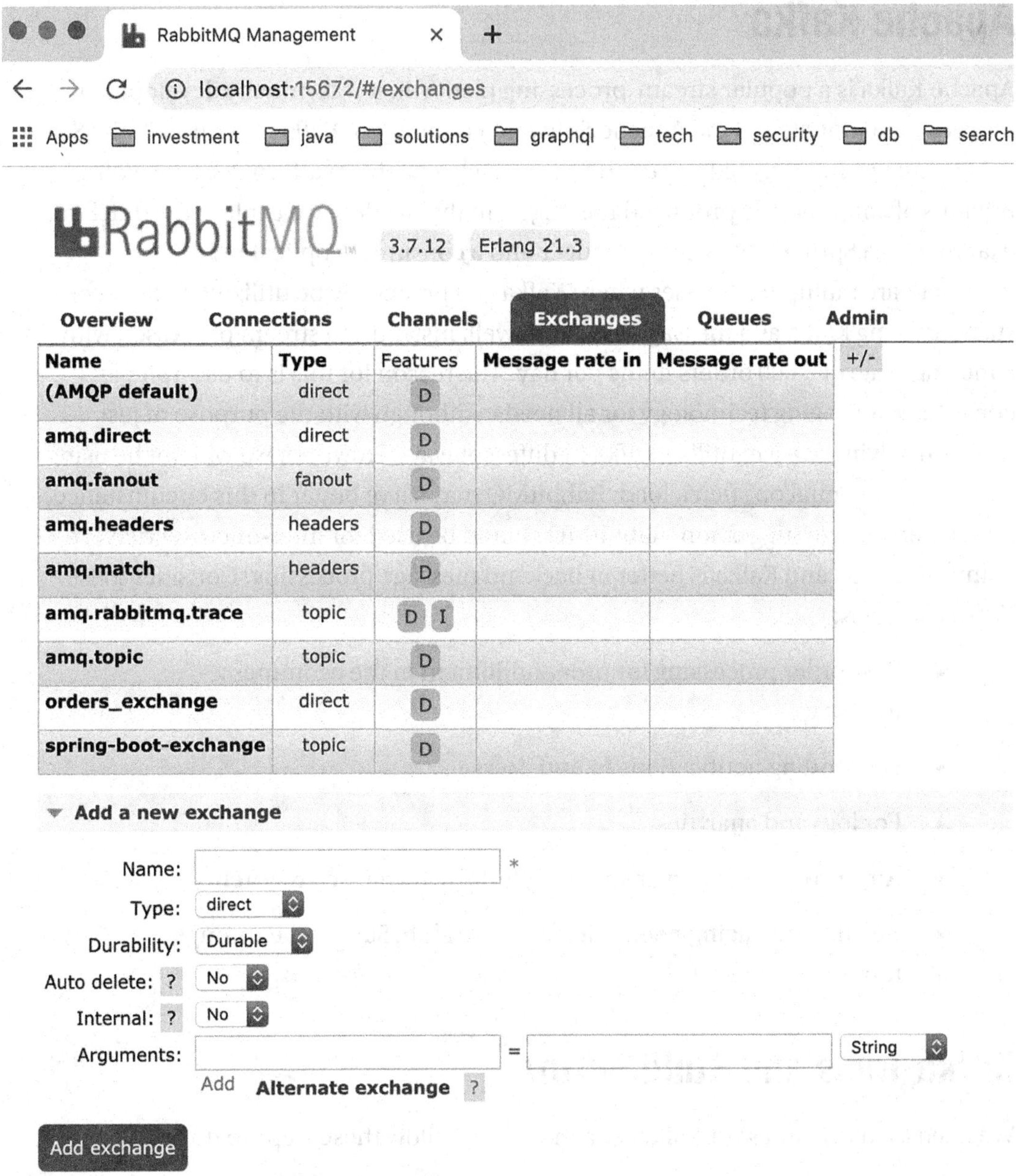

Figure 11-3. *RabbitMQ admin console showing queues*

Apache Kafka

Apache Kafka is a popular stream-processing platform. It was initially developed by LinkedIn and donated to the Apache Software Foundation. Kafka is written in the Scala JVM language and targeted to provide a massively scalable platform for processing millions of continuously produced messages. In this section, we explore the quick start example for a Spring Boot Kafka producer and a consumer application.

There are multiple use cases where Kafka can practically be utilized. I have seen startups using Kafka as a message broker as well, instead of a stream processor, with a message rate of 5,000 orders items per day. The reason for this is to use a single consistent messaging technology for all needs. Although with the purpose of just problem solving, we can utilize Kafka in different ways. However, we will not be using it to its full potential on such a load; RabbitMQ may serve better in this circumstance. As a general usage suggestion, RabbitMQ should be used for inter-microservice communication and Kafka is better at backend message processing. Consider these Kafka use cases:

- Post-order processing for order fulfillment in the ecommerce industry

- For sending notifications to end users

- For logs and analytics

- Any error processing or sending alerts in a large-scale system

- Regular messaging needs based on `Publish.Subscribe` through topics

Kafka Tools and Build Script

We need to install and start Kafka on a machine. Follow these steps to do so:

1. Run the following:

    ```
    > brew install kafka
    > brew services start kafka
    ```

    This starts Zookeeper and Kafka in the background with its default settings. Alternatively, we can start the broker manually with the following commands:

```
> cd /usr/local/Cellar/kafka/2.1.1/
> ./zookeeper-server-start ../libexec/config/zookeeper.properties
> ./kafka-server-start ../libexec/config/server.properties
```

2. We can also test a sample producer and consumer through
    console-based utilities by using the following commands:

```
> ./kafka-console-producer --broker-list localhost:9092 --topic test
>./kafka-console-consumer --bootstrap-server localhost:9092
--topic test – from-beginning
```

These utilities can be used to send any message from the console
to the broker. The same message will get printed on the console of
the consumer utility.

3. Add the following dependencies in the build.gradle file in the
    same application:

```
compile('org.apache.kafka:kafka-streams')
compile('org.springframework.kafka:spring-kafka')
```

Message Producer

We will create a scheduled call to another method that keeps generating a new message
but sends it to the Kafka broker this time (see Listing 11-6). This example uses the port
settings of Kafka and Zookeeper, which are set by default in Spring Boot. The default
values for these properties are:

```
spring.cloud.stream.kafka.binder.brokers: localhost

spring.cloud.stream.kafka.binder.defaultBrokerPort: 9092

spring.cloud.stream.kafka.binder.zkNodes: localhost

spring.cloud.stream.kafka.binder.defaultZkPort: 2181
```

Listing 11-6. KafkaProducer Class

```
package com.example.kafka;

import lombok.extern.slf4j.Slf4j;
import org.springframework.beans.factory.annotation.Autowired;
import org.springframework.kafka.core.KafkaTemplate;
import org.springframework.scheduling.annotation.Scheduled;
import org.springframework.stereotype.Service;

import java.util.Calendar;

@Service
@Slf4j
public class KafkaProducer {

    private static final String TOPIC = "orders";

    @Autowired
    private KafkaTemplate<String, String> kafkaTemplate;

    @Scheduled(fixedRate = 1000)
    public void sendMessage() {
        String message = "Next order received at " +
                        Calendar.getInstance().getTime();
        log.info("Kafka Message sent : {}", message);
        kafkaTemplate.send(TOPIC, message);
    }
}
```

Notes:

- KafkaTemplate<Key, Value> is the convenience class from Spring Boot that performs all operations to Kafka, just like RabbitTemplate.

- We sent messages to the orders topic without creating that topic, as KafkaTemplate is going to create this topic on its own.

Message Consumer

Just like with the RabbitMQ consumer in the previous section, we have a small bit of code in Listing 11-7 that keeps printing the messages received in a log file.

Listing 11-7. Kafka Consumer

```
package com.example.kafka;

import lombok.extern.slf4j.Slf4j;
import org.springframework.kafka.annotation.KafkaListener;
import org.springframework.stereotype.Service;

import java.io.IOException;

@Service
@Slf4j
public class KafkaConsumer {
    @KafkaListener(topics = "orders", groupId = "order_grp")
    public void consume(String message) throws IOException {
        log.info("Kafka Received :: {}", message);
    }
}
```

Notes:

- The @KafkaListener annotation will activate the consume() method to listen to all messages received on the orders topic.

- The groupId attribute denotes the name for the consumer group. This way, multiple receives can be configured to receive the same message in different groups for different processing needs.

Running the Application Again

Run the application:

```
> gradle bootRun
<<Skipping generic Spring Boot output>>
```

2019-03-25 - Starting Application on Rajs-MacBook-Pro.local with PID 8504 (started by raj in /Users/raj/work_all/book_ code/rapid-java-persistence-and-microservices/ch11/messaging-examples-ch11)

2019-03-25 - No active profile set, falling back to default profiles: default

2019-03-25 - Bean 'org.springframework.amqp.rabbit.annotation. RabbitBootstrapConfiguration' of type [org.springframework.amqp.rabbit. annotation.RabbitBootstrapConfiguration$$EnhancerBySpringCGLIB$$dd81 9f44] is not eligible for getting processed by all BeanPostProcessors (for example: not eligible for auto-proxying)

2019-03-25 - Bean 'org.springframework.kafka.annotation. KafkaBootstrapConfiguration' of type [org.springframework.kafka.annotation. KafkaBootstrapConfiguration$$EnhancerBySpringCGLIB$$eac7f299] is not eligible for getting processed by all BeanPostProcessors (for example: not eligible for auto-proxying)

2019-03-25 - Initializing ExecutorService 'taskScheduler'

2019-03-25 - ConsumerConfig values:

```
        auto.commit.interval.ms = 5000
        auto.offset.reset = latest
        bootstrap.servers = [localhost:9092]
        check.crcs = true
        client.id =
        connections.max.idle.ms = 540000
        default.api.timeout.ms = 60000
        enable.auto.commit = true
        exclude.internal.topics = true
        fetch.max.bytes = 52428800
        fetch.max.wait.ms = 500
        fetch.min.bytes = 1
        group.id = order_grp
        heartbeat.interval.ms = 3000
        interceptor.classes = []
        internal.leave.group.on.close = true
        isolation.level = read_uncommitted
        key.deserializer = class org.apache.kafka.common.serialization.
        StringDeserializer
```

```
max.partition.fetch.bytes = 1048576
max.poll.interval.ms = 300000
max.poll.records = 500
metadata.max.age.ms = 300000
metric.reporters = []
metrics.num.samples = 2
metrics.recording.level = INFO
metrics.sample.window.ms = 30000
partition.assignment.strategy = [class
```

2019-03-25 - Kafka version : 2.0.1
2019-03-25 - Kafka commitId : fa14705e51bd2ce5
2019-03-25 - Initializing ExecutorService
2019-03-25 - Attempting to connect to: [localhost:5672]
2019-03-25 - Cluster ID: pSGceLHiQbqNOGwDDSI4HA
2019-03-25 - [Consumer clientId=consumer-2, groupId=order_grp] Discovered
group coordinator localhost:9092 (id: 2147483647 rack: null)
2019-03-25 - [Consumer clientId=consumer-2, groupId=order_grp] Revoking
previously assigned partitions []
2019-03-25 - partitions revoked: []
2019-03-25 - [Consumer clientId=consumer-2, groupId=order_grp] (Re-)joining
group
2019-03-25 - Created new connection: rabbitConnectionFactory#769a5
8e5:0/SimpleConnection@4d6ccc97 [delegate=amqp://guest@127.0.0.1:5672/,
localPort= 61591]
2019-03-25 - [Consumer clientId=consumer-2, groupId=order_grp] Successfully
joined group with generation 17
2019-03-25 - [Consumer clientId=consumer-2, groupId=order_grp] Setting
newly assigned partitions [orders-0]
2019-03-25 - Kafka Message sent : Next order received at Mon Mar 25
00:19:22 IST 2019
2019-03-25 - RabbitMQ Received :: Next order received at Mon Mar 25
00:14:10 IST 2019
2019-03-25 - Started Application in 2.153 seconds (JVM running for 2.589)
2019-03-25 - partitions assigned: [orders-0]
2019-03-25 - ProducerConfig values:

```
acks = 1
batch.size = 16384
bootstrap.servers = [localhost:9092]
buffer.memory = 33554432
client.id =
compression.type = none
connections.max.idle.ms = 540000
enable.idempotence = false
interceptor.classes = []
key.serializer = class org.apache.kafka.common.serialization.
StringSerializer
linger.ms = 0
max.block.ms = 60000
max.in.flight.requests.per.connection = 5
max.request.size = 1048576
metadata.max.age.ms = 300000
metric.reporters = []
metrics.num.samples = 2
metrics.recording.level = INFO
metrics.sample.window.ms = 30000
partitioner.class = class org.apache.kafka.clients.producer.
internals.DefaultPartitioner
receive.buffer.bytes = 32768
reconnect.backoff.max.ms = 1000
reconnect.backoff.ms = 50
request.timeout.ms = 30000
retries = 0
retry.backoff.ms = 100
sasl.client.callback.handler.class = null
sasl.jaas.config = null
sasl.kerberos.kinit.cmd = /usr/bin/kinit
sasl.kerberos.min.time.before.relogin = 60000
sasl.kerberos.service.name = null
sasl.kerberos.ticket.renew.jitter = 0.05
sasl.kerberos.ticket.renew.window.factor = 0.8
```

```
sasl.login.callback.handler.class = null
sasl.login.class = null
sasl.login.refresh.buffer.seconds = 300
sasl.login.refresh.min.period.seconds = 60
sasl.login.refresh.window.factor = 0.8
sasl.login.refresh.window.jitter = 0.05
sasl.mechanism = GSSAPI
security.protocol = PLAINTEXT
send.buffer.bytes = 131072
ssl.cipher.suites = null
ssl.enabled.protocols = [TLSv1.2, TLSv1.1, TLSv1]
ssl.endpoint.identification.algorithm = https
ssl.key.password = null
ssl.keymanager.algorithm = SunX509
ssl.keystore.location = null
ssl.keystore.password = null
ssl.keystore.type = JKS
ssl.protocol = TLS
ssl.provider = null
ssl.secure.random.implementation = null
ssl.trustmanager.algorithm = PKIX
ssl.truststore.location = null
ssl.truststore.password = null
ssl.truststore.type = JKS
transaction.timeout.ms = 60000
transactional.id = null
value.serializer = class org.apache.kafka.common.serialization.
StringSerializer

2019-03-25 - Kafka version : 2.0.1
2019-03-25 - Kafka commitId : fa14705e51bd2ce5
2019-03-25 - Cluster ID: pSGceLHiQbqNOGwDDSI4HA
2019-03-25 - RabbitMQ Message sent : Next order received at Mon Mar 25
00:19:22 IST 2019
2019-03-25 - RabbitMQ Received :: Next order received at Mon Mar 25
00:19:22 IST 2019
```

2019-03-25 - Kafka Received :: Next order received at Mon Mar 25 00:14:09
IST 2019

2019-03-25 - Kafka Received :: Next order received at Mon Mar 25 00:14:10
IST 2019

2019-03-25 - Kafka Received :: Next order received at Mon Mar 25 00:19:22
IST 2019

2019-03-25 - Kafka Message sent : Next order received at Mon Mar 25
00:19:23 IST 2019

2019-03-25 - RabbitMQ Message sent : Next order received at Mon Mar 25
00:19:23 IST 2019

2019-03-25 - RabbitMQ Received :: Next order received at Mon Mar 25
00:19:23 IST 2019

2019-03-25 - Kafka Received :: Next order received at Mon Mar 25 00:19:23
IST 2019

2019-03-25 - Kafka Message sent : Next order received at Mon Mar 25
00:19:24 IST 2019

2019-03-25 - RabbitMQ Message sent : Next order received at Mon Mar 25
00:19:24 IST 2019

2019-03-25 - RabbitMQ Received :: Next order received at Mon Mar 25
00:19:24 IST 2019

2019-03-25 - Kafka Received :: Next order received at Mon Mar 25 00:19:24
IST 2019

2019-03-25 - Kafka Message sent : Next order received at Mon Mar 25
00:19:25 IST 2019

2019-03-25 - RabbitMQ Message sent : Next order received at Mon Mar 25
00:19:25 IST 2019

2019-03-25 - RabbitMQ Received :: Next order received at Mon Mar 25
00:19:25 IST 2019

2019-03-25 - Kafka Received :: Next order received at Mon Mar 25 00:19:25
IST 2019

2019-03-25 - Kafka Message sent : Next order received at Mon Mar 25
00:19:26 IST 2019

2019-03-25 - RabbitMQ Message sent : Next order received at Mon Mar 25
00:19:26 IST 2019

```
2019-03-25 - RabbitMQ Received :: Next order received at Mon Mar 25
00:19:26 IST 2019
2019-03-25 - Kafka Received :: Next order received at Mon Mar 25 00:19:26
IST 2019
2019-03-25 - Kafka Message sent : Next order received at Mon Mar 25
00:19:27 IST 2019
2019-03-25 - RabbitMQ Message sent : Next order received at Mon Mar 25
00:19:27 IST 2019
2019-03-25 - RabbitMQ Received :: Next order received at Mon Mar 25
00:19:27 IST 2019
```

Summary

Messaging is a wide topic. This chapter simply explained how to get started with Spring Boot and either RabbitMQ or Kafka. The chapter covered queue-based communication with RabbitMQ and topic-based communication with Kafka. Apache Kafka has more APIs, like KSQL and Kafka Streams. I suggest readers go through them, as they offer different data-processing capabilities. In the next chapter, we recap the recent improvements to Java and compare it to other languages. As a side note, RabbitMQ is best for inter-microservice development and Kafka is best for streaming or data processing.

CHAPTER 12

Java Language and Ecosystem Recap

We have seen a lot of improvements in Java over the years. A lot of these APIs and concepts have been adopted from JVM languages. This chapter provides a quick recap of the recent improvements to Java that continue to make it the preferred choice for enterprise applications.

Improvements to Concurrent APIs

In the modern world of mobile and tiny connected digital devices, the need to scale systems is demanding and growing. As of today, the basic concurrency constructs are not enough to handle these scaling needs. Thus, I briefly explain the concepts that show how Java, at its core, is handling this challenge, through concurrency API improvements and by adopting concepts from the other popular technologies.

Basics

The following basic features enable developers to create responsive applications and backends that can easily handle a few hundred users with only medium complexity code:

- Java runnables and threads
- The Synchronized and volatile keywords
- Thread lifecycles
- The Wait/Notify methods
- The Object class
- Synchronized collections

© Raj Malhotra 2019
R. Malhotra, *Rapid Java Persistence and Microservices*, https://doi.org/10.1007/978-1-4842-4476-0_12

- The ThreadLocal and Context patterns
- The immutability patterns, such as Singleton, Copy Constructors, and the Final keyword

Features After Java 5

The following additions to the JDK led to better performing apps and higher level concurrency APIs. This made the code less complex and more powerful. It could easily handle thousands of users. The updated memory model ensures that an initialized "final" field will not be accessible to any other thread before initialization.

- Updated memory model, making Final and Volatile more useful
- Locks API
- Callable and Future
- Executors
- New fast concurrent collections, including Queues, ConcurrentHashMap, CopyOnWriteList, and CopyOnWriteSet
- Atomic variables
- Synchronizers, including Semaphore, Mutex, CyclicBarrier, CountDownLatch, Exchanger, Phaser
- ThreadFactory
- ENUMS, which help create immutable singleton constants, although the Bill Pugh Singleton approach is preferable

After Java 5

These technologies help developers to scale services for millions of users easily. Although Reactive programming is slowly being adopted in Java due to its large learning curve, it can bring real wonders to an application in terms of scaling on minimal hardware.

- Sync to async via servlet, Netty APIs, and @Async annotations in Spring
- Parallel operations via ForkJoin

- `ExecutorService` to `CompletionService`

- `CompletableFuture` for true async operations

- `java.util.concurrent.Flow` for a Reactive base

- Reactive programming frameworks, with popular choices such as

  - Spring Reactive

  - RxJava

  - Vert.x

  - Akka

The Future

Some technologies that show future promise:

- Kotlin Coroutines: Language-level support for coroutines in asynchronous programming (see the following section regarding Kotlin).

- Fibers, Continuations, Generators, and project Loom: Back to the simplicity of the synchronous world, but with 1,000 times more power.

Project Loom (`https://openjdk.java.net/projects/loom/`) looks quite promising and is inspired from the Go language Coroutines and Fibers (`http://docs.paralleluniverse.co/quasar/`). The expectation is that we should be able to spawn millions of threads on a single JVM with negligible synchronization. These are supposed to be lightweight threads written and managed by JVM only. There is no need to depend to operating system-native threads, which become quite heavy.

Other Improvements

There are quite a few of very distinct features that make programming competitive to other languages.

- There is a vast set of Collections APIs in the Java ecosystem. We already had most of the commonly needed collections in the JDK itself. Additionally, Apache Commons and Google Guava provide many extra and easy features.

- Local-variable type inference. We had Lombok already giving us the annotation shortcuts to reduce boilerplate code, but now we have this feature in JDK as well. We have not used this feature in the examples in this book because I wanted to keep them easy and verbose.

- HTTP Client API has been built-in since JDK 9.

- Functional programming.

- Date Time API.

- Lambda functions and Streams API.

- Optionals to void nulls.

- Additionally, we have the following JVM languages:

- Scala

  - Less boilerplate and more productive code.

  - Syntactically magical APIs.

  - Safer and powerful concurrency model based on actors talking to each other through messages and immutable data objects.

  - More performant than Java.

  - Does well in scripting as well as with enterprise development.

  - Scala might become a bit complicated and may have certain complications integrating with Java code.

- Kotlin

  - Full compatibility with Java APIs.

    - Data classes provide a precise syntax. For example, `data class Customer(val name: String, val email: String)`

  - Immutability a first class citizen.

  - Type inference and functional programming.

  - Faster compilation.

There are probably many more features in these languages and their frameworks. The idea here is to flesh out the overall richness of the Java ecosystem.

Tools and Tips for Productivity

These tips are mostly based on my personal experience and should not be taken as the final say:

- Choose functional versus imperative programming wisely. Functional programming may look attractive but will be more complex and require more work and forethought.

- If you are working on a big enterprise application, working with a single language (preferably Java) rather than several is best.

- In terms of performance, we have seen success with Java through Kafka and Spark-like platforms, and many success stories from the industry. Thus, we don't have to prove Java's worth again with self-generated benchmarks.

- Java 10 onwards has type inference support, but I still suggest including Lombok, as it has many other annotations that improve productivity.

- Use JVM languages effectively whenever appropriate in your project.

- Use IntelliJ or Eclipse Java as the IDE. Working on just RESTful microservices does not require most plugins related to J2EE in Eclipse.

Summary

In this chapter we reviewed the Java APIs and feature set that has been improving productivity every year. We also examined the benefits of JVM languages, along with a few productivity tips.

I created this book to cover most of the topics that are required to build applications with today's practices. Additionally, it included brief coverage of all the essential topics in enterprise development.

Index

A

Actuator, 195, 199
Apache Kafka
  build script, 296
  consumer, 299
  definition, 296
  @KafkaListener annotation, 299
  message producer, 297, 298
  run, application, 299–305
Apache OpenWhisk, 280
API gateway, 206
  configuration, 208, 209
  @EnableZuulProxy, 209
  gateway-service, 207
  microservice, 206
  run, 211, 212
  Zuul filter, 210
ApiInfo, 203
APIs
  concurrency
    features, 307–309
    JVM languages, 310
    Kotlin, 310
    tools for productivity, 311
    updated memory model, 308

B

BeanPropertyRowMapper class, 122
broadcastMessage() method, 271

C

CascadeType.ALL, 48
  Cascade type, 49
  DataGenerator, 51–53
  defined, 49
  entity changes, 49, 50
  entity corrections, 56, 57
  TestCase class, 54–56
CascadeType.REMOVE, 49
Code reuse
  Grade file, 212
  Java, 212
  microservices, 212
  multi-module
    project, 212
  package managers, 213
  product-catalog, 213
  uploadArchives, 213
CommandLineRunner
  interface, 23, 24
Command Query Responsibility
  Segregation (CQRS), 223
Common base repository
  implementation, 69, 70
  @NoRepositoryBean, 71
  saveAndFlush()
    method, 69
convertToDatabaseColumn
  method, 104
CrudRepository, 29, 30, 123

313

T

U, V

W, X, Y

Z

Printed in the United States
By Bookmasters